OFF THE MAP

Stephen Hume
OFF THE MAP

Western Travels
on Roads Less Taken

HARBOUR PUBLISHING

Published by
HARBOUR PUBLISHING
P.O. Box 219
Madeira Park, BC Canada
V0N 2H0
www.harbourpublishing.com

Cover, page design and composition by Warren Clark
Edited by Irene Niechoda
Front cover photo of the Dempster Highway, just north of the Arctic Circle in the Northwest Territories, by Pat Morrow
Back cover photo of author by Wendy Kotilla
Printed in Canada

Harbour Publishing acknowledges the financial support of the Government of Canada through the Book Publishing Industry Development Program (BPIDP) and the Canada Council for the Arts, and the Province of British Columbia through the British Columbia Arts Council, for its publishing activities.

THE CANADA COUNCIL | LE CONSEIL DES ARTS
FOR THE ARTS | DU CANADA
SINCE 1957 | DEPUIS 1957

National Library of Canada Cataloguing in Publication Data

Hume, Stephen, 1947-
    Off the map

    Includes index.
    ISBN 1-55017-239-5

    1. British Columbia—Description and travel. I. Title.
FC3817.4.H85 2001   917.1104'4   C2001-910919-9
F1087.H85 2001

This book was printed using low-VOC vegetable-based ink on acid-free paper containing 100% recycled, post-consumer fibre and was processed without using chlorine. This 100% old-growth-free paper was provided by New Leaf Papers.

I have always known
That at last I would
Take this road, but yesterday
I did not know that it would be today.

Ariwara No Narihira

Acknowledgements

A number of the informal essays in this collection first appeared in different form in the pages of the *Vancouver Sun* and I am grateful to editor Neil Reynolds for permission to include them here. No wise person goes off the map without a guide. I'm grateful to the many who have given so freely of their time and advice over the years. They know where they are, even if I don't.

Contents

Prologue:
Roads Less Travelled

Western Canada sprawls across an area that is only slightly smaller than the continental portion of the United States, which is more popularly known as the Lower 48. It's a region that spans three time zones, ten parallels of longitude, almost eight parallels of latitude and, if superimposed on a map of Europe, would cover an area extending from Moscow to the Atlantic and from Scandinavia's Arctic to the Mediterranean Sea. From prairies as flat as a billiard table to some of the most corrugated terrain on the planet, from the highest point in Canada to the lowest, from the mildest climate to the most extreme, from harsh, treeless barrens to lush rain forests that grow the world's largest conifers, it's a region of exotic and even bizarre polarities. Yet where Europe teems with 480 million people and the continental US is home to 265 million, the vast expanse of Canada's west remains almost uninhabited. Its overall population is 25 percent smaller than that of metropolitan Los Angeles, most of it huddled in a few major urban centres and virtually all of it within a few hundred kilometres of the US border. Beyond those manicured urban boundaries, the relatively few paved corridors between population centres rapidly fray into gravel, then dirt, then peter out in the wilderness. Look to the fringes of your road map and your finger will find scores of places that can genuinely claim to lie at the end of the road.

I've always been fascinated by what lies off the map, both physical and psychological, by the unusual people who prefer to live there and by the overlooked histories that reach back to the dawn of time in a country that often claims to have no history or, at best, a boring history. To get to this landscape you have to be prepared to take the roads that few Canadians choose to travel, you must be prepared for the unexpected and you must want to hear the stories of people who for the most part remain invisible to and unheard by the larger society. Where did this fascination first arise? Perhaps with my own arrival here more than half a century ago, the unwitting companion of parents who were themselves striking out into an enigmatic future that lay beyond the map of their own knowledge and sensibilities.

My faint first memory is of the bite of chill air against flushed skin, scratchy wool fabric against my face, being hoisted into the air at the end of powerful arms and hearing a raspy voice say something like: "They must have heard you were coming. See, they named a mountain for you. That's Mount Stephen." That had to be in 1948. It had to be on the railway platform at Field, British Columbia, where the transcontinental trains would stop in a hiss of steam and weary passengers would get off to stretch their legs. And that voice, my mother tells me, most likely belonged to the Negro conductor from Winnipeg. Negro. I still catch up short on my mother's use of these now largely abandoned terms she learned in another country a couple of continents, an ocean and three-quarters of a century ago. I try to guess what old-fashioned phrases will forever anchor me in a place and a time that is alien to my own daughter, her granddaughter.

On that train, soon to be the first down the Fraser Valley following the disastrous floods that spring, my mother was eight months pregnant with my brother Timothy, had a sick toddler—me—to deal with and was bound for the complete unknown. The conductor had befriended the fresh-faced immigrant mother, a woman younger then than most of the innocents who come to the writing classes I teach at the University of Victoria. The conductor told her he had kids himself.

Or perhaps the voice that sounded the way the coarse cloth feels in my memory was the soldier who was on his way home, leaving behind the desolation that was post-war Europe, a man hungry for the domestic dream he saw in that young English couple. The soldier had a mechanical monkey. He'd wind it up and distract me with the toy. Then he'd walk me down the swaying aisle of the railway car, giving my swollen mother and worried father some respite. Certainly the two of them—conductor and soldier—in their respective uniforms stuck in my mother's memory for the rest of her life and this little fragment of their unsolicited kindness is now mingled with mine, too.

How did my mother come to be on that train, clickety-clacking through the days and nights of the Canadian Shield, the Prairie wheat fields and the Rocky Mountains, traversing a vastness her English country girl's senses couldn't begin to encompass? When I asked her, she had to think awhile.

Those thoughts took her back to 1946 and the winter that had left a brutal casing of ice on the smoking ruin that was Europe. She'd spent her war in the Women's Land Army and watched the night horizon glow with burning cities. She'd celebrated VE Day and VJ Day with everyone else, but a year later the shadow of the war still fell on everything. The first general assembly of the United Nations had been held in London, but Winston Churchill had just warned that police states now ruled in Eastern Europe behind an "Iron Curtain" that extended from the Baltic to the Adriatic. Technically, the war was still going on. A final proclamation declaring the cessation of all World War II hostilities would not be declared by US President Harry Truman until December 31, the final day of 1946, just a few hours before I was born.

My mother was carrying me through all this, her war baby, conceived that first spring after her marriage in 1945, her first contribution to the baby boom and the unspoken faith in the future that this resurgence of life represented. Her strength sapped by rationing, she had gone into the hospital's maternity ward well before Christmas and was still there as the end of 1946 approached. The Victoria Hospital in Blackpool, a resort town on the Irish Sea not far from the village where her father lived, was still occupied by wounded soldiers. The hospital had been expanded in anticipation of war casualties in 1939 and I read somewhere that the waterbed as we now know it was developed there in the treatment of severely burned air crew.

My father had been through the Blitz at Coventry. He told me how he'd been restrained from bolting to his first-aid post on that awful night when the Luftwaffe first turned its attention from RAF airfields to civilian targets in an attempt to shatter national resolve. The whole skyline erupted with the subsequent firestorms. His own father, wounded in the landings at Gallipoli in the Great War and rendered unfit for further service after an Imperial army career that had taken him from India to Egypt, had made his son wait to report for duty. They'd need stretcher-bearers soon enough, but not in the middle of the bombardment, he'd said. A good man did nobody a service by getting himself killed trying to reach his post before he was needed. His father's home was bombed, too. And now, on the final day of the war, his own son was being born next to a ward filled with men who had wreaked the same kind of havoc upon German targets.

After thirty-six hours of labour, I came into the world around 1 a.m., the first to be born in that hospital in 1947. There was an epidemic sweeping the maternity wards. Even my father was denied a visit. But the soldiers and airmen next door were another matter. The nurses bundled me up and while my mother got her well-deserved rest, I was paraded before the troops. When I returned, my mother says, my little feet were dangling, blue and cold, from the swaddling clothes. She chided the nurse. There was no stopping it, the nurse replied. Those men who were able would reach up and take my tiny feet in a hand and hold them as though they were reaching out for life itself. In a sense, I suppose they were. Later, those lingering casualties of the world's bloodiest and most destructive conflict had pooled their Red Cross parcels from Canada and sent my mother a special gift: a whole juicy box of bright red Okanagan apples. When my father decided that the future lay elsewhere than England, somewhere with elbow room, my mother told him she thought she'd like to go wherever those apples came from. And so a box of BC apples is how I came to be on the first train to the coast after those terrible floods of 1948.

My mother brought no special skills to Canada, nothing that would directly contribute to the country's economic needs. She was a children's nurse who had spent the war milking cows and mucking out barns to keep the country fed when U-boat flotillas had tried to seal off the supply routes across the North Atlantic. She'd married a truck driver with itchy feet and aspirations to write. But she gave her new country five sons and they all grew up straight and strong and contributed to Canada on her behalf— writing ten books between them, working as loggers and fisher- men, carpenters and journalists, public servants, farmers, home- steaders and artists.

And what son could ever thank his parents enough for that fateful decision to take the road less travelled, a road that led them into a country as wondrous, vast and full of hope as this one and who set me on my own adventures—journeys that have led me again and again to the urban boundary that defines everyday life for most Canadians and then beyond it, to encounters with the people who live out there, off the map.

The Perfect Cup
of Coffee

Several lifetimes ago, when I was a University of Victoria student struggling to make his mark in the campus newspaper, a girl who occasionally came into the cramped, paper-strewn cubicle that passed for *The Martlet* office asked one evening if I'd like to go for a coffee. It was late but a girl offered far more interesting prospects than my nagging editor and, anyway, my story was rapidly going nowhere. I gratefully abandoned my assignment and headed for the cafeteria. The evil coffee in UVic's Student Union Building was legendary, exceeded in vileness only by the soggy, microwaved hamburgers and a permanent cadre of neo-conservative student politicians (the Maoists preferred the seedier ambience of Hong Minh's in Chinatown) endlessly plotting their takeover of the paper. Still, I was going to need something to get me through to deadline. This offer of coffee came wearing a heady perfume and a tight sweater. Whatever the conversation turned out to be, it already promised to be superior to anything I might expect of my acne-tormented colleagues at *The Martlet* or their furtive foes in the basement corner.

But she surprised me. We didn't stop at the cafeteria. Instead, she led me through the Student Union Building with its ceaseless games of hearts and the pathetic undercover narcotics detective whom everybody knew as The Narc, and who knew, sorrowfully, that everybody knew, but who sat stonily in his corner like a Zen monk, conducting his surveillance over books that never changed.

I sometimes wondered what policeman's sin he had committed to merit such a lonely posting, though my sympathy evaporated when a flinty RCMP sergeant appeared miraculously during the October Crisis of 1971 to seize *The Martlet*'s "seditious" front page from beneath the noses of its editors, one of whom would later be appointed a provincial court judge.

I was never much of a SUB rat, so it was with a sense of relief and anticipation that I followed the mystery girl out to where she was illegally parked in the faculty lot of the Classics department and clambered into her battered blue Volkswagen. "We are looking," she said, "for the perfect cup of coffee." Forty-five minutes later, speeding down the Patricia Bay Highway with Victoria receding in the distance, I ventured to ask exactly *where* she was looking for this "perfect" coffee. "Seattle," she said. "It's only 300 klicks. Don't worry, I'll get you back for your lectures." I knew she meant that part from the way she was speeding. We raced up the ramp at Swartz Bay, beetled over the gangplank and onto the last ferry for Vancouver, then went up on deck to watch the stars wheel overhead and the phosphorescent glow of moonlight unfolding its ribbons in our wake.

Of our wind-buffeted conversation, I remember only that we talked of Archilochos—his name means First Sergeant of the Ash Spears—the Greek poet and mercenary. He was slain 2,500 years ago, some say by a man named Kallondes, brawling over a woman in a tavern. Of his poems, so powerful and true to the human condition they might have been written today, only fragments remain. Some were gleaned from literary references, most were recovered from scraps of papyrus used to stuff third-class mummies in Egypt—the dead men wrapped, perhaps, in the pages of treasured books from their own libraries. I've often thought since how most of us are destined for the same fate that claimed Archilochos, lingering only as fragments of ourselves, scattered across the dwindling memories of friends, enemies and acquaintances. Leaning on the rail, gazing out into the dark nap of Galiano Island and listening to the deep music of Active Pass, I became acquainted for the first time with Guy Davenport's stunning new translation. It was an ancient description of the warship carrying the half-forgotten poet to somebody else's fight and perhaps to a dusty, unmarked grave. And, more poignant, the Greek mercenary's landscape seemed so similar to our own Gulf Islands, scattered like bits of broken amber across the western sea. The words resonate with the sound of hornets in fig trees, of crows on the sunburnt rocks with their tawny, wind-tossed grass, and with his universal lament for all lonely travellers by sea, "their souls in the embrace of the waves," foam-streaked and curling like a god's hair. These words from 700 years before Christ, seemed to blend our own feelings into his, a kind of bright alloy binding hearts across the dark ocean of the generations.

From the deck of the *Queen of Esquimalt*, watching the black islands glide by in a blacker sea, talking with my companion about the random tides of posterity, I wondered how a poet who left such tiny fragments of himself could remain so compelling and contemporary—and so little known that when he was first translated even classical scholars thought it a hoax by a modern poet. For the first time it dawned on me that there were serious holes in my education and that university lectures could address only a few of them. Along that ferry rail were planted the seeds of my retreat from the conventional course of study I'd so carefully laid out. Over the side went Psychology 101 and Economics. Exchanging the Oedipus Complex for *Oedipus Rex* turned out to be less of a leap than I'd imagined. And how was I to guess that the trials of Orestes would lead me to understand people with names like Ivaluardjuk and Attuat and provide insights into the still-present reality of intergenerational blood feuds on the frozen seas of the High Arctic? Changing horses cost me an extra year of school in the end, but what's a year in twenty-five centuries?

Yet all this lay behind the featureless screen of the future. For the moment, my whole bemused attention had focussed on my guide's night progress in search of the perfect coffee. At the Tsawwassen ferry terminal we swung east on the King George Highway, then south onto Interstate Number 5, barrelling along with the freeway to ourselves, the heavy truck traffic and the early morning DJs. Three hours later, with the morning mist rising off Puget Sound, arms and legs tingling with that curious lighter-than-air feeling that comes from staying up all night, I got my first look at the earthy wonders of the Pike Street Market. I felt deranged. This seemed a surreal polarity from obscure poetry at the ship's rail.

A smoke-blackened hangar of a building, the market teetered on stilts stuck into a hillside above the battered waterfront. Grimy windows looked out on a lead-coloured sea. It rolled greasily away to the fog-shrouded mysteries of Bremerton naval yards. Along the whole blighted stretch of First Avenue, the only people stirring seemed to be winos too late to get into the Harbour Light Mission and tough-looking guys in navy watch caps who swaggered by like press-gang bosses from *Captains Courageous*. My elegant companion reassured me: I wouldn't be Shanghaied. She worked her summers not in some law office but on the canning line with the Songhees ladies at Oakland's fish-packing plant; these were just your basic stevedores heading for the docks at the first crack of daylight.

Vancouver might make its waterfront a playground for the wealthy; Victoria might turn its Inner Harbour into a garish, illuminated postcard picture for tourists; Toronto's lakefront might throb with the sophisticated tastes of the emerging yuppie class. This part of Seattle's waterfront was strictly calloused working-class and somehow had evaded the architects and urban planners so busy sanitizing the rest of the city core. The foreshore had been the most convenient place to build the now-decrepit freeway called the Alaskan Way Viaduct, so that's where it went, sealing the towers of the moneylenders off from the dirty origins of their wealth. Below it bristled the soot-stained piers and brick warehouses where barquentines and square-riggers once dumped their cargo from the Vancouver Island collieries. Above it, the long, seedy tenderloin of First Avenue, with its porno theatres, junk stores, army salvage depots and its crowning glory: the Pike Street Market.

The market that opened before me was a two-block rabbit warren of dim passageways. They formed a kind of Pacific northwest version of the *souk*. It was an open-ended caravanserai of booths and tables, boutiques and barrows. Street silversmiths were laying out their turquoise-studded belts, filigree settings for chips of jade and blood-red garnet. The wiry arms of sunburnt men and women gestured and threatened, indecipherable arguments swirled in and around their beat-up trucks in languages I could only guess at— fragments of Greek, Croatian, Cantonese. Crates of parsnips, bundles of leeks, a cataract of cut flowers—the produce poured into the market booths. Among the white splash of carnations and yellow chrysanthemums, the prim sheafs of roses and the crisp eruption of gladioli, the scent of flowers mingled with that rising from the snowy trays of the fish merchants. Silver salmon fresh from the trollers below were being layered in beside crimson mounds of snapper, red Dungeness crabs were buried in crushed ice next to yellowtail rockfish and the lethal blue bullets of albacore tuna.

My companion took my hand and led me, a bit dazed, through this amazing montage of strange sounds and rich stinks, through the ornate, visual textures of a swirling, changing tapestry, forming and re-forming before my eyes. I've been back to Pike Street many times since, but nothing has ever matched the vividness of that first morning with the light breaking over my shoulder, mist on the naval basin, the young woman's cold hand in mine, and the hem of night trailing on the western highlands. On the side of the market that juts out over the harbour, we found a place that sold hot drinks and slid into a booth. The bare planks had been worn glossy by the buttocks of how many generations of sailors and troller-men? The coffee came strong and black as pitch. It seemed like the perfect cup of coffee to me, but then, I was a neophyte. "They always taste perfect at a time like this," she warned. "Later on you'll realize it wasn't."

She was right about that as well. And so I began to learn the endless lesson: that while the search for perfection is what makes life worth living, the object of that search is seldom as satisfying as the seeking after it; that it is during the spontaneity of seeking that we open ourselves to the possibility of experiencing, and being changed by, the new. It is the process of search that brings intensi-ty to experience and makes a celebration of that shared continu-um—that connection between Archilochos and the Pike Street Market, between his islands and mine—from which our own brief existence is shaped. That's what is best about it. It hurls one in the way of the unexpected, and it is through the prism of the unantic-ipated experience that one is best able to see the world without those blinders of stereotype and assumption that constrain the perceptions of our everyday lives.

Since that trip to Seattle, the impulsive search for the perfect "cup of coffee" has taken us places I would never have dreamed of going if I were being my responsible self and actually planning a vacation. It has taken us up the south fork of the oyster-grey Nahanni River to a perfumed sleep in a Persian prince's carpet of sulphur-yellow buttercups. We breakfasted on bloody chunks of caribou cooked over an open fire. There, surrounded by the aching quiet of the Tlogotsho Range, I listened to the wisdom of a Slavey trapper named Ted Trindell, now long buried. Sitting among wild strawberries, we compared the fate of Archilochos and the defiant vanity of Crazy Horse. I began to appreciate that wise old Dene's warning that Shelley was right: cities and civilization are passing baubles, but his enduring wilderness contains the whole of Canada—our past, our present and our future.

The same impulse took me haring off to the west of France, a willing companion in the search for the source of a fleeting image in a medieval Norman troubadour's romance. We used his 850-year-old verses as a road map to the magic forest of Brocéliande. The imperfect charts of the troubadour turned out to be only a road map to the human heart. Like Robert Wace, who died in 1170, I didn't find the magic woods, although we found the forest of Paimpont, which seemed magic enough at the time. And we did find a basement full of passionate Breton students, rough wine served in unglazed earthenware cups and directions to the perfect bottle of cider. It came from the cellar of a black-clad grandmother who charged two francs for the litre. I helped drink it in the ruins of a convent at the heart of Europe's last remnant of primeval forest, careful not to disturb the lovers who were occupied at the holy spring, surrounded by their pre-Christian circle of yew and beech, hawthorn, elder and oak.

Following directions from the memories of a man born before World War I, the perfect cup of coffee led me into a maze of unmarked Vancouver Island logging cuts in search of the lost town of Bevan, once so famous it was the subject of music hall songs, where the streets were said to ring to the perfect pitch of Welsh spoken by miners. I found no miners, not even a ghost town, but I did walk the eerie network of streets and driveways leading to the foundation holes of vanished houses, subsiding now into the enduring power of the scrub and underbrush that will outlive us all. And if the slow Welsh airs under the dogwoods were only the conjurings of memory, the story had been foretold by the British poet Meigant a thousand years before, lamenting his own return to a country emptied of its people: "carrion birds befriend them."

Going for a coffee has led me into a Yukon hotspring, drinking Liebfraumilch from a bottle stuck into a snowbank, listening to the ice crystals hiss in the 115-degree waters, and discussing how Plato's cave might relate to the imminent problem of getting out, getting dry and getting dressed at 48 degrees below zero in mixed company. It's led me to a midnight hike on Hadrian's Wall, the Roman border beyond which lay Hyperborea and the mysterious Picts. I watched the full moon rise over the cavalry fort at Housteads. Below me, three horses, the steam rising from flanks as white as frost, thudded home through the gathering dark and I wondered about those ancient border guards standing where I stood, looking out across the same landscape and thinking—what?

Going for a coffee has led me to the Cable Café, constructed entirely of heavy logging cables; to the top of a rocking, rolling coker at the Syncrude plant in Fort McMurray, mortally aware of the thousands of tons of super-heated steam churning under my feet; to Dot's truck stop, where the perfection was found in the lemon meringue pie; with my friend David, ten years dead now, to Mary's Café at Halfmoon Bay, where you order your shrimps by the bucket; to the Alaskan panhandle's Red Dog Saloon, with its sawdust floors; to the old Wheatsheaf at Cedar, where the Confederate raider Quantrill is said to have drunk on his way north to hide at Quatsino; and the fire-blackened foundations of the Bucket of Blood at Fairview, a town that blossomed and petered out with the gold.

It's led me to the wonderful place names of Tomorrow Country that you find scattered along the back roads of Canada: Blue Sky, Westward Ho, Bonanza, Eden Valley, Golden Days, Gilt Edge, Paradise Valley, Sunset Prairie, Valhalla. It's led me to Highway 43 near Little Smokey, where the Cree kid working on the front-end taught me that you don't need store-bought lanolin or gas-soaked rags to get the grease off: you just go down in the ditch and find yourself a fuzzy bunch of dock leaves. And to the view from the front door of the 49 Motel at Spirit River in the Peace River. In August the colours across Highway 49 are blinding. To the west, the gold leaf onion dome of an orthodox church blazes against a blue sky that stretches from horizon to horizon. Beneath the enormous sky, a vast patchwork of intense green fields and the acid yellow of canola in bloom. Out back, the owner's pride and joy—a glorious patch of the most enormous blue-green cabbages.

I've drunk what seemed like the perfect cup of coffee at Romulus Lake on Ellesmere Island, spitting distance from the North Pole, and on the shoulder of Highway 63, south of Boyle, Alberta, watching the wall of cloud that marks the leading edge of a fast-moving arctic front. The rolling tops of these clouds are luminous, amber and magenta, the undersides flat as rock, heavy slabs of darkness. Beethoven is playing on the radio. The clouds sweep overhead and in an instant, freezing rain coats everything with a lacquer of clear ice. Trees, grass, barbed wire fences, everything glitters. The road is treacherous and I spin out twice before I stop, calm my nerves with coffee from the steel thermos I still carry, then slam my Jeep into four-wheel drive and churn the rest of the way to Lac la Biche with two wheels in the ditch, listening to Beethoven all the way, music that for him existed only in his questing mind.

All this I owe to Susan, the young woman who took me looking for that first perfect cup in Seattle and led me to forgotten Greek poets who spoke like gods and set me on this meandering path, so long ago.

And yes, she got me back for my first lecture.

Promises, like quests, are made to be kept.

A Way into
the Hearts of Men

It is winter in Fort Simpson and the rivers groan beneath their burden of ice. All along this flat alluvial plain, wedged as it is into the confluence of the Mackenzie and the Liard rivers, the ice squeals and cracks. Already the pressure ridges are heaving truck-sized blocks up over the low-lying banks; by spring they will scour out new channels through the gravel bars, create and destroy islands, change the whole contour of the silt-laden foreshore. Up in the old settlement, the big, square-sterned freighter canoes and flat-bottomed river skiffs wallow in the drifts. Their dark-sided whale humps are everywhere, canopied with snow between snug log cabins. Windows cast small, butter-bright squares of light into the long blue shadows of the sub-arctic night 1,400 kilometres north of Vancouver. Sled dogs curl in the snow and the wolf ruff that trims my parka hood bristles with frozen exhalations. It's cold enough, in fact, that the natural moisture in my breath changes to ice crystals on contact with the air. When I talk, my words hang glittering for a moment, then fall as snow.

One set of senses takes detached note of all this, scrawling cryptic shorthand into notebook margins, the ink congealing in the pen to create its own strange, lumpy calligraphy. The rest of my mind listens to the old man I've really come to see in this winter of 1971. He grins. He's courteous, hospitable, but he doesn't want to talk about himself, his past, or anything on my agenda. He can barely read or write, never attended school, but he slips around the conversation with the grace of a trained diplomat. Disarming non sequiturs, ingenuous arabesques, the final resort of questions that are direct to the point of rudeness—all the standard interview techniques loop back into his small talk. Then, sharp and sudden as the blaze left by a trail axe, his voice cuts across the chat. He waves an arm in the direction of the river. "It's there," he says abruptly, parchment-yellow hand extended, so skinny it looks like an owl's claw. "It's there," still pointing. I nod knowingly. The old prospector means the motherlode he's never found, the object of a search that spans more than twice my own lifetime.

Three years later, contemplating the terse message announcing his death, I find myself idly sorting through old notes, staring into the gathering night of these northern latitudes as though the con-juring of memory might foster some denial of the hard-edged fact of his final, indisputable disappearance. "Tough as a wolverine, perhaps a little tougher," his friend Fred Sibbeston had said of him. And suddenly, reading these spare entries, I am flooded with the knowledge of what the old man was really pointing out for me. In the mind's eye, tracking back into that absent landscape, it becomes absolutely clear. He is not talking about gold. He is point-ing toward a black shimmer in the river ice, pointing to the belt of open water where a powerful, unseen eddy boils up, eating away the ice from below. Even back at that meeting years before, at some unconscious level I must have noticed the black water. The ink was already beginning to freeze in my cheap ballpoint pen, but my notebook is graced with two faint and obscure mnemonics: "jet slick" says one; "sluice gate" says the other. Later, the image will coalesce into a poem, but now, replaying the tapes of memory at the close of his life, I stand again behind the outstretched arm. I understand at once: it is death he is pointing at. The relentless black current is his metaphor for what will sweep his life's prospects away. His beloved river has led him not to Eldorado, but to the final canyon, the cold chasm between stars.

This is New Year's Day, 1974: morning of the night that I came into the world. After a life spanning eighty-five years, Albert Faille has departed on the same night. I find myself bemused by this final irony that connects us. There's even a curious coincidence of numbers wrapped up in the event. The year of his death, 74, is the reverse of the year of my birth, 47. The two dates are separated to the day by 27 years. It was in 1927 that his strange quest began. A nonsensical linkage in the age of science, or maybe not.

Yet looking over my notes from that last encounter with him, I realize how precisely he saw the end of his long trail just ahead. A life in the bush demands an attention to detail as meticulous as any urban intellectual's; all that differs is the currency. Blinded by academic assumptions, all that I could see of Albert Faille was the residue of a life full of dreams; the words he had painted on the splintered planking of his river boat, readying it, we thought, for a last, impossible trip—"Nahanni or Bust." The trip for which he prepared was another one entirely. The weathered words represent only the trappings, a parody of the quest that became legend in his own lifetime, and in turn a tiresome encumbrance. In his old age, the reputation of the man who loved seclusion became a magnet for pilgrims and supplicants, would-be disciples, reporters, rubbernecks and glad-handing politicians. His fate must have seemed a final joke. Half a century he strove in anonymity for Eldorado; in the end, he found only an odd fame in the persistence of his failure, tinsel for a National Film Board documentary and the final knowledge that the river had won. He was found leaning in his old privy. The fatality report listed age and heart failure as the cause of death. Those who came to know him also knew that whatever failed Albert Faille, he didn't quit this life for want of heart. Even in defeat, he was defiant, pointing at it, staring it down.

His story begins as an enigma wrapped in uncertainty. He claimed he was born in New Salem, Pennsylvania, in 1888, but

American researcher Norm Kagan of St. Paul, Minnesota, wonders whether he didn't add a few years to his age to qualify for a US Army veteran's pension. The army accepted his claim and so it stands as the official version. In any event, birth records in New Salem were destroyed in a courthouse fire in 1904. Faille told people in Fort Simpson that he'd run away from home at the age of nine, that the only school he attended was in the hobo jungles where he learned to fend for himself. Later, he enlisted with the US Army and served in France—"just a support unit, behind the lines." Army enlistment records that might have yielded a clue to his origins apparently perished in another fire the same year he died. One thing is clear without the records, however. By 1917, when Albert Faille and 73,000 other Americans enlisted, even pioneer battalions had been sucked into the bloody maelstrom of the Great War.

An exhausted Britain teetered at the brink of collapse. The Canadian government forced conscription when no more men would volunteer for what seemed certain death. The French commander was convinced his army could fight only one more battle because, even with conscription, there were no more able-bodied men left in France to replace the slain. Fifty-four divisions of the French army had mutinied or suffered what officials glossed over as "collective indiscipline."

All this was before the allied offensive at Arras, where 10,000 wounded were expected. Instead, in the first ten days 150,000 casualties descended on field hospitals equipped for less than a tenth that number. Six weeks later came Passchendaele and 650,000 killed, wounded or missing. Albert Faille arrived just in time for the great German offensive of 1918. General Ludendorf's advance inflicted the greatest defeat in the history of the British army and claimed another 100,000 casualties. By now there were 10 million dead and another 30 million missing or wounded. Both sides paused, collecting the exhausted remnants of their shattered, depleted armies. The newly arrived Americans shored up the lines for Götterdämmerung.

Perhaps it was during the carnage of the St. Mihiel salient and the Meuse offensive that Albert Faille developed his longing for solitude and a green wilderness that was not all stripped trees, tangles of barbed wire and pale corpses surfacing in the mud. Certainly, he would not have been alone in wanting distance from the senseless fellowship of slaughter. More than one soldier watched the skylarks above the trenches and dreamed of the absence of his fellow man. The Peace River district to the south of Fort Simpson was settled by many war-weary British veterans simply because of its name and the fact that it was the farthest reach of the Northern Alberta Railway, as far from the charnel house of Europe as they could get. Perhaps, like many others in that curious migration from Wisconsin, Minnesota and the Dakotas to homesteads at the fringes of western Canada, Albert found a lure in the stories set loose by people like Stephan Stephansson, Alberta's greatest poet—writing about the promised land for an audience in Iceland. Norm Kagan wonders if he cut his teeth in childhood on the romance of the Klondike gold rush. What is known is that sometime after Albert Faille's return from the war, he abandoned a wife and civilization for a trapper's life of solitude, drifting northward until he reached the Beaver River watershed where it drains toward Great Slave Lake. There, harvesting the rich furs to pay for his few store-bought needs, taking the rest of his requirements from the bountiful land, he lived for almost a decade.

And then came a sea change. Did he hear stories over some campfire in the sub-arctic bush? Did it hit him swapping tales at one of the trading posts while picking up his rations of flour and tea? Whatever triggered his decision, old-timers later told me they all remembered that summer. It was one of peculiar lassitude, strange hot days when the lakes and rivers of the northern wilderness seemed cast in molten brass. The trout sank into the deepest shadows and the browsing moose took siestas amid the eelgrass and lily pads of silent rivers and trackless muskeg. Only the insects were in action, rising from the tangled undergrowth in the whining, blood-sucking clouds of gnats, midges, blackflies and mosquitoes that have come to symbolize the Canadian North as much as the dog team or the polar bear. For the skinny young man wearing garish red trousers made from Hudson's Bay Company trade stroud, the bugs were a nuisance to be put off with grease and campfire smoke when possible and endured when not. In any event, Albert Faille was in the act of closing a chapter in his life and embarking on a course that would eventually rewrite the rest of it as completely as if he had taken a trip to Mars.

In the rest of the world, it was the height of the Roaring Twenties. The stock market was going wild, paper empires of finance expanded and greed blossomed everywhere, there were moving pictures and 12-cylinder automobiles. Even in the north, the impact of industrial technology was making itself felt. Near Fort Nelson a Dene trapper shot a caterpillar tractor, mistaking the belching, roaring machine for some mythical beast. Bush pilots and their flimsy, fabric-covered craft were transforming the frontier that had swallowed Franklin's expedition without a trace.

The pilots and their planes seemed miraculous. There were only sixty aircraft registered in all of Canada and Wop May's first airmail flight down the Mackenzie River to Aklavik was still two years in the future. The grand total of airmail hauled for 1927 was eight tons for the whole country. Navigating with the skills they had learned as pilots in the war—acute perceptions, sharp memory, instinctive common sense and a quickness in dead reckoning— the bush pilots provided a springboard to the burgeoning search for the new ores demanded by dawning technologies; molybdenum, tungsten, radium, as well as the traditional base wealth of copper, lead and zinc, and the always precious metals of silver, platinum and gold.

Albert Faille was called Red Pants by the aboriginal Dene: *Tl'a-e detsili* in the liquid syllables and glottal stops of southwestern Slavey, *Ttatsik ethli* in the harsher Tukudh language farther north. The more literal translation from Slavey is "scarlet bum dress." The gentle humour suggests a general remarking of the excess of his garish trousers. But Red Pants remained as oblivious to the joke as he was to the harbingers of the modern age. He quietly folded up his trapline and abandoned his cabins and caches in the dense spruce and pine forest of the Beaver River country, striking out westward, plunging deeper into the wilderness. He had decided to attempt what conventional wisdom of the day said was impossible. Albert Faille was out to cross the mighty Funeral Range and penetrate to the heart of a blank spot on the maps that had earned its place in pulp fiction and newspaper stories as The Valley of No Return.

This seems romantic nonsense today, when bush pilots triangulate position by computer and satellite while Yellowknife bureaucrats worry about whether their expense accounts will stand the escargot and the second Rémy Martin. Today the unknown country that drew Albert Faille is mapped to the centimetre and patrolled by federal park wardens. But in that winter of 1926–27, as Albert Faille considered his expedition, it was country as uncharted as any on the planet. Even the bush pilots had yet to fly across it. Charles Lindbergh was still working up to his own solo flight across the Atlantic. Yellowknife did not exist, even as an idea. The capital of the Northwest Territories was distant Ottawa, and would remain so for another forty years.

The landscape Albert Faille sought was charted better in the imagination than in reality. Maps of the day show simply white space marked "unknown," or at best, crude guesses at the physical features of the remote and rugged triangle enclosed by the northern boundary of British Columbia, the eastern border of the Yukon and the Mackenzie River. "Mountains," they might say. Or "river," with a whimsically dotted line. The *Royal Atlas* of 1927 does not even acknowledge the existence of one of Canada's most beautiful and spectacular rivers, the south fork of the Nahanni. The whole region was not yet surveyed and what skimpy maps did exist were the informal renderings of memory and the records of trappers operating out of settlements like Fort Liard, Trout Lake and Nahanni Butte.

In a way, although he didn't think of it in such terms, Albert Faille's journey was a voyage away from the present and into a simple, austere archetype of the past. It was an anachronism, the kind of personal search that had its origins with Coronado's hunt for Cibola and the Seven Cities of Gold—the kind of quest that had launched the California rush, and the Cariboo rush, and the stampede to the Klondike only thirty years before. More and more, such prospecting would pass from the passionate to the methodical; from the kingdom of high adventure into the realm of the newly emerging earth sciences—geophysics and seismology, geology and geomagnetism—all measurement, statistical incidences and probability theory. Albert Faille's dream cast back to his father's generation. It lay in his conviction that a fantastic motherlode of gold was buried somewhere in the distant and mysterious mountains on the border of the Yukon and the Northwest Territories. He believed it had been found once before, then lost again, shrouded in bloody violence and betrayal in the dark canyons of the world's last great corner of unmapped wilderness. His one-man gold rush would last half a century and he would never find his motherlode. The legend was to grow out of his ceaseless striving.

The source of his conviction can never be known now, but its fountainhead is likely found at the turn of the century when George Carmacks and his two companions, Skookum Jim and Tagish Charlie, reported gold on Bonanza Creek and launched the rush to the Klondike goldfields. From 1897 to 1905, the world was delirious with a peculiar kind of fever. Men and women poured into the Yukon by the tens of thousands. A few struck it rich, either on their claims or working the dance halls. Kitty Rockwell is said to have left with a steamer trunk full of nuggets. Most found not gold, but grinding labour, privation and a cold grave. They are buried by the thousands on the aspen-clad slopes of the Midnight Dome, where it rises behind the relics of a Dawson City only recently tarted up by governments less caring of our heritage than tourist dollars. Once the biggest boom town in Northern history, then a near ghost town, Dawson City was always a priceless cultural artifact. Yet for generations it was neglected by foolish Whitehorse and dull-witted Ottawa while smarter Yankees stripped it to the bone. Only after much of that rich past had already been looted and wrecked did federal and territorial bureaucrats take steps to restore a fragment of what was left.

Ultimately, inevitably, the Klondike rush had been transformed from gold pans and sluice boxes to the brutal pragmatism of industrial engineers. The unrestrained rape of the environment with massive dredges and hydraulic mining did not simply blight landscape, it killed it, churning the thin mantle of northern soils under wastelands of sterile gravel. Even at that, even after the stampede had ebbed into the perverse satisfaction many Yukon residents still take in environmental pillage, a few prospectors kept searching in the old way. A few others, too young to participate in the great march over the Trail of '98, were still infected with gold fever at a time when the rest of the world slowly turned its thoughts back to more sensible commercial ventures: securing empire and building battleships for the coming apocalypse. Three of these were among the sons of Murdoch McLeod, factor at the Hudson's Bay Company trading post on the Liard River, upstream from Fort Simpson and the Mackenzie. His sons were the first to be reported lost in the Nahanni Valley and are clearly the source of the modern legend, although the legend itself is only an accretion upon prehistoric myth.

Never more than a wilderness outpost, Fort Liard remains a tiny settlement today, although its strategic location in 1804 had made it the object of intense competition between the Hudson's Bay and the North West companies. The Dene people of the area were fierce and independent, and the competing fur traders did not hesitate in exploiting any warlike propensities to their own advantage. Fort Liard was burned at least once and sixteen of the residents butchered before the merger of the two companies put an end to the rivalry in 1821.

This potential for violence was not new to the region. Early Hudson's Bay Company reports observe overt hostility from the "Russian" Indians who traditionally traded into Catherine the Great's outposts in Alaska. Indeed, there is ample evidence of ferocious inter-tribal warfare. Father Adrian Gabriel Morice records in his *History of the Northern Interior of British Columbia* that hostility between Dene and Carrier, Sekani and Beaver, resulted in horrifying massacres that he dates to 1745 and 1780 on the basis of the age of his informants. Even the tough Father Morice shudders at the atrocities: children and infants with their ribs chopped loose from the spine, spread and spitted on poles like drying salmon and left as battle trophies by the dozens. It is from the xenophobia that reasonably accompanies such events that fearful myths arise. Alexander Mackenzie's journals record his own inability to induce any of the Dene he encountered on his voyage to the Arctic Ocean in 1789 to guide him past the mountain range he was told separated his great River of Disappointment from another vast and fabulous river running westward to the sea. Mackenzie wrote of his certainty that the Natives had far more knowledge than they would share and although he longed to explore to the west, neither bribes nor threats could budge the Natives' resolve. Their fears, he said, revolved around belief in a tribe of gigantic stature whose members had the power to kill men with a stare from their terrible eyes.

Hudson's Bay Company and North West Company fur traders

made sporadic contacts with nomadic mountain peoples they referred to as Nahany Indians, but it wasn't until 1837 that Fort Liard factor Robert Campbell made significant contact. Dispatched by HBC Governor George Simpson to explore the headwaters of the Liard River, Campbell encountered "such a concourse of Indians I had never before seen assembled." It was the trading camp of the great chief Shakes from the mouth of the Stikine, gathered for the annual exchange of goods with the Russians. In this camp, Campbell met the chief of a tribe he called the Nahanies: "She was a fine looking woman above the middle height and about 35 years old. In her actions and personal appearance she was more like the Whites than the pure Indian race. She had a pleasing face lit up with fine intelligent eyes, which when she was excited flashed like fire. She was tidy and tasteful in her dress...At our first meeting, she was accompanied by some of her tribe and her husband, who was a nonentity." In mid-winter, when Campbell was in danger of starving and "perfectly destitute," she personally intervened to provide dried salmon and fresh caribou meat. She must have been a powerful and respected leader, because she openly defied Shakes, who had ordered the gathered tribes to harass Campbell's party and trade only with the Russians, for whom he was the middleman. The others were fearful enough of the Nahanies and the woman Campbell called the White Chieftainess that they left the Hudson's Bay party alone.

Fifty years later, exploring on the Yukon side of the mountains for the Hudson's Bay Company, William Ogilvie's Exploratory Survey from the Pelly–Yukon to Mackenzie River by Way of Tat-on-duk, Porcupine, Bell, Trout and Peel rivers reports similar fears among tribes in the Interior. Ogilvie's trek took place in 1888, the apparent year of Albert Faille's birth. The expedition took Ogilvie as far as a high plateau on the western ranges of the mountains that sweep down the present Yukon–Northwest Territories boundary. His Native guides would go no further. "These people have a great dread of a tribe who, they suppose, dwelt at one time in the hills at the head of these streams and still exist somewhere in the vicinity, though exactly where they do not know..." Ogilvie names this mysterious tribe with its mythical powers as "Na-hone" or the "Na-haune" and speculates that it occupies territory around the headwaters of the Liard and Pelly rivers.

Obviously, the term *Na-hone* or *Nah'aa* is the root from which the present anglicized word *Nahanni* derives, although it is no longer used by anthropologists to describe any culturally or linguistically distinct tribal grouping. The Nahanni tribe, however, was clearly distinct in the minds of Ogilvie's guides, and he was sufficiently impressed by their apprehension to inform his superiors that "this dread appears to be lively, so much so, that I believe only some pressing necessity, such as hunger, would induce them to remain in this locality for any length of time, and then only if they were in strong force.

"They described them [the Nahanni] as cannibals, and living altogether outside, without shelter from the cold, and believed them to be such terrible creatures that they required no cover, but could lie down anywhere to rest, and did not need a fire to cook their food, but ate it raw. They seemed to ascribe to them supernatural powers." It is interesting to note that many Native people of the Mackenzie Valley, the direct descendants of those who warned Mackenzie of the dangers of the west country, still believe greater powers of medicine, both for good and for evil, may be ascribed to the Montagnard peoples or Mountain Indians, as those groups are now described by anthropologists.

Nick Sibbeston, the Metis from Fort Simpson who rose to become government leader of the Northwest Territories and now sits in the Senate, recalls sitting on his grandmother Embe's knee as she approached her hundredth birthday. She told him of her mother, who lived when the Nah'aa beyond the mountain canyons still struck fear into the Slavey settlements. Yet even today, in the age of computers, almost nothing is known of the expressive culture of these Mountain Indians. But then, the first field expeditions of anthropologists did not penetrate that remote and wild area until 1957, three decades after Albert Faille ventured there.

In 1973, at Trout Lake, about 160 kilometres east of Fort Liard by air, I visited a village terror-stricken by sightings of a Nahkah, a wild man of the woods. Dogs barking frantically at night, glimpses of a pale face at cabin windows, unexplained gunshots echoing through the bush, unexpected footprints in the snow—these, I was told, were the signs of his presence. I talked with children and adults who claimed close encounters with the Nahkah, who described him for me along with his familiar, a funny little dog-like creature. Where did the Nahkah find shelter in the winter? Nobody knew.

But, listening to 77-year-old Chief Joseph Jumbo itemize fish stolen from nets and dried meat mysteriously vanished from caches too high for dogs and children, there was no doubt that whatever I and the RCMP constable might think, the Nahkah was a tangible threat for the 51 villagers. Nor did it take a linguist to notice the structural similarities between the word *Nahkah*, meaning a human being who has reverted to the wild state of an animal, and the fierce, mysterious Nah'aa described by Embe. Or between *Nahkah* and *Nahanni*, which today is explained as meaning "the people who live way far away over there," but was also the word Ogilvie's informants gave to describe the mythical cannibal tribe of the mountains that needed no shelter and slept on the ground in the winter cold.

Out of the myth-based aboriginal fears recorded by Mackenzie and Ogilvie was constructed the framework upon which the wider world embroidered an enduring legend of a mysterious northern Valley of No Return. "A land of terror and mystery," the *Edmonton Journal* called it in 1929, in a story that touted the Nahanni as a place where a prospector could kick the gravel bars and "see the gold gleaming like butter." It would take a brave explorer, however, to venture into a land "haunted by horror and strange tales of witchcraft and torture." This journalistic excess was less an outright fabrication than a replay of the generally accepted folklore. Hidden behind high cliffs, deep canyons and roaring, impassable rivers, it was said to be a place of bizarre tropical growth and perhaps a lost tribe of headhunters. White men venturing into it simply disappeared, went the story, and every teller could no doubt supply a personal anecdote to cement upon the conglomerate of Native myth, frontier folklore and mis-remembered history. None of this was true except in the imagination. Although, paradoxically, all of it had foundation in truth.

The southwest corner of the Northwest Territories that has now been set aside as Nahanni National Park reserve does indeed remain one of the most dangerous parts of Canada. The danger springs not from cannibals and wild men, but from the ruggedness of the terrain and its remoteness from sources of help in the event of accident or injury. It is a land that is unforgiving of the slightest mistake or miscalculation, even for experienced outfitters and wilderness experts. Slashing through mountain wall after mountain wall, the pale grey South Nahanni snakes through canyon walls higher than the world's tallest buildings, rising sheer from the riverbed. In places, the canyons narrow to 100 metres and the river hurtles through like water from a high-pressure hose. Falling thousands of metres over 200 kilometres, the turbulent South Nahanni current rips past at 12 knots. The steepness of the watershed and narrowness of the canyons make the river subject to sudden and dangerous fluctuations in flow and depth. An unheard thundershower beyond a mountain range can turn a tributary stream into a treacherous jet of whitewater, blasting unexpectedly from the canyon side to swamp a canoe; a large eddy can be transformed into a sucking vortex by what seems an innocuous little rain. The list of those who have drowned over the last forty years is a testament to the hazard.

It was to this country that Murdoch McLeod's sons turned in the winter of 1904. There are still McLeods at Fort Liard today, although now they live down the dusty road from the post their ancestors once ruled like Persian potentates. Willie, Frank and Charlie McLeod were tough, seasoned, bush-wise young men who had been raised as Indians. Their life was that of the trapline and the hunt, the fishnet and the dog team. Maybe it was the slowness with which news travelled in the days before telegraph and radio, or maybe the McLeod boys were first stung by tales still floating around from the Cariboo stampede that had swept through northern British Columbia a generation before. At any rate, they apparently heard that somebody had a showing of gold on the Flat River, the main tributary of the South Nahanni. Initially, they set out by heading south and then booking steamer passage to the Alaska Panhandle. Instead of going over from Skagway and then down the Yukon River to the Klondike, the McLeod boys struck inland, up the frozen Stikine River by dogsled and into the mountains of the southeastern Yukon Territory. Somewhere they ran into a group of Cassiar Indians who were carrying coarse placer gold they had taken from a creek further into the mountains. The story goes that the brothers over-wintered and the following spring built sluice boxes on the Flat River. They are said to have collected enough nuggets and dust to fill a large bottle, lost it in a boat accident, sluiced out more, then run down the Flat and the South Nahanni on the way back to Fort Liard.

The prospects were strong enough that Frank and Willie, accompanied by a Scottish mining engineer named Robert Weir, decided to try again for the big strike. This was in the spring of 1905. The party is said to have retraced its steps through the forbidding canyons of the South Nahanni and a band identified only as "Little Nahanni Indians" later told an RCMP investigation that the missing men had been encountered and supplied with fifty pounds of flour and five pounds of tea. That was the last time anyone saw the three men alive.

According to RCMP reports, a five-man party that included two other McLeod brothers journeyed up the South Nahanni in 1908. On or around July 24, the party found the headless remains of two men lying in the spruce bush not far from the river. An examination of the bones revealed evidence of fire and the tattered remnants of clothing appeared to have been burned, particularly the shirts. Nothing remained to positively identify the bodies, but with them were found two .44-40 rifle shells, a bone-handled pocket knife, a ring and a gold watch that was later identified as having belonged to the missing men's mother. Charlie McLeod, who had been on the first expedition, told police that hair found near the site was similar to that of his brother Willie. Of Robert Weir there was no sign. Charlie was later said to have put about the plausible speculation that perhaps Weir had murdered his brothers to keep knowledge of a rich gold strike to himself. Men had been killed for far less.

An official police report was not filed until 1909. This four-year delay between the men's disappearance and the formal report to authorities is evidence not of uncertainty, but of the difficulty both of investigation and of communication in such a remote region. It was during this silent period between 1905 and 1909 that rumours regarding the McLeod deaths and a mysterious Headless Valley began to set their hardy roots. They found fertile ground. It had, after all, been well cultivated by the aboriginal myths first recorded more than a century earlier. The formal dispatch of RCMP Corporal Arthur Mellor, however, provides a cool and clinical alternative to the popular folklore that was springing up. He says unequivocally that the McLeod brothers were not murdered, but starved to death. Of the headless state of the bodies, we can deduce the ravages of carrion-feeding animals. Corporal Mellor's judgement is corroborated by interviews with local Natives and by RCMP reports that Native hunters travelling up the river had located the remains of a third man, believed to be Robert Weir. Yet this was only an opinion. Nothing conclusive had been proved. The discovery of yet another headless body up the South Nahanni River provided even greater impetus for the developing legend. This man, too, was said to have struck it rich, only to be found dead with no trace of either his gold or his rifle.

Once again, RCMP reports indicate a more prosaic end. Martin Jorgensen had last been seen on the Flat River in 1913, where Indians found him camped with a good supply of meat. The next year, a prospector named Osias Meilleur reported finding a burnt-out cabin on the South Nahanni about a mile upstream from its confluence with the Flat. Meilleur told RCMP that in front of the shack he had found a long-barrelled .22-calibre revolver and a badly rusted but still loaded .30-55 rifle. He had also found a bundle of clothing that he recognized as the missing Jorgensen's. The following year, a party of three prospectors reported to RCMP that on September 28, 1915, they had found and buried skeletal remains in the same vicinity. The Mounties were not able to investigate until the summer of 1916, when they exhumed and made an inventory of the grave's contents. The bones were human and most of them were recovered, the reports say, with the exception of the skull, "which judging from the close proximity of other bones to the riverbank, might have fallen into the river. Some of these bones had been gnawed."

The next death on the Nahanni was that of May Lafferty. She strayed from a hunting party in 1921. Although the bush-wise trappers followed what seemed to be a girl's tracks for nine days, they were never able to catch up with her in the rugged terrain. A Little Girl Got Lost Creek commemorates the tragedy. The following year, according to the RCMP, a returned soldier named John O'Brien froze to death on his trapline. He was found huddled over the twigs with which he was trying to light a fire. There are no formal reports of deaths in the region over the next decade, but the *RCMP Quarterly* observes that the force's records for that period have been destroyed. It draws attention to unverified newspaper accounts that indicate another five deaths from 1922 until 1932, when an RCMP patrol did confirm that the bones of Phil Powers, a prospector missing since the previous year, had been found in the burned rubble of his cabin. The only other item in the ashes was a rifle with a piece of wire attached, apparently as a mechanism designed to trip the trigger automatically. Dick Turner, who visited the burned-out site not long after, reports a never-explained sign nailed to a tree which read: "Powers—his finis." On June 1, 1936, two more prospectors, William Epler and Joseph Mulholland, were reported missing. An RCMP expedition found no trace of the men but did find their cabin burned to the ground. It was officially assumed the two had either drowned in a river accident or been swept away by an avalanche while attempting to cross the mountains near the junction of the Flat and South Nahanni rivers. There is one interesting common denominator in all these instances of death, the RCMP point out: in each of them, fire of unexplained origin appears as an important factor.

Much of the mythology of Headless Valley had been debunked by R.M. Patterson in his book *The Dangerous River*, an account of his own solitary season on the South Nahanni in 1927. Yet when Albert Faille first travelled up the river, publication of Patterson's narrative lay twenty years in the future. The stories that attracted him were still powerful, the country still a blank space on the map. Today, the names on the charts speak to the strength of those legends: the Coffin Range, Deadmen Valley, Sunblood Mountain, Twisted Mountain, Broken Skull Creek, the tiny notch in the Funeral Range known as The Gate and the peculiar rock formation called The Pulpit, brooding like a sentinel over the narrowest canyon. All these add mystery and an eerie sense of the unknown, even to the modern cartographer's problems of elevations, scales of measure and reference grids.

When Albert Faille decided to search the hidden reaches of the Nahanni Valley for the lost gold of the McLeod boys, he was challenging a legend that had been growing steadily for a full generation. Anyone who has travelled the South Nahanni by canoe understands the magnitude of the solo expedition he undertook in the face of disturbing tales and little accurate information. Cascading down from Virginia Falls, a waterfall twice the size of Niagara, the river boils through canyons a thousand metres deep. They are the only chinks in three towering mountain ranges.

Starting at the tiny settlement of Nahanni Butte, which boasted a population numbering only sixty-five people when the first of my three treks through the Nahanni had jumped off in 1971, Albert Faille headed upstream through waters made treacherous by sweepers. These toppled trees, with their roots still embedded in the bank, are swept under by the strength of the current. Submerged, bent like enormous bows, they can lash to the surface and smash any canoe unlucky enough to be over them. From these deep channels, he moved into The Splits, where the plunging river strikes flat ground and branches into thousands of overgrown channels, most of which are blind cul-de-sacs. At the best of times it takes a skilled navigator to read the riverbed and choose the real channel where it twines amid rapidly shifting sand and gravel bars. Faced with a host of dead ends it demands a special sense of the water. Beyond The Splits, as contemporary river travellers do today, he encountered the lovely, flower-filled meadows surrounding the hot springs, where mineral water bubbles up and collects in pools dug out by wayfarers. At a constant 110 degrees Fahrenheit, the water is hot enough to stay ice-free even during winter temperatures that plunge to 65 below. Gus Krause and his wife Mary lived here for decades. Mary is famous in her own right for dropping a grizzly bear with a single-shot .22 short when it threatened her child. Gus and Mary pulled up stakes when the river got too busy with park tourists. The canoe traffic drove them deeper into the wilderness, farther north to Little Doctor Lake.

In the hot springs lies the not-so-mysterious origin of stories about a tropical valley. Above these meadows loom the dark faces of the First Canyon, with the whitewater of Lafferty's Riffle beneath. This is a long, straight rapid where the South Nahanni swirls across the mouth of a tributary creek and boils for half a mile along a sheer rock wall, the turbulence creating a series of standing waves or haystacks. Beyond this canyon, the land opens into Deadmen Valley where the bones of the McLeod boys were found. From here, Albert Faille edged his way into the Second Canyon, through George's Riffle where tons of water smash into the cliffs at a sharp right-angled turn in the channel. Lining his canoe from shore where possible, fighting the current where he had to, he continued past Pulpit Rock, a 100-metre pillar of free-standing stone, through the Hell's Gate and the Third Canyon and on to his destination at the mouth of the Flat River. Perhaps the nature of Albert Faille's journey into that country where the maps were simply stamped "mountainous" can best be measured by a modern comparison. When a highly trained and well-equipped British army commando team made the same voyage, travelling in their high-powered rubber rafts and depending upon resupply of food and fuel by parachute drop, its leader described the expedition as a nightmare.

For Albert Faille it was simply the beginning of a dream. There, in the shelter of a birch thicket near the Flat River, he built the snug little cabin where he was joined by fellow woodsman R.M. Patterson for a housewarming dinner in 1927. Patterson never forgot the simple act of generosity. All that he learned about canoeing the river, he later wrote, he learned from Albert Faille. Twenty-four years later, returning for a last look at the country that had claimed his own youthful heart, Patterson wrote that he found his comrade of the woods still camped on the Flat River. "So you've come back," Albert said, stayed for dinner and a slug of rye, and the next morning was gone like a ghost into the high country.

From his base on the Flat, Albert Faille searched the river bars and fault lines for the McLeod brothers' lost glory hole. His one-man gold rush was to last for forty-six years and in the end, he became a bigger legend than the one he challenged. Prospecting in the summers, trapping and hunting in the winters, sometimes for two years at a stretch, travelling alone down the wild river to the "big town" at Fort Simpson to trade his furs, he left a trail of stories to match any mythic figure. Stories of how he would make the journey to Virginia Falls, dismantle his skiff and pack it and a full ration of supplies up a portage the height of a forty-storey building, then rebuild the boat from scratch and continue on into the wilderness. The way he broke his back in an accident, took himself to bed and walked out again the following spring. The way, weakened by scurvy and hunted by a pack of timber wolves, he held them off with his rifle in one of the few recorded incidents of its kind. Most of all, the way he kept returning from the Nahanni when so many others succumbed to the hazards of brutal cold, whitewater and isolation in a desolate and unforgiving country.

Almost half a century later, when I visited the Flat River myself, the cabin was still there, dry and immaculate, awaiting the old man's return. Yet if it was gold that Albert Faille sought, his quest was not a failure. The gold he found was of a different sort, but no less precious than the kind that the legends award to the McLeod boys. At the old prospector's death, friend and long-time Northerner Dick Turner said: "Oh, Albert Faille found gold all right. He found a way into the hearts of men."

Only as Sharp
as Your Knife

Most of us know the proverb about beating swords into ploughshares. Up here in the biblically austere landscape of British Columbia's northern bush, another grizzled craftsman named Joe Breti is making his international reputation doing exactly the opposite. Joe, who lives at Mile 15 of the Alaska Highway, scavenges discarded steel planer blades from Louisiana Pacific's oriented strand board plant, about 25 kilometres down the highway in Dawson Creek, and then recycles them into stunningly beautiful knives that draw custom business from all over the world.

Prices for his knives start at around $130 and rise to $200 and higher depending on the materials. If you want 40,000-year-old mammoth ivory from the Arctic in the handle, you'll pay a lot more than you will for mountain goat horn or moose antler...or wood. "My personal preference for a handle is wood," he says. "It's tougher and it's more functional." It's also an aesthetic wonder. Joe has found a way to dye the grain so that different layers take on different hues. The knives become art objects in themselves, the whole contoured into a shape that weds an eye-pleasing form to utilitarian function. Pick them up and the heft and feel is, well, satisfying, even sensual.

"You have to be a refugee from the twentieth century to take up this kind of thing," he says. "The only thing I buy is some sheep horn for my handles. This is not everybody's piece of cake. There's an art to this. Some people have it and some people don't.

"If you wanted a knife it would take me a day to come up with the blade and scabbard—but it would be a damn long day. I make about $5 an hour here. But I'm happier 'n a tick making my $5, let me tell you."

He proudly brings out a wooden display case. The blades inside glimmer in the dim light of a suitably untidy shop that's pungent with the smell of dust and smoke and quenched iron. The handles of ivory, antler and wood are burnished to a rich sheen and the leather scabbards are buffed to a soft lustre, even along the hand-sewn seams. Yet these are all true working blades, not display pieces. There's little ornamentation and nothing simply for show. They are all designed for skinning beaver, flaying big game, filleting fish or butchering a moose carcass for the winter—according to the advice of the hunters and trappers. The grateful users of his knives bring Joe offerings of horn and antler for future handles, and more than a few plan on leaving the knives he made for them to their sons.

"You can either buy a good knife or you can pay the same money for a piece of assembly line junk," he says. "The steel I use in my blades has a Rockwell hardness of 63, which means it's damn hard and it has phenomenal edge-retention. This steel cuts other steel. These knives are guaranteed to skin a whole moose without stopping to sharpen or I want the knife back."

Joe, who was born 135 kilometres north of Regina—"Section 23, Township 27, Range 17, West 2, Saskatchewan"—made his first knife at the age of twelve but says he didn't really get serious about it until 1991, when he began looking for something to keep him busy after thirty years working in the northern gas fields, where he wound up as a tool crib operator, "not so much knowing the tools, but knowing where to find specialized tools." It was knowledge that proved surprisingly useful in his new trade, since he had to design and build most of the specialized equipment that fills the weathered cabin that serves as his knife-making shop out behind the neat white house overlooking the Alaska Highway.

"In 1991, I had a chance to go to Vancouver," he snorts. "In my view that wasn't even an option. That was just a big, fat zero." Instead, he went to Edmonton to learn the basics of his new vocation, making his first knives entirely by hand but, more importantly, soaking up information about the kind of equipment he'd need to do the kinds of difficult things he wanted to do.

"I got into this business to make knives for working people," he says. "Each of my knives has a precise function." He holds up a stubby, relatively short-bladed specimen: "Beaver knife. When you are skinning a beaver, the fat really sticks to the pelt. In the old days they left the fat on the pelt when they stretched it. When it dried they get it off. This blade lets you get all that right at the start, so you bring home a clean pelt.

"Now a skinning knife," he says, holding up another, "it's got lots of arc in the blade. A drop point, not quite the same arc. A caping knife, it's designed so you can hold it like a pencil. Here's a gutting knife. And here's a skinner with a point, a bit more general purpose. Filleting knife—I'm usually way behind in filleting knives."

Who buys what? That was a bit of an eye-opener. "Your German hunter prefers a deep drop point," he says. "Your Canadian wants his basic working skinner. I guess the German hunter who comes over here sure as hell don't plan on skinning no moose. He just shoots it. I figured that the Germans, being traditionalists, would want bone [handles]. But I got it backwards. The Germans like wood. The Canadians, especially Indians who spend a lot of time in the bush, they want bone." What about Americans? It turns out that they are taken with oversized, extremely ornate and, in Joe's opinion, essentially useless Bowie knives, which are basically weapons and not working tools. "What the hell do they want with it? This kind of knife has only one purpose and it sure as hell ain't to skin a buffalo. Still, if a knife-maker makes only the knives he likes, he's going to be an awfully poor knife-maker."

To work with these materials, especially the world's hardest industrial steel, Joe says he wound up having to make much of his own equipment. He had to modify a drill press, slowing it down so the drill tip would cut the steel. He designed and built his own table saw with a wheel that permits him to cut knife blanks from the planer blades. He scrounged a piece off a farmer's junked combine to make specialized buffing wheels. And he haunts the farm auctions for the bits and pieces he needs. "Necessity has been the mother of invention," he says. "You know, half the farm equipment that actually works was designed by some Saskatchewan farmer out in the back shed. For example, to drill this stuff you have to use a solid carbide drill bit. The problem is that nobody in Canada sharpens a carbide bit—except me. I made my own sharpener."

Once he's cut a blank from a template and made the blade, he prepares the handle. If it's to be bighorn ram, for example, he cuts plates off the curved horn, boils them, puts them in a special press and cures them for a month.

"When it goes up against the steel it has to be absolutely flat, zero tolerance," he says. "It's measurement by feel not by the eye. Then, before I sharpen the knife, I make the scabbard—I've found it saves a hell of a lot on fingers." Even there he's improvised, designing a mechanical, spring-loaded awl that makes precise, neat holes in the thick hide he uses to sheath the ultra-sharp blades.

Joe came north as a teenager and he doesn't figure on ever leaving. "I came up here in 1959. Best move I ever made," he says. "I can walk up to the mayor and call him by his first name and he knows who I am.

"And if you're a nonconformist, this is heaven. If you don't fit in one little hole, well, then you carve your own. You can do anything here, and the damnedest people wind up doing the damnedest things." Of which Joe Breti and his marvellous blades are but one example, living proof of the saying they have up here that no matter how sharp you are when it comes to surviving in the bush, you're only as sharp as your knife.

Batman and Faye

Late in the day the western sun flares against the exposed rocky faces and grassy uplands of the island the Haida call Gandlak'in brightly enough that you don't need a chart to know that you've arrived at the one place in a hundred miles where you can get a hot bath. After a week of sleeping on a steel deck and bathing (as seldom as decorum permitted) in sea water cold enough to—well, use your imagination—a soak in the hot mineral springs that bubble up from deep in the earth's crust just off the coast of South Moresby Island seems just the ticket. So we anchor behind what's popularly known as Hot Springs Island, radio the Haida watchmen for permission to come ashore and hike through the gloomy forest along trails outlined by luminous white clamshells to the series of rock pools that overlook the spectacular scenery of Ramsay Passage and Juan Perez Sound.

There's a rough bathhouse, the cedar planking gone silver in the weather, where you can shower before choosing your pool. These rocky basins that catch the trickles from mineral springs can range from tepid to near-scalding. I work myself up the temperature scale gradually. Night is falling fast and I've hauled myself out and I'm sitting on a bench in the shadows watching the stars emerge as silver frosting on a sky that slips from peacock blue to ultramarine when I hear what sounds like the clicking of a Geiger counter. Squinting into the darkness I can just make out what appears to be a man pointing some kind of equipment at the sky.

Then, looming out of the underbrush behind him comes a shapeless figure that has not a face but an...apparatus.

Nope, not an episode of "Star Trek and the Borg." Meet the Batman and his faithful sidekick, Faye. Doug and Faye Burles—he's a soft-spoken Parks Canada warden, she's a lively junior high school teacher at Sandspit—are studying bat colonies here in the remote mid-coast of Gwaii Haanas National Park Reserve. Both are working on their masters' degrees at the University of Victoria. During their long stints of field research, they live in a tent, often sleeping by day and working by night when their nocturnal subjects venture out. And if this sounds like a vaguely troglodyte existence, they are strictly high-tech when it comes to the science. The Borg-like apparatus that gives me such a start is Faye's set of military night-vision goggles, the only way to see the small creatures in their own natural habitat. By day the bats are roosting in the trees or hidden clefts in the rock. At night when they come out to hunt insects, the goggles enable her to observe them in the eerie, phosphor-green landscape of the electronically enhanced sniper.

Doug, on the other hand, tracks the bats using radio telemetry. The clicking device is a receiver that picks up the darting creatures' echolocation transmissions as they navigate like miniature stealth fighters through the trees and rocks. "They are the most amazing creatures," he says. "Their echolocation systems are fantastically specialized and they are among the most successful creatures on the planet. Did you know they are one of the most differentiated mammals on earth? There are 975 different species of bats. Only rodents have more species. And they are extremely beneficial. A pregnant or lactating female bat will eat her body weight every night, which is five or six grams of insects."

This site is a key research point for Doug and Faye precisely because of the hot springs. It's a kind of giant maternity ward for bats. He explains: "Bats have such a high rate of metabolism that it's very difficult for them to maintain their body temperature.

Different animals evolve different strategies to solve this problem. Shrews just eat all the time. Others put on a fat layer. But bats have to fly, so they can't put on fat. Their strategy is to use periods of torpor when they slow down their metabolism.

"A bat's normal body temperature is about 37 degrees, just about the same as a human, but in its torpid state that temperature drops to 20 degrees. Here at Hot Springs, pregnant bats congregate and use the same geothermal energy that heats the water. They roost in clefts in the rock where there's steam and in large rubble piles where the rocks are hot. Then, when they've stopped lactating and the babies have flown, they leave again."

There are two groups of bats in which he's primarily interested, both the common little brown bat, which is found in almost all forested habitats in BC, and the much rarer and more solitary Keen's long-eared bat, of which only a few specimens have ever been collected. Knowledge about this species, which is named after the Reverend John Keen, who collected the first specimen more than 100 years ago, is limited to a scattering of sightings ranging from southeast Alaska to the Olympic Peninsula. Only three or four specimens are recorded in BC, mostly from Vancouver Island and around Bella Bella. And, of course, here in the Queen Charlotte Islands. Officially red-listed by the provincial government, Keen's long-eared bat is under active consideration for designation as either an endangered or a threatened species. And this colony at Hot Springs Island is the only known maternal breeding population, which makes the research conducted by Doug and Faye of enormous importance.

What *do* we know?

"Well, I have no idea what they are foraging on right now. There's a fair abundance of moths that they might be foraging on. They may well feed on mosquitoes. But I don't know. It seems to be a coastal species," he says. "The males are solitary. They roost in different trees every night. In 1991 bat researchers estimated the numbers here at about seventy. I'm not getting that. I'm getting the feeling there are maybe half that number."

How can he and Faye tell these tiny, darting creatures — some of them barely larger than your thumb—apart in the dark forest night? That's where the radio telemetry comes in. The different bat species have quite distinctive echolocation transmissions. And to corroborate, there's visual identification using the night goggles. "Keen's long-eared bat flies like a plane evading radar," Doug explains. "It follows the contours of the ground just a foot or so above the underbrush." So he monitors the bat's sound signals while Faye scans the near horizon.

What's the main objective of the research? First: a study of the actual numbers of bats that come to the Hot Springs site to breed and rear their babies and an evaluation of any future risk to their unique habitat and the specialized behaviour they've evolved to exploit it. As the number of visitors to Gwaii Haanas increases, there is likely to be pressure to develop the hot springs from their rustic splendour. There's talk of a Haida big house near the site and improvement to the pools to accommodate more visitors. "Is there [going to be] any impact on that bat colony? There are plans to develop this site further. That might change the thermal flow, which could be critical for the bats. Before any development goes on we should fully understand the ecology of Keen's long-eared bat at this site," Doug says.

Second: where does this rare, solitary animal fit into the elaborate ecology of bats in the province? "We have the northern long-eared bat and the western long-eared bat and they appear almost identical. Are Keen's a separate species? Have these bats been isolated here on the Queen Charlotte Islands for 10,000 years? Are they evolving into a separate sub-species?" His research clearly has implications not only for the province's management of a vulnerable species, but also for our fundamental understanding of the mechanics of evolution itself.

It's now well after sunset and the real work is about to begin. Doug has managed to get a radio tag onto a roosting bat and, when it comes out to feed at night, he's hoping to track it with a hand-held direction finder so that he can understand its range and its roosting behaviour.

"Wanna come?"

So from sunset until close to three in the morning, we clamber into his boat and speed through the narrow passages and along the shorelines of a maze of islands. Doug steers and reads the radio monitor while his passenger holds the direction-finder up into the slipstream and points it where instructed. There are a few clicks and bleeps from other bats, but this target is evasive. "He must be a teenager," says Doug, who has two of his own. "He's only found when he wants to be found." And, indeed, he never is found—until the next day when he turns up in a rock cleft, uncharacteristically roosting with the females.

Doug's career with Parks Canada has taken him and Faye through seven national parks postings including Kluane in the Yukon, Nahanni in the Northwest Territories, Banff and Kootenay parks, and the last nine years here in Gwaii Haanas. How deeply they care about these small, largely misunderstood creatures is evident from their commitment. The couple, married for twenty years, took self-paid leaves of absence from their jobs to carry on with their chronically underfunded research. "I could use another automated bat detector," Doug says. "We need funding for DNA research. I guess we need about $10,000 to do everything that needs to be done." Meanwhile, working with what's available, spending their summers on some of the most remote seascapes in the country, the Batman and his sidekick Faye are laying down the scientific baselines for all that will come after them.

No Wonder
He Took it to Town

The wind whips in across the bow of Torleiv Wold's steel skiff as it skims past what looks like a landscape imagined for *The Lord of the Rings*. The low pressure system that brought heavy rain has layered the sky with overcast and the subtle light that penetrates has an odd quality, as though it were filtered through opals. Masses of cloud are piling up against the mountaintops here on the rugged northern end of Vancouver Island. They tear loose into ragged pennants of grey and white. Beneath them, an incredible palette of greens descends to an iron-coloured sea. There's the vivid green of new growth across old logging cuts, the sombre greens of ancient stands, the verdant green of wet-footed alder marching down the creek beds, the acid green of ground maple and salmonberry crowding the forest edge, the green of grassy meadows just glimpsed among the trees. To get here, I left my truck parked not far from where the arched jawbones of a blue whale commemorate Coal Harbour's reeking past as one of the last of Canada's active whaling stations. Then I strolled to the end of the government dock, killing time by watching deckhands ice down tonnes of ling cod, yellow eye and banded rockfish bound for Vancouver's trendy fresh markets.

Out here, Mother Nature still governs the appointment book. Torleiv said he'd pick me up if the weather was good, otherwise I might as well drive back to Port Hardy and wait. The weather co-operated. Now we're bucking a strong current through the narrows and his 50-horsepower Yamaha kicker slams us through ripples and sends us skittering down the cross chop. In a way, we're passing through barriers of time, returning to a culture and a way of life that's vanishing from British Columbia and its historic coast. Quatsino, where we're bound, is one of the last of those communities that's happily not connected to civilization by the pervasive umbilicus of Canada's road net. Isolation, some call it. Enriching, say the people who live here. Life in Quatsino demands self-reliance and the cultivation of a generalized genius that's vanishing from much of our compartmentalized, specialized, urban, phone-an-expert lives. If your car breaks down in Quatsino, you learn to fix it yourself. If your roof blows off, you figure out how to put on a new one fast. In August, the topic of conversation over dinner is not Senate shenanigans in Ottawa but the flow rate into your well. Nothing in Quatsino is anonymous, faceless, dehumanized. Whether it's for a death or a birth, the whole village, friends and enemies—who ever said you had to like *all* your neighbours?—will be there with genuine grief at a subtraction from the community's collective wisdom or real joy over a new addition to the roll at the one-room, one-teacher school.

Quatsino must be the longest, narrowest community in Canada, a necklace of homes strung along the beach. Eighty-six people live here on the far west side of Vancouver Island, 340 kilometres as the crow flies from the bustle and clamour at Granville and Georgia. And as for national affairs—why, Ottawa is closer to Panama City than it is to Quatsino. Fishing, logging and catch-as-catch-can are the economic mainstays of a community that maintains its fierce independence from the wider world. Yet here you'll also find computers, electronic pianos and satellite dishes. They serve loggers like Andy Hansen, who commutes to work every morning across 10 kilometres of open saltchuck by speedboat, and the last of the West Coast's day fishers—trollermen so confident of their skill that they run without ice and come in to sell fresh-caught salmon each nightfall. I won't get a chance to talk to any of these hardy free-market buccaneers on this visit; they've all departed for Winter Harbour and the summer salmon opening on the open Pacific.

Aboard the skiff, Torleiv sits impassive in a bright-hued canvas deck chair. He's been doing this for most of a long, rich lifetime. But some of us—Doris Wold for one—still find it awesome and exhilarating. Doris is at the wheel today. Torleiv is nursing a heavy plaster cast, having broken his arm in a fall on the treacherous beach boulders. Spray flecks our glasses and her teeth flash as we peel into a long, slow curve to follow the shoreline. The cedars, their dense skirts drooping to the waterline, give way to a sudden clearing and what looks like an abandoned schoolhouse, its windows broken and paint scabbed. This is all that's left of the Quatsino Native village, its people relocated to Coal Harbour and road links to Fort Rupert and the east coast of Vancouver Island. Next a boat house. Then the home of the Russian Old Believers, a small sawmill, smoke curling from the chimney of Annie Howich, Quatsino's reigning elder and for now the settlement's most valued treasure at ninety-four. Finally we're nosing into the log floats and flexing cold, stiff limbs for the walk up to the snug house Torleiv built with his own blunt, calloused hands when Doris was a bride forty-five years ago.

I ease back into the overstuffed sofa of Doris's parlour—and parlour seems the right term in this insufferable age of living rooms, family rooms, dens, studies, lofts and studios—and tickle Ninja, the cat. Brindled in brown and black, the cat has shrewdly decided the visitor on best behaviour is good for at least an hour of mushing up and Ninja is now buzzing like a Pioneer chain saw. I survey photographs of children and grandchildren crowding the top of the upright piano and, having lived in twenty-six houses or apartments in my peripatetic life, contemplate the comfort that comes of dwelling in the same house for forty-two years. Popular culture propels us into the age of mobility where people may pick up and move at the drop of a hat. It's sold as freedom, yet everywhere the price is a sense of rootless ennui. To sell the family home in one city and move to another is routine. "Willingness to relocate" is often part of the job description in a corporate world of management components. And who these days thinks twice about selling and moving across town to a neighbourhood offering just the right schools and services? So, when Doris told her husband Torleiv it was time to pull up stakes in their remote fishing village and move into town for a few years while their three kids went to high school, he took the matter under serious consideration. Some choice. Either the kids did high school by correspondence, or they boarded in town and got up to who knows what—or the family moved.

Torleiv thought about it, then the answer came to him out of the blue. He hitched choker cables to the house he'd built Doris back in 1951, skidded it down the beach and hauled it out onto a barge. Next he floated that house through Quatsino Narrows and around to Coal Harbour on Holberg Inlet. At Coal Harbour he enlisted a donkey engine left over from the days of A-frame logging camps and winched the family home back up the beach to a nice central location in town. Eight years later, when the kids were done with high school, he reversed the process, returning Doris and her house to Quatsino and putting it back into the neat garden with the picket fence and chicken run they occupy today.

Express amazement at this commitment to home and hearth and you draw quizzical looks in a village where families recite genealogies that go back to the first Cape Scott homesteaders a century ago. Doris and Torleiv's son Tony lives next door with his wife Shirley, grandsons Samuel, 5, and Leon, 1, and the granddaughter (everyone devoutly hopes) who's on the way. Some families celebrate fourth generations on the same site. Some individuals have lives that span the four generations, for example Annie

Howich and her sister Helen Sorensen, ninety-one.

Still, to an urban fellow like me, even one who's seen just about everything, it's an astonishing tale. The Canadian Hydrographic Service's sailing directions for these waters are full of warnings about the tidal velocities off Hecate Cove and down through Quatsino Narrows. Swells and weather from the open Pacific funnel down this deep west-coast fjord, arriving finally at a notch in the mountain wall that separates Quatsino Sound from the sheltered inland sea of Holberg Inlet and Rupert Arm. The narrows are one cable wide at the gut, a nautical measure of just over 180 metres. It might be a model for the venturi effect. Flood and ebb tides jet through this opening at high pressure and currents reach almost eight knots. The sailing directions warn of frequent heavy rip tides off Ohlsen Point, Makwazniht Island and Quattische Island. Ask Torleiv about the marine hazards he navigated to move his house and he just shrugs, the way a Toronto taxi driver might if asked by a wide-eyed Quatsino kid about the perils of negotiating the 401 in heavy traffic.

Torleiv came to Quatsino from Norway as an eight-year-old boy in 1929 when the northern end of Vancouver Island was linked to the outside world by steamship or shank's mare. Like most early settlers in these outports, he did a little logging and a lot of fishing, or a little fishing and a lot of logging as circumstances warranted. But he never thought of leaving and if there was ever a man for quiet determination, Torleiv Wold is it. Just ask Doris.

She met him on April Fool's Day, 1948. She was a fresh-minted nurse from New Westminster on duty at the little hospital in Port Alice, a pulp mill town up Neroutsos Inlet. Torleiv came in as an emergency—and a pretty grave one, at that—after a log had rolled on him and smashed both legs. But he took a shine to his nurse— or she did to him, it depends on whom you ask—and on August 28 that same year they were married. "That was a whirlwind romance, considering I spent a good part of the time in Vancouver

General Hospital," he says, waving for emphasis the plastered arm. It took a long time for Torleiv to recover, but he had his obligations to his new bride. He had a house to build. "He was still on crutches when he built this house," says Doris with a shake of her head. No wonder he took it with him when he went to town.

Panhandle Pete

Almost a thousand kilometres north of Vancouver's high-tech steel and glass, past industrial Prince Rupert and the A-B Line that marks the boundary between British Columbia and Alaska, the primeval salmon coast just keeps on going. Shrouded in drifting fogs, pounded by some of the continent's heaviest rainfalls, clearing occasionally into a stunning panorama of forest, ocean and sky that is edged with a glittering wall of snowy mountains, this coast twists away into a maze of narrow, glacier-fed channels between thousands of islands. Ospreys stoop to take fish from the sea just off the Ketchikan docks, porpoises ride the bow waves of fish boats, humpback whales blow and, a little farther up coast, some of the world's biggest bears can be seen padding the shoreline between high water and the dense, gloomy tangles of spruce and cedar. But it's here, in a deceptively simple world that seems insulated from politics and the boardroom, beyond the control of far away Ottawa or distant Victoria, that the complicated future of the Canadian fishery may be shaped.

This is the Alaska Panhandle. It droops 800 kilometres southward from "Seward's Folly," the vast Alaskan peninsula that the United States purchased from the Russians for two cents an acre in the same year that Canada was founded as a country. Twice the size of Ireland, measured inland from tidewater to the height of land according to an acrimonious 1905 border deal, southeast Alaska's coastline is almost as long as the BC coast that stretches from

Victoria to Dixon Entrance. Eight great rivers carve through the mountains that crumple skyward out of the slow collision between the Pacific and North American plates. Their immense, still pristine watersheds in the BC Interior produce the salmon with which these nutrient-rich northern waters teem. But harvesting the silver bounty is not without risk. The narrow canals of southeast Alaska can act as weather funnels, accelerating winds and six-metre tides from the North Pacific. The combination can transform open crossings between islands into a maelstrom of wicked tide rips and cross chops that make them among the most treacherous on the planet.

A rangy, red-haired forty-six-year-old, Peter Knutson is one of the men and women who fish these icy waters for a living. He's had friends drown. His own boat sank under him. He has been on the rocks, been scared spitless by the elements and endured the vicissitudes of uncertain runs and even less certain market prices. He's been doing this for thirty years. "This" means one of the most hazardous occupations in the modern United States, sleep deprivation, cramped accommodations that Knutson likens to "living in a tool shed," physical labour that would daunt a hod-carrier and separation from his family in Seattle from June to September. Yet when he talks about it, diffident about the intensity of his feelings for the hard life he's chosen, Knutson doesn't sound so different from his Canadian counterparts south of the A-B Line.

"Hey," he says, "what I hear in the bar in Prince Rupert is the same talk that I hear in the bar in Ketchikan. How are we going to make it?

"My most vivid memory of the bar in Prince Rupert is a guy vomiting and the bartender spraying him with Lysol. I can tell you from Ketchikan that the smell of Lysol is the same on both sides of the border.

"I'm not trying to get rich. I don't want a bigger boat or a bigger house or more debt. I just want to make a sustainable living from a sustainable resource. The dream of small boat fishing is a great dream," he says. "It's a dream of autonomy. It's a dream of living in harmony with these amazing, incredible creatures."

To achieve that dream, he chances the stormy weather, running his small 10-metre boat hundreds of kilometres to openings, setting and hauling nets up to seventy-two hours at a stretch with little or no sleep, dressing his catch on a pitching deck with razor-sharp knives, then racing for home while the fish are still fresh enough to bring premium prices in Seattle fish markets. "When do conditions preclude me fishing? Basically, only when I stop catching salmon in my net—that's when I stop fishing. Half to two-thirds of my season is fishing in heavy weather." Taking risks with the weather, he says, knowing how and where to catch fish when others head for harbour—that's his edge.

In some ways, for all the satellite navigation aids, cruise ships and jet traffic linking the Panhandle to outside civilization, the salmon coast that Knutson fishes resembles the BC coast of half a century ago. The state's population is half of Greater Vancouver's and the entire population of the Panhandle's eight towns and scattered outports would fit into BC Place with seats to spare. While the raw patches of clear-cuts and the haze of the odd pulp mill can be seen, the landscape has so far largely escaped the habitat-gobbling industrial development and urban sprawl that put BC's Georgia Basin and the south coast at risk—which is one reason these waters still teem with almost unbelievable numbers of coho, chinook, sockeye, pink, chum and steelhead.

The astonishing abundance of Alaska's salmon resource dwarfs BC's. Although the oil-rich state obtains 90 percent of its revenue from petroleum that accounts for 25 percent of US production, the largest private sector employer is still fishing. In 1996, Alaska's catch was over 175 million salmon, 86 million of them from the waters where Knutson fishes, with a total landed value of $366 million. That compares to a 1996 catch of 15 million salmon in BC, with a landed value of $96 million. Historically, about five percent of the Alaskan catch has been coho, predominantly in the panhandle fishery, while chinook have accounted for an even smaller proportion—often less than one percent. But percentages are deceptive. In real terms, the Alaskan fishing pressure on coho has increased almost fivefold, from about 1.5 million fish in 1970 to the present average of 6 million.

This increase in fishing pressure on a migratory species that originates in Canadian as well as American waters is the source of much of the present tension between the two countries. In recent years, degraded by overfishing on both sides of the border and by poor ocean survival rates attributed to the El Niño phenomenon, coho stocks returning to northern BC rivers have declined steeply and the declines appear to occur in direct inverse proportion to increased fishing pressure in Alaska. Canadian scientists are blunt. They say up to 70 percent of the mortalities suffered by the deeply depressed Skeena River stocks are directly attributable to the fishery in southeast Alaska. The Alaskans counter with claims that apparent increases in their percentage of the catch are a function of declines in the Canadian catch. Furthermore, they say, a brutal Canadian bycatch while fishing for Skeena-bound sockeye is to blame for coho declines. There seems to be some truth on both sides. Even Canadian figures show Alaska's interception of Canadian-bound coho declined steadily from 1.1 million in 1994 to 450,000 in 1997.

In any event, Knutson argues, while Canadians cry about Alaskan interceptions of their fish, many of those salmon caught in Alaskan waters are taken by boats working for big BC companies that straddle the border. "These corporations don't have any national interests. There are very large Canadian processors here in southeast Alaska. Canadian processors are buying salmon up here. A BC Packers guy said to me, 'If you have a good season, we'll have a good season.'" Knutson says that when Canada imposed a transit fee on fish boats travelling to Alaska from Puget Sound, "the Canadian companies they fish for up here paid their transit fee for them."

He has a point. Even the BC government's fisheries statistics acknowledge that in 1996 almost half the 990,000 cases of canned salmon exported from the province consisted of fish caught in Alaska but processed by BC companies. In fact, Knutson points out, Canadian companies are big in the Noyes Island and Tree Point fisheries—precisely the spots identified by Canadian government scientists as key chokepoints where most BC-bound coho and sockeye are intercepted. Is it valid for Canadian and Alaskan fishers to point fingers at each other, the Alaska skipper wonders, or are they really allies in a bigger confrontation between a transborder corporate model of vertically-integrated industrial efficiency and small independent operators like himself?

"We have to start thinking about the fish," he says. "We have to get beyond the institutionalized greed that resides at an almost unconscious level. We have to get beyond the sideshows and circuses that our governments are propagating.

"In southeast Alaska we've had massive centralization. We now have two or three companies controlling everything. Things can't go on as they are, driven by industrial priorities rather than ecological sustainability. I think these elements are responsible for prolonging this so-called salmon war. It's in their interests to pursue an industrial strategy where they are not constrained by concerns for the survival of weak stocks.

"If they are allowed to pursue their drive for greater and greater industrial efficiencies—which are social inefficiencies—it will lead to the destruction of the resource."

In the meantime, he acknowledges, there is a lingering resentment of the Canadian government's decision to use the safety of fishing crews bound for Alaska as leverage in the fish wars. Everywhere you go you hear anecdotes like the one about the

Brenda K, passing through Johnstone Strait when four Canadian fish boats began forcing her to the side of the channel.

"He had his young son on board and he was frightened to death," Knutson says. "That's not right. When Glen Clark starts coming in and advocating that small boat operators should risk their lives at sea—this is really bizarre, a union man calling for increased danger for workers in what's already the most dangerous occupation in the country—my blood just boils. The NDP is supposed to be a socialist government, isn't it? It's more like National Socialism. I don't mean to compare them to the Nazis, just to point out that socialism gets pretty ugly when it's nationalistic.

"On both sides of the border, these guys [politicians] who are posturing and throwing nationalist rhetoric about have to be responsible for their actions, they have to be held accountable for saying things that can have huge impacts on individuals."

But Knutson doesn't have much time to debate the fine points of blame on this occasion. He's scrambling to get his boat ready for the first opening of the season, which takes place at 12:01 p.m. the next day. He has grub to get aboard, gear to check and last-minute gab with fellow gillnetters like Mike Duncan, whose boat the *Paula D* actually has a figurehead, a plastic dinosaur, "leading us to extinction"—by which he means the small boat fishers, not the fish. Knutson's boat *Loki,* which he bought for $33,000 in 1979, is a slender blue and white vessel that might serve as a metaphor for what her owner calls "the unitary culture" of the salmon coast that stretches from California to Alaska: *Loki* was built in New Westminster in 1959.

Powered by a World War II landing craft engine, she's strictly a work boat with a cramped single-bunk foc's'le—he and his deckhand will hot bunk during openings, otherwise one will grab his catnaps on the deck—and a wheelhouse that's jammed with electronic navigation aids, depth-sounders, digital monitors, radar screens, an auto-helm, radio gear and the ubiquitous cell phone. A big metal drum with 600 metres of hand-tinted gillnet—some panels of mesh are green for sockeye, some are pale blue for coho—hydraulic winches, the motorized lead-line kicker and net levellers crowd the stern. Amidships are a tangle of hoses the size of your forearm and two large fish holds, their hatch covers customized as gutting tables. This is the technological innovation that permits Knutson to survive and prosper as an independent operator. The hoses, using a pumping system designed and installed by himself, flush fresh seawater into the holds where two huge chilling coils let him cool the water to temperatures below the freezing point of fresh water.

Salmon are dressed as they are caught and immediately immersed in a bath of freezing salt water. When he gets back to port after an opening the fish are packed into insulated boxes and flown out fresh to Seattle markets on the next plane. That's the reason for the cell phone. He's in constant touch with his wife, Hing, in Seattle, informing her of the precise details of his catch as it comes over the side. She's the marketer. "Our fish are sold even as they go into the hold," he says. "And we can take custom orders right on the boat." Want a case of chum for the smoker? A big chinook for a wedding buffet? Fresh coho for a backyard barbecue? He delivers. That agility and pinpoint accuracy in responding to high-end niche market demand is something no big corporation can achieve, he says. The inertia of size condemns them to mass-marketing and lower quality.

This first opening of the 1998 gillnet season will take Knutson about 125 kilometres out of Ketchikan, the former Tlingit village whose 8,000 residents now sprawl down the east side of Tongass Narrows, a sheltered gut between Prince of Wales Island and Revillagidedo Island. To get to the remote fishing grounds at *Loki*'s seven knots means a nine-hour run to the north bucking the tide. It's a rough run. A northwest wind battles the current and the waves stack up into a steep chop, changing in colour from steel grey to gunmetal blue. It buries the stem in creamy foam, splattering the wheelhouse with spindrift and frosting the glass with patterns of salt. "See that shore." Knutson points northeast to the cliffs and 2,700-metre outcrops of the Cleveland Peninsula. "There's no place to hide from the weather there. The hills act like a funnel for the wind and you get these monstrous tides. Just under the surface it's a jungle of reefs and shoals. Tides from three directions meet here. You get weather from the southeast over a tide running the other way and this is the most God-forsaken place on earth. It's just hellishly evil when the wind is blowing."

The son of a Lutheran minister, Knutson got himself kicked out of Stanford University in 1972 for his anti-war protests and made his way to fishing, first as a deckhand on purse-seiners, then to his own boat. Along the way, he completed college and even took a Ph.D. in anthropology at the University of Washington. "I wrote my dissertation on my life as a fisherman, an analysis of language and power," he says. During the off-season he even teaches a course in American culture at an inner-city college in Seattle, but every summer he's back at his real occupation.

With night falling and many kilometres yet to go, Knutson decides to duck into Meyer's Chuck, a tiny pocket of calm that provides the only safe moorage on this stretch of coast. The harbour entrance is a narrow, almost invisible notch in the rock that requires a sharp right-hand turn at the entrance. "It's pretty scary trying to get in here when it's really blowing," he says. "You basically have to ride this huge surf and try to shoot the hole. But man, it's nice in here when it's blowing 60 knots outside."

It's now midnight, but there's to be no sleep yet. A coupling on the power take-off that runs *Loki*'s refrigeration system has disintegrated. If it can't be fixed there's no point in fishing. Knutson disappears into the grimy bowels of the boat and re-emerges with a rotting cardboard box. In it is the replacement coupling he's been carrying for a decade for just such a crisis. Then, with help from

Mark Johansen whose *Cora J,* another New Westminster-built gill-netter, is tied up alongside, he spends the night tearing down and refitting the damaged coupling.

At 6 a.m. he's underway again, clearing out to make way for the float plane that's due in on a sched run. By noon, Knutson is on the fishing grounds, *Loki* positioned within a few metres of the boundary thanks to the precision placement permitted by a global positioning system that triangulates from satellites in stationary orbit. There are only two other boats. All this high tech is one thing, he admits. The fish are another thing entirely.

"Are they going to be here, that's the gamble," he says. "You can't out-think the fish but you can out-think the other fishermen. That's the fun of it.

"I tell newcomers, don't run around trying to catch fish. Learn one beach until you know it like the back of your hand. If you know every reef and rock, every eddy of tide and what the wind does to it, you can always scratch out something. But some of these new guys, they don't even know how to mend a net and they don't want to know. They just buy a new net.

"You know, I've got an old boat, but I know every system on her. She's like an extension of my body. I can take this boat apart and put her back together with my eyes closed. And I don't have a lot of capital tied up in her. I own her. I don't have to catch huge volumes of fish to service my debt. I can go for value-added and small volumes and make it quite nicely."

Starting his sets within a boat-length of the rocky shoreline, he pays out 300 fathoms of net, curving it into the tide and letting it drift for ninety minutes. He'll do this for the next seventy-two hours, changing position to adapt to winds and currents, grabbing brief catnaps between sets. If the fish come fast, there's little sleep at all because they have to be dressed and chilled right out of the nets. Meals are wolfed on the run, but there are two hedonistic concessions. There's a microwave oven adapted to run off the engine—and an espresso machine.

"Nothing like a hot latte at first light," he grins. "My last deckhand, we were fishing halibut out in the gulf [of Alaska]. I hired that guy full-time after he made a perfect latte in that six-foot swell."

Then, with the sea a bowl of brushed pewter reflecting a mother of pearl sky, he dons his oilskins and goes back to haul net, picking out the perfectly proportioned sockeye and the blunt silver bullets of coho. He drops the fish into tubs of chilled water to bleed, sets a new drift and dresses the salmon. At night, the deck starkly illuminated by floodlights, the dark swells alive with flashes of phosphorescence, he keeps on fishing. "You see strange things out here," he says. "Once my net filled with dogfish, so many I couldn't pull it in. I had to cut it loose as they dragged it under. All you could see was this glow of green eyes spiralling down in the dark."

What about the accidental bycatch of other species? Knutson says a gillnetter who knows his beach and currents should have almost none. Indeed, in this seventy-two hours of fishing his bycatch consists of two steelhead, one of which he releases alive—the dead one he keeps to give to a cargo-hand at the airport—a tommy cod, a Dolly Varden trout and a sea bass, all of which he'll eat himself. Later that night, a sea lion is in his nets. No panic, though. He starts the engine, pulls the net taut and pops the big sea mammal out like a tennis ball.

Knutson's last set comes out of the water three minutes before closing. His catch is 269 coho, 195 sockeye, 33 chum, nine chinook, eight pink and two steelhead—about four tonnes of salmon dressed and ready to ship, with a gross value of around $10,000. Then it's the run "back to K-town" and a long night of packing fish into boxes and trucking them to the airport. Tomorrow he'll sleep. But not for long. There are boxes to make for the next shipment, nets to mend, gear to fix, and then it's time for the next opening.

Behind *Loki* a following sea hisses under the stern. The wind is with her this time and she surges forward. Suddenly, the sun breaks through the clouds, gleaming off the mountains. The sea turns brilliant blue, every wave crest a tossing white plume. "Yeah," Knutson grins. "Another tough day at the office. How do you like the view from the executive suite?"

The Soul
of British Columbia

Every summer about 500 kilometres southwest of this austere ridge atop Fraser's Pass, the dusky sandstone ledges at Russell Beach ring with laughter as the kids of Saturna Island gather to cavort like gleaming porpoises in the warm plume of the Fraser River. The plume swirls out across the Strait of Georgia and eddies southward along the tilted sedimentary plates of Galiano, Mayne and Saturna islands, sliding over the colder, denser marine waters from the north Pacific like a cup of coffee spilled over a green glass tabletop. For the children who come down from Winter Harbour or over the hump from Breezy Bay, the milky sheen that accompanies the Fraser's freshet signals another brief opportunity to swim where it is usually cold enough to freeze the knuckles off a brass monkey.

If it seems a stretch of the imagination to contemplate a swimming beach in the Gulf Islands from a vantage point amid the snowfields crowning the Rocky Mountains along Alberta's border, it's not. These places are vitally connected. They are the terminal points of this great river that is a manifestation of the hydrological cycle upon which all British Columbians depend for life. A flow that rises on the massifs between Casemate Glacier and the Hooker Icefield finally passes out of Canadian territory just beyond Boiling Reef off Saturna's arid East Point. To scientists like Otto Langer, who's spent the last decade worrying on behalf of the federal government about the Fraser and its future, it's a reminder of the profound way in which all the streams, creeks and rivers that empty into Georgia Strait form the meshes of an ecological web. The complex interlacing of waterways is most evident from the kind of detailed satellite mapping conducted for the environment ministry's geographic data branch by geographers like Malcolm Gray, the senior image analyst in Victoria. At a scale base of 1:50,000, the spidery network of river and streams whose drainage sets the boundaries for 952 watersheds in the Georgia Basin, is enough to overwhelm the eye. "How many streams in total?" Gray laughs in response. He knows the answer is both arbitrary and relative. "Depending on the scale you use, probably almost infinite." In the case of the Fraser, its fluid strands bind the fate of the inland sea to an interior ecosystem so vast at 235,671 square kilometres that it dwarfs some European countries. If it begins as a few icy droplets of fresh water in the high country, the Fraser eventually pours out across the shoals and mud flats of the Sandheads in such volume and force that it affects everything from the chemistry to the physics of Georgia Strait. The Fraser's plume dilutes the adjacent ocean, reducing salinity, while the drag of the river's current passing above colder layers creates an upwelling of nutrient-rich water from the deeps just off the estuary, providing for a teeming catalogue of species from cetaceans to molluscs. As many as 800 million juvenile salmon migrate down the Fraser to the sea each year and up to 20 million salmon can be in the estuary on any given day. The muddy shoreline, the sloughs and side channels, the bogs and marshes of its delta are an essential component in the great migratory bird corridor that links South America to the Arctic. Approximately 750,000 waterfowl and 1.2 million shore birds share the mud flats, beaches and sloughs with more than 300 species of invertebrates.

Increasingly, as scientists like Langer learn more, they speak less and less in terms of discrete marine, riparian and terrestrial ecosystems, and more often in terms of how all these biomes are linked together into one astonishing ecology that extends from ocean floor to mountain peak. From hot-blooded grizzly bears to cold-blooded salamanders, from soaring eagles to bottom-hugging sturgeon, from woodland caribou browsing on the lichens of ancient forests to the rare and seldom seen ghost pipes fungus of the Lower Mainland, from the solitary steelhead to the more than three million human beings crowded along the Fraser's banks to the billions of nearly invisible invertebrates in the bottom ooze—all are part of a complicated and only partially understood equilibrium in which what affects one must ultimately affect all. The strands that most obviously link these organic components are the glittering ribbons of moving water which replenish the oceans and are replenished in turn by the seasonal cycle of rain and snow; which create corridors of vegetation through a desert land-scape; which provide habitats for species great and small. But this miraculous tapestry is at risk of being torn irreparably by a host of threats including industry, agriculture and urban sprawl generated by the three million people who have come to live in the watershed in the last hundred years.

For the year 2000 the Fraser River was ranked third on the endangered rivers list that's compiled annually by the Outdoor Recreation Council of BC. Two other rivers among those consid-ered most at risk are the Coquitlam—a major tributary of the Fraser—and the Englishman River on Vancouver Island. A fourth is the Tsolum at Courtenay, which means that four of the five most endangered rivers in BC are found in the Georgia Basin. Yet this is not a localized phenomenon. It's part of a growing global trend. Even up in the thin air of the high alpine, this pristine snow is already polluted with heavy metals, hydrocarbons and pesticides like DDT. Banned in Canada because of the toxic effects for fish and birds outlined by Rachel Carson in her seminal work *Silent Spring*, DDT is still used in some places, and it is only one of many chemicals blowing in from Asia on the jetstream. Although the phenomenon is now attracting the worried interest of scientists, fish boat crews off the Queen Charlotte Islands were warning a decade ago that when the wind was right they could smell the dead, metallic stench of China's factories.

More than half the world's major rivers are now deemed at risk by the World Commission on Water for the twentieth century. The commission is a collection of international agencies under the umbrella of the United Nations, which is concerned that overuse and misuse of fresh water is now so severe that not only are the rivers themselves in jeopardy, but also their surrounding ecosystems and the people who inhabit them. Only 10 percent of the Nile's flow actually reaches the floodplains that were the cradle of Egyptian civilization for 5,000 years; the Yang-tze, which waters China's most important agricultural region, ran dry in its lower reaches for 226 days in 1997; 97 percent of Russia's Volga is unsafe to drink; and even the Ganges, the holy river of India, is so depleted as to threaten the mangrove forests of Bangladesh. In 1999, the number of refugees from various ecological crises in watersheds— about 25 million people—exceeded those fleeing military conflicts for the first time in known human history. If the current trend holds, the report warned, the number of persons displaced by water-related environmental disaster could reach 100 million by 2025. This is not just a third-world problem. The commission, which was chaired by World Bank vice-president Ismail Serageldin, concluded that North American freshwater species now face a risk of extinction five times higher than for terrestrial species because of the mismanagement of rivers like the Colorado, in which 90 percent of the flow is diverted for irrigation or lost to evaporation behind dams.

From the scientific evidence, it's unequivocally clear that no serious discussion of the fate of the Strait of Georgia can ignore the collective fate of the rivers that feed it, nurture it, provide marine corridors into the heart of the continent, shape its weather and create a complex series of interfaces between mountain and valley, land and sea, earth and sky—and, of course, connect the present and the future to the past. But to find the true story of the Fraser, one must go to the source—in the stark shadows of an immense arc of mountains known as the Ramparts. They curve along the Alberta border, as remote from the alluvial flats of Lulu Island as anything in British Columbia. The icy trickles seeping from the snowfields will eventually water the otherwise arid valleys of BC's cordilleran rain shadow and bring the simple joys of summer to a bunch of Gulf Islands kids. For it is with these clear, already polluted droplets that the Fraser begins its incredible journey to the sea.

To find the Fraser's source I work backwards from tidewater, travelling up-country through landscapes so different they might serve as metaphors for the Asian concept of yin and yang—wet to dry, low to high, flat to rugged, warm to cold, lush to stark, civilization to wilderness, big city clamour to places that know only the sound of wind and water. It's also a trip through time. The Fraser carves its own 12-million-year-old fault-line through geological epochs, from the newly deposited sediments of its delta that are the bedrock of the future to high-elevation formations so ancient that some of them bear traces of the origins of life itself. In its descent to the sea, the river also marks off the whole brief history of the human presence in BC.

Everywhere you go on the Fraser River you can hear it talking, but to heed its stories, you have to look as well as listen carefully. Near tidewater, the river slides seaward past the landings of the Greasy Grass people like a muscular, coffee-coloured python, coiling down the hulls of tugboats struggling upstream. Curling along the log booms and tearing at the islands of silt near the Musqueam Indian Reserve, the slick hiss of the current makes a permanent undertow of sound, as insistent in charter skipper Paul Kendrick's ears as the eternal noise of the ether is from an astronomer's radiotelescope. Behind the undulating noise of traffic on the Port Mann bridge, punctuated by the squeals of cranes dropping bales of crushed cars onto barges and the rhythm line of piledrivers, the voice of the river is always there, whispering in the background. In the canyons above Yale, amplified in the echo chambers of solid rock that the Fraser has carved from the hearts of the upstart coastal mountains, the river speaks to awestruck tourists and Pacific Salmon Commission biologists alike in a thunderous, earth-shaking, godlike bellow that drives all but the simplest thoughts from the mind. At Lytton, where its confluence with the clear-running Thompson creates a brief window of green, translucent light in the muddy torrent, tree planter Ingmar Lee swims in the clear eddy, submerges, listens in wonder to the millions of tonnes of silt particles whispering past in the opaque wall of the main current and finds a transcendent experience. From Roy Howard's meadow near the village of Dunster in the Rocky Mountain Trench, the river sings a throaty melody behind a bright, crisp chorus of trembling aspen, willow, poplar and snowberry rustling in the high mountain breeze. Beyond this deciduous fringe along the Fraser are the gloomier stands of the world's most extensive examples of a rare "antique" inland rain forest, thought by lichen scientist Trevor Goward to contain one of the longest unbroken biological traditions of any forested inland region in the world.

Up here in the Selwyn Range, a few hundred metres from the Alberta border and two-and-a-half kilometres higher than Vancouver, the voice is not one but a myriad—the shrill, bright laughter of water sprites where icicles drip, snowbanks slump into meltwater and everything is in motion. We all know instinctively what the Fraser is saying, although most of us might find it difficult to express. That's because the language we share with the river is one not of words but of profound archetypes buried deep in the primordial unconscious. For all our advanced technology and sophisticated self-assurance, these archetypes still connect us to our humble origins in the natural kingdom. The river calls us to all that is untamed, reminds us that there are still forces at work that may dwarf our achievements, forces that might sweep them away in the twinkling of an eye, as even the supposedly domesticated Red, Mississippi and Yellow rivers did in recent years when they breached their levees—and the Fraser has done and still threatens to do on occasion. Could the floods of 1894 and 1948, when much of the Fraser Valley was inundated, happen again? The answer, even with our twenty-first-century dikes and levees, channels and spillways, is yes. As recently as 1997, a greater volume of water passed through the Fraser in the midsummer freshet than came downriver during the devastating flood half a century before. Luckily for the Lower Mainland, weather conditions co-operated to average the flow instead of sending it seaward in one spike that would have overwhelmed the dikes.

If the river carries an inherent threat, it also carries an intrinsic promise. In every culture on the planet, from ancient Celt to modern Hindu, from Babylon on the Euphrates to the Nlaka'pamux on the Fraser, whether on the Nile, the Congo, the Amazon or the Mekong, the river remains the enduring metaphor for the recurring miracle of life. To the ancient Egyptians, the great river at the heart of their civilization sprang from the loins of the sun god Atum, himself, and the Nile's annual flooding that brought nutrients to replenish the croplands was seen as heaven's act of procreation. Mesopotamians believed the same of the mythic figure Enki and the Tigris. If these beliefs seem far-removed from the Fraser, archaeologist Timothy Taylor points out that beliefs like these are among the often unacknowledged footings on which the whole edifice of our collective human psychology is built.

The river is still perceived as a purifying force that rises, like the Ganges, from the sacred source of godhead itself. And the river marks the boundary between temporal life and the spiritual dimension. The Styx separates our world from the old Greeks' idea of Hades just as Japan's Sanzu-no-kawa, the river of three ways, brings the dead to their fate. Marcus Aurelius sees life itself as a flimsy leaf carried past our vantage point on the current of a river that rises somewhere beyond our vision and passes away from us into the unknown and beyond understanding. Homer's *Iliad* personifies the river Skamander in the form of an immortal supernatural warrior. From the Romans, the crossing of the Rubicon by Julius Caesar and his legions has entered the Western canon as the metaphor that represents an irreversible decision. In our time, Aleksandr Solzhenitsyn uses the river as a symbol of the irrepressible will of the Russian people and C.S. Forester uses the river to conceptualize the nature of time itself. Aboriginal peoples belonging to the eight linguistic groups of the watershed know the Fraser as the bringer of fertility to barren landscapes, the eternal cauldron of abundance from which her children may forever dip their sustenance. Not so different from us, perhaps.

Dave Marshall, executive director of the Fraser Basin Council, an organization charged with finding ways to implement policies that will reconcile environmental, economic and social values in the basin, points out that 80 percent of BC's economy and 10 percent of Canada's gross domestic product are generated each year in this one river's watersheds and floodplains. To scientists, the river is the spine of an ecosystem that extends from the bottom of the sea to the summits of the mountains. If the hydrological cycle of evaporation and precipitation is the breathing of the earth, gathering water from the oceans and depositing it as rain or snow, then the river is its pulse, the pulmonary artery by which nutrients are carried to the sea, the land is replenished and the process renewed all over again.

Perhaps it's not surprising, then, that the Fraser River, draining a watershed as big as the state of Washington but contained entirely within the province—a throbbing 1,399-kilometre-long umbilical cord that connects the Strait of Georgia to the high peaks of the Rocky Mountains—is so often characterized as the soul of British Columbia. "No man stands beside the Fraser River without sensing the precarious hold of his species upon the earth," observed the Vancouver *Sun*'s Bruce Hutchison in his matchless biography of the river, authored more than fifty years ago but as fresh as anything written today. "In this grisly trench, bored out of solid rock through unimaginable time by the scour of brown water, the long history of lifeless matter, the pitifully brief record of life, the mere moment of man's existence, are suddenly legible."

Nowhere is the gathering power of the river more evident than at its mountain source. Getting to the beginning means chartering a $900-an-hour helicopter at Valemount, flying south with pilot Keith Westfall along Canoe Reach where the Columbia River backs up behind the Mica Dam, then turning east through clear-cuts that seem puny in contrast to the 30-kilometre-long gorge that Ptarmigan Creek has carved between 2,700-metre-high ridges. At the end of this vista of hanging valleys, glaciers, naked rock faces and avalanche chutes where huge grizzlies browse on new growth, there's a brief rise of land and then you're over, into the remote trough gouged between the Brule Hills and the Ramparts by the Fraser and its ancestors, the ice age glaciers that are still in retreat. It's a reminder that the river we see appears as it does only for our moment of time. Considered on the geological scale, the Fraser is the swiftest of shape-shifters, sometimes a raging cataract, other times bulked up by eons of snow into a slow-moving tongue of ice powerful enough to pulverize entire mountain ranges.

Another 35 kilometres to the south the slope steepens and the turbulent mountain stream dwindles, stutters, vanishes under midsummer snowdrifts, emerges again farther up, until it's a trickle that's almost invisible from the air. This is Mount Robson Provincial Park and landing is not permitted in the fragile alpine meadows, so we circle west, land on a ridge just outside the boundary and hike back to find the highest seep, where the Fraser can truly be said to begin. The ridge is anchored at one end by the crags of Black Rock Mountain, at the other by the uplands on the other side of Fraser Pass. Land falls away in three directions from here. To the east, it drains into Alberta's Athabasca River, to the southeast into the Columbia and to the northwest thousands of streamlets converge to create the mainstem of the Fraser. That source we're seeking is at the highest point, a tiny trickle barely the span of a hand, which oozes from the hummocky sedges of this alpine tundra. For this is an Arctic landscape not so different from the one once inhabited by mammoths and cave bears. There is nothing but snow, ice, scoured rock, the scudding shadows of clouds and the sound of wind and moving water.

Even here in this austere landscape, life is amazing in its abundance and adaptability. Plants here have evolved special thermal insulation, huddling together in communities that maximize their hold on the thin soil, trap air and moderate their temperatures. Surprisingly, this high altitude expanse of naked stone, searing ultraviolet radiation, extreme temperatures, violent winds and deep snow is one of the most ferociously sexy places on earth. Because summer is so short, flowering alpine plants must complete their entire reproductive cycle in a matter of weeks, which explains the explosive annual eruption of mountain wildflowers so beloved of photographers and naturalists. The spectacular bloom on otherwise small and drab plants is evidence of a heavy investment in the strategy of sacrificing overall size and strength for the relatively large, prolific, briefly displayed and extremely showy flowers that adorn their reproductive organs. It's here from a humble beginning among the sedges, lichens and wildflowers that the river gathers its momentum toward the sea, swollen by the contributions of its tributaries large and small—the Raush and the Goat, Stuart, Nechako and Quesnel, Chilko and Horsefly, the mighty Thompson, the Bridge, the Anderson, the Pitt and the Coquitlam—until, at peak flow, it can be moving as much as 1.2 million cubic metres of water a minute into the Strait of Georgia. Try visualizing the volume this way: imagine the water in blocks the size of a football field cubed, with one of these massive objects moving past your front door every sixty seconds. It's against this seemingly irresistible force that the silver-sided hordes of salmon swim each year in one of those natural miracles that seem commonplace on the Fraser.

Not far downstream from the source—barely 90 kilometres as the crow flies and still more than 1,200 kilometres from tidewater—the river plunges over a ledge of harder rock, cascading into a deep pool with a thundering resonation that can be heard more than a kilometre away. This is Overlander Falls, the last insurmountable challenge to the few mighty chinook strong enough to pass the barrier of Rearguard Falls a few kilometres downstream. They and the sockeye of the Stuart River are the farthest travellers of the salmon nations that inhabit the complex network of tributaries and lakes that made the Fraser the greatest natural salmon factory in the world. Before the ravages of European industrial exploitation, the Fraser is thought to have produced as many as 150 million salmon a year at the peak of their cycles. Musqueam, Straits

Salish, Sto:lo, Nlaka'pamux, Stl'atl'imx, Chilcotin, Carrier, Secwepemc, in all more than forty aboriginal nations relied—and still rely—on salmon runs considered so central to their cultural existence that the Supreme Court of Canada has ruled that they have a prior constitutional right to the fish for food, ceremonial and social use.

Even today, in the aftermath of overfishing, mining, shoddy logging in the watersheds and the degradation of water quality with pulp mill effluents and sewage, the drainage basin is still home to hundreds of genetically unique salmon stocks. It still produces 60 percent of the salmon caught in BC waters. The river is also home to 41 species of non-salmonid fish and another 46 species that are distinct to the slower-moving estuary with its tidal flows. Some of these species are in a state of ecological crisis. The mysterious green sturgeon, one of only three saltwater sturgeon species in the world and the only one in the Pacific, has been in a steady state of decline for three decades; eulachon returns to the Fraser are dwindling; and a rare and distinctive race of chum salmon from Jones Creek near Hope is thought to have become extinct as recently as 1998.

Ross Howard, now co-ordinator for the Fraser Headwaters Alliance, a non-profit organization whose mission is "to maintain and restore the ecosystem health and the natural beauty of the Canoe and Robson valleys and all the watersheds associated with them," homesteaded on the banks of the upper Fraser twenty-seven years ago. "Jill and I brought our first-born right from the maternity ward in Prince George to a shack. My mother wasn't very impressed," he laughs. Today they live in the comfortable log house they built and have even mellowed enough to let the highways department graders plow out the drive so Jill can get to her teaching job in McBride. "This is really a unique headwaters area," he says of the landscape that gripped his imagination so long ago.

"We have four of the biggest rivers in North America—the Athabasca, the Columbia, the Thompson and the Fraser—all rising within 50 kilometres of each other." Squeeze into the cab of Howard's battered four-by-four pickup, with the rolls of duct tape and baling wire hung on the stick shift for emergency repairs, and he'll take you down for a look at the Fraser you seldom see. The slick green expanse is right up to the edge of its banks, seething and slithering under the dip and splatter of willow leaves, churned here and there by sweepers—semi-toppled trees that are dragged under by the current until they work loose and come back to the surface with a shuddering, churning, canoe-destroying roar. "To me, the Fraser is the heart and lifeblood of BC," Howard says. "Whatever you do to the headwaters, you do to the whole river. Most people in BC live in the Fraser River watershed and it's the basis of much of their economic prosperity.

"The biggest threat to the river here in the headwaters is over-harvesting of forests in the watershed. The long-term harvest level here is 340,000 cubic metres of wood per year, but the annual allowable cut is around 650,000 cubic metres. It will ultimately have an effect on fish. It hasn't happened yet, but it will. Where they log the steep slopes we're seeing siltation and slope failures. Sustainability of timber resources is just a huge issue for me."

From Howard's homestead, the river meanders through the gentler terrain of the Robson Valley in a series of loops and oxbows that seem more appropriate to a lazy prairie river. But it's just a brief rest from the headlong plunge to the sea and it picks up the pace again as it approaches Prince George. If there's a symbol of the impact of manufacturing on the Fraser, it's here, in the plumes of steam towering above the pulp mills that stud the skyline of this city of 75,000, which is the brawny industrial hub of northern BC.

In some ways, these mills represent a success story. After a billion dollar province-wide clean-up of processing infrastructure, the pulp and paper industry has dramatically reduced the levels of dioxins and furans—among the most toxic and persistent pollutants in their effluents—entering the Fraser and other provincial waters. Also reduced dramatically were discharges of substances that consume oxygen in the water and fibre that accumulated into dense mats. But these mills still represent an enormous industrial footprint on the Fraser Basin ecosystem. The pulp and paper mills located on Fraser River watersheds account for 35 percent of the total permitted volume of effluents discharged every day, according to a sustainability study of the basin by the federal Department of Fisheries and Oceans. And the pulp mills near Prince George together with mills at Quesnel and Kamloops contribute 75 percent of the permitted volume of discharges to the Fraser River upstream of Hope. Dry cleaning plants, cement plants, petroleum and natural gas refineries, breweries, fish processing plants, car washes and wood preservative plants all contribute their waste to the Fraser system, too. For example, the study points out, wood preservation facilities use approximately 4,500 metric tonnes of chemicals each year, many of them highly toxic to aquatic life. Among the worst are pentachlorophenol, ammonia copper arsenate and chromated copper arsenate, which lead to both acute and chronic effects in fish and are chemically and biologically persistent. Even a widely-used substance like creosote, applied to prevent rot in timbers used in river and marine environments, is now linked to lesions in the livers of fish species.

Overall, the federal study concludes, the total amount of pollutants entering the Fraser is still not properly documented—and disturbing research, by geneticist Michael Easton, found in 1997 that even low levels of supposedly non-toxic pulp mill effluents were causing serious damage to the DNA in baby chinook salmon. The mill effluents Easton studied at Prince George—he used the sophisticated diagnostic technology developed for human cancer research—met all current provincial and federal standards and were being discharged into the Fraser at a rate of 1,500 cubic metres per day. But toxic compounds aren't necessarily the most immediate major threat to fish habitat in the river, the federal scientists say. That threat comes from the discharge of water used to cool industrial processes. Even when clean, it can raise water temperatures to the detriment of species like salmon and trout that require colder water. And if it's contaminated, a warm discharge in winter months can attract fish right to where the harmful chemicals are concentrated.

Here at Prince George, the upper Fraser watershed divides into a tilted "T" shape with one arm extending southeast to the Rockies, the other northwest up the Nechako and Stuart rivers that drain a landscape characterized by short, hot summers and the fierce cold of snowbound winters. It's an important divide. This western branch of the upper Fraser supports approximately 25 percent of the total run of commercially valuable sockeye salmon, among them the highly prized Stuart River runs that occur in early summer and fall. Among the most beautiful of salmon with their silver streamlined bodies and metallic green heads, their bodies shaped by millennia of natural selection to provide the least resistance to the current, these elegant, highly adapted sockeye travel farther to spawn than any other salmon species in the river. Each year, returning salmon battle the currents for 1,150 kilometres to the rivers draining into Takla and Trembleur lakes. In fact, except for the Chilako system, sockeye spawn in all the major watersheds west of Prince George with the biggest runs returning to the Stellako River. Fraser Lake, where juvenile Stellako stocks spend a year feeding on rich concentrations of insects and plankton, is the most productive lake in the Fraser Basin. Slab-sided chinook salmon are also an important species in the upper Fraser. They spawn in virtually every watershed west of Prince George, with the Nechako and Stuart rivers rearing the largest populations.

Chinook populations were adversely affected by development half a century ago of an Alcan Aluminum project that required the damming of the Nechako and the diversion of its flow through Cheslatta Lake to re-enter the river nine kilometres downstream. Reduced water flows and subsequent increased water temperatures in the Nechako had an impact upon the historic abundance of the upper Fraser chinook and sockeye populations. Plans to extend the project resulted in some of BC's bitterest environmental battles over the last decade. But after Alcan shelved the Kemano Completion Project in 1995, industry, provincial and federal agencies, aboriginal people and environmental groups began talking about how to mitigate the destruction on the Nechako and restore salmon abundance.

Farther north is Fort St. James, established by Simon Fraser in 1806, where the Stuart River drains out of Stuart Lake. It was once considered so remote that it was known as the "Siberia" of the fur trade. Today, with its nineteenth-century buildings largely intact and the blood-red Hudson's Bay Company ensign flapping over the hand-squared timbers of the trading post, Fort St. James is a National Historic Site that provides twenty-one-year-old Nicole Robert with a good job interpreting her Carrier people's turbulent and dramatic history for tourists. More pragmatically, Hudson's Bay records show that the company bought 60,000 dried salmon a year from aboriginal people, points out Sharon Bird at the Nak'azdli treaty office down the road. "That's over and above what we took for our own sustenance," she says. "Last year my sister fished—she got nineteen salmon. That tells you how much it's declined."

Declining salmon runs are a crucial part of the Fraser's story. How will history judge those who inherited such natural abundance and frittered it away, converting salmon into disposable aluminum pop cans and the garish neon signs advertising casinos, strip joints and movie malls? Bird is under no illusion that to those who lived here long before the fur traders put up their palisades and built the factor his big log house with its stunning view down Stuart Lake, the importance of these salmon was more than as a simple economic commodity. Salmon, she says, are still at the cultural and spiritual heart of her people's existence. Perhaps the fish are even entangled in their very physiology, a curious symbiosis that links them to an ocean that some of them have never seen. "I believe that genetically we're dependent on the oil in these salmon," Bird says. "We've been studying this with nutritionists in the States. We believe access to these fish is a longevity issue for us. This is a big human issue here, never mind treaty. I often wonder if they'll try to negotiate salmon oil capsules into our treaty instead of our fish."

Down at the lake front, Francesa Antoine, eighty-six, devout parishioner of Our Lady of the Snows Catholic Church, is getting her smokehouse ready for the salmon harvest. Tut-tutting over a torn net—"I must make a binding for that!"—and explaining how the poles for the drying racks have to be a certain type of willow, she likes to reminisce about the joys of fishing as a little girl with her mother, Ellie Cho, now long-dead, at the opening of the twentieth century. There's a crucifix over the door and a picture of Mother Teresa on the wall and the smokehouse does have the air of a holy place. Sunlight lances into the velvety shadows through chinks in the unpeeled logs and the air is redolent with the musky, mysterious, incense-like scent of smoked buckskin, dried venison, racks of deer ribs and the bales of dried salmon left from last season. "The old people used to do everything through smoke," she explains. "When we get sick in our house, we come to the smokehouse for the day and get better. That smoke is good for chasing away sickness."

Right now, just as the new season begins, she says, is when the preserved meat is most flavourful—one more bit of lore that's lost on the younger generation, the ancient knowledge drowning in an avalanche of television celebrity worship, Nintendo and Internet chat-room trivia. "[Young] people clean the meat out of their freezers at the end of the winter," she says. "I always ask them to give it to me. I dry it. It's very good. Very good. I don't like to see them wasting food." Then she laughs, remembering how some young men had come around earlier. They'd caught a huge sturgeon and didn't know what to do with it. "It's big and they were scared to cut it up by themselves." Granny Antoine shakes her head. "The biggest was caught by my grandmother, it was twelve feet long. Anyway, they had smashed the sturgeon's head. You're not supposed to do that. It's easy to put the head in the pot, you know. We used to kill them very gently. We tied a rope around the tail. When you tie the rope, it can't feel its body. It just goes very still. But it's hard to teach these young men. They think we don't know anything."

The elders' stories about salmon and sturgeon, the central place the smokehouse still occupies in so many lives in the Stuart and Nechako watersheds, the emerging scientific research are all evidence of how the ecology of the Fraser Basin involves people as well as plants, animals and hydrology. These distant tributaries of the Fraser tie the remote peoples of BC's Interior to aboriginal nations at the coast. "Our bones are made of fish," elders from the Sto:lo and Nlaka'pamux are fond of saying. The proverb turns out to be fact. Scientists have been tracing compounds that originated in marine organisms and later migrated into human bone samples. They suggest that people living along the Fraser for at least the last 5,000 years derived about 90 percent of their protein from marine sources and in every sample tested, salmon proved to be the major component in aboriginal diet. Yet there are contemporary biological links that tie coast dwellers at the mouth of the Fraser to those who live along its Interior banks, too.

At Big Bar Creek in what's known as the mid-Fraser Basin, the stretch of river extending from Prince George to Lytton passes through the great, arid plateau between the Coast Range and the Cariboo Range. It's here that Lawrence Joiner runs a cattle ranch that's right out of the 1800s, except for the pickup trucks, tractors and other mechanical implements.

A successful farmer from the Fraser Valley—look for the sign for Joiner's Corn on the Trans-Canada Highway near Chilliwack— Lawrence and his wife, Joan, bought 6,000 hectares of ranchland in the south Chilcotin and abandoned mixed agriculture in the Lower Mainland to the next generation of Joiners, the progeny of which are creating a minor hurricane on the rambling front porch. Grandsons Lee, 9, Braden, 10, and Kyle, 12, are up for a visit—the granddaughters came separately several weeks earlier—and still hyped up over a day hunting frogs in the swampy creek bottoms below the pasture.

Driving out from Highway 97 to the Joiner ranch west of Clinton means an hour of dusty gravel before the forest gives way to an immense vista of grassland that sweeps away to the steep, eroded banks of the Fraser. Across the benches on the other side of the canyon, the prairie breaks against rugged mountains. At dusk, with a golden glow on the prairies and the first brilliant star of evening drooping in a lilac sky shot through with amber-tinted streaks of cloud, it's easy to see why there's not a lot of pop art on the homestead walls in this country. What print could compete with that? The Joiners run just over seven hundred head of beef cattle on the 775 square kilometres of grass to which they hold a combination of deeded title and grazing leases. The bronze panorama of bunch grass is punctuated by the vivid green of irrigated fields where he crops the hay and alfalfa that's stored for winter feed.

This is classic rain shadow. Average annual precipitation here in the Fraser Plateau region can be as little as 30 millimetres, a far cry from the average of 1,100 millimetres that falls on the facing slopes of the Quesnel Highlands to the west. The dry soils and unusual climatic conditions intrigue Joiner, who brings his experience from the coast to bear. He explains as we bang down through the ruts and dust to the lush riverside fields that also sustain a herd of up to eighty bighorn sheep. "It's a curious thing," he says, "but here we have almost the exact reverse of the Fraser Valley. We have acid soils at the coast and we build ditches to carry excess water away from the fields. Interior soils are alkaline soils and we build ditches to bring the water to the fields for irrigation. At the coast we have to lime the soil. Here the mountains are about 99 percent limestone but the soil lacks nitrogen. So I grow alfalfa, which fixes nitrogen in the soil."

On a flat-topped promontory that juts out above the huge gravel shoulder in the Fraser that gives Big Bar its name, he stops his truck beside a pile of black soil. Except it's not soil, he says, kneeling to run it through his fingers. Joiner is experimenting with what the marketers prefer to call biosolids—otherwise known as the sludge from the Greater Vancouver Regional District's sewage plants. That sludge was once discharged raw and untreated into the Fraser by the billions of litres. Indeed, over thirty municipal sewage treatment plants still discharge wastes into the Fraser Basin. Today, however, the largest plants in the Fraser estuary have been upgraded and with greater emphasis on treatment, the Lower Mainland now produces about 700,000 tonnes of biosolids every year. In this large-scale experiment, Joiner has been applying it to some of his forage crops at the rate of 1,000 kilograms per hectare. He's using about 35 tonnes per year and the results have made him an enthusiast. Joiner now sees it as a crucial step in recycling that can only reduce stress on the Fraser Basin landscape. "When you are farming, your soil is like your bank," he says. "You have to put in what you take out. This stuff is just like black potting soil. Putting it on the fields helps create topsoil that will hold the moisture better. And it is biologically inert. All the pathogens have been killed. It's sterile." That's important because one of the traditional methods of replenishing soil is spreading manure on fields. Whether used as natural fertilizer, piled up around feedlots or left to concentrate where livestock winter in creek bottoms and coulees, manure has been identified as a threat to waterways, particularly where runoff collects contaminants and introduces high levels of nutrients, fecal coliforms, oxygen-consuming substances and ammonia.

So far, Joiner says, except for the silly natter from people who seemed ideologically opposed to the idea of Vancouver sending its sewage to the Interior, everything about the use of human biosolids on his land has been positive. Hay yields increased tenfold and the protein content in the feed more than doubled, an important factor since plants with higher protein content are better able to withstand the frequent drought conditions in the region. There's a downside, of course. Joiner says that once the notion catches on, the price for biosolids will soon be bid up in the market. But he sees an upside to that, too. "When it is perceived as a value-added commodity, then there will be an incentive for all these communities that don't treat their sewage to treat it and then recover their costs by extracting the biosolids. Then we will have a really sustainable cycle," Joiner says. "It will be good for the communities, good for the waterways, good for the land and good for the people who live on the land."

South of the Joiner ranch, past the frothing punch bowls of the lower Stein, where the river tumbles toward the Fraser through car-sized boulders polished as smooth and round as if they'd been turned for eternity in God's tumblers, the saskatoons are showing their first golden leaves, the wild rosehips are crimson and the

Oregon grape is dressed with acid-blue fruit. The dusk comes early and the dawn comes late on the dusty west side of the river where the hillsides close in. The Fraser is moving here from the open plateaux of the Interior toward the canyon and the coast. If anything, the country seems even drier now. At Texas Creek, a near-vertical notch in the cliffs descends to a startlingly verdant grotto of alder and willow that's as welcome as a cool desert oasis. Here, when the sun comes up over Blustery Mountain with an eye-searing glare so harsh you suddenly remember that sunshine is radiation from a thermonuclear reaction, the Fraser is a blinding arc of silver in a sere country of sun-blasted rock, burnt sagebrush flats and lodgepole pine. Yet down by the river, Gordon Scheller and his dog Snoopy, move through an iridescent mist in a field so green it hurts the eyes. He's moving a line of sprinklers and setting up "the gun," as he calls the big one on the end that sends its jet half the length of a football field. "Yeah, this qualifies as irrigation pasture, all right," he says, gesturing to Cat Creek where he draws the water. A zoology graduate from UBC, Scheller's been ranching for more than thirty years. "It's all gravity feed," he says, "the silt in the Fraser is so abrasive that it would ruin any pump in no time." That clean water, spilling toward the river from the hills, drives BC's $2.2 billion agricultural industry. And although only 5 percent of the province's land mass is considered capable of supporting a farming operation, 40 percent of BC's best arable land and 75 percent of its best pasture are found in the Fraser basin where water is readily available for crop irrigation and watering livestock.

Even though BC is the only province where family farms have been on the increase—there were more than 20,000 in 1996—along the Fraser some farmers are still finding it necessary to turn to other innovative sources of income. David Jones is the third generation to farm his 2.5-square-kilometre spread on the banks of the Fraser River not far from Lillooet. His grandfather, Dr.

Oswald Jones, a respectable Victoria surgeon who had come around Cape Horn under sail in 1889, bought the land from a homesteader in 1906. The family's been farming it ever since. In fact, Jones will take you into the house, past the original stove from 1908, past the original Jack Shadbolt painting of Clinton—"Grandfather had a weakness for art"—up the wooden stairs with the age-blackened balustrade and show you the bedroom where he was born sixty-seven years ago. "The first ten years before the crash of the 1930s they made good money. He [his dad, D.C. Jones] kept it together raising flower and vegetable seeds during the war. He went into sheep. He went into dairy. Then he wound up in beef and hay." Jones took over the operation more than thirty years ago and returned to sheep ranching. "Golfing in our family goes back a long way," Jones says. "I thought, I've got these sheep out here and the coyotes are harvesting as many as I do. I know, I'll build a golf course and the sheep will mow the greens while the golfers keep the coyotes away." It worked. Which is why, in the company of 65 wool-ly ewes and up to 90 frisky lambs, you can shoot a round at the Sheep Pasture Golf Club on one of the oldest pieces of registered land in the Interior. "It's pretty laid back," Jones says. "We're not exactly up-scale. We don't have golf carts. On the other hand, just over the hill at Whistler the green fees are in the $150 to $175 range. Here you can shoot a weekend round for $10—$9 on a weekday—and there's no marshal out there yelling at you to play through or clear the green. I've done pretty well. It's cut my preda-tor loss right down to zip. There are people out there at all kinds of hours with no set pattern and the coyotes stay away."

If innovation is the way of things on the Jones ranch, tradition is the engine of events just north of Lillooet where the Bridge River jets out of its twisting canyon of metamorphic rock to collide with the Fraser in a massive stretch of whitewater. This is the country of Sts'wan, the wind-dried salmon, and the aboriginal peoples that

Simon Fraser met on his voyage down the river in 1808 have been gathering at family fishing sites here since before Moses went up Mount Sinai to get the Ten Commandments. This is the place where the humid air of the coast really gives way to the hot, dry air of the rain shadow, says Gerald Michel, a fisheries manager for the Bridge River band. It creates perfect conditions for drying salmon on open racks, just when the salmon reach the ideal state for preservation. Once they begin their migrations upriver, salmon stop feeding and live off the fat they've been accumulating in the last ocean phase as they approach the estuary. "At this point, most of their fat is gone—they are just perfect," Michel says. "Downriver by Spuzzum, the flesh falls off their skin because it's still too rich, there's too much fat. Farther up the river they are too far along and the wasps come and eat the flesh before they can dry it so they have to cut their fish up at night."

Below, agile as cats on the spray-slicked rocks, deafened by the thunder of millions of tonnes of water boiling past, muscular young men sweep long-handled dip nets through the back eddies where the fish idle, and have always idled, gathering strength for another attempt to move upstream. Michel points to one dark swirl of current behind a dripping rock. "There's a ten- or twelve-foot sturgeon there in that eddy. He'll come up and nudge the net every once in awhile. I saw a fourteen-footer there one year. I heard a big slurp and there he was, staring right at me." Behind the dip nets, finding precarious footing in the ledges, two other young men work swiftly to gut the fish, cut out the backbones and score the flesh for hanging on the drying racks that stud the drab banks of the Fraser. At Michel's drying shed, the silver-backed sheaves of dark red salmon rustle in the furnace wind like strange leaves. They perfume the air with the scent of—not fish, but something for which the English tongue can't quite find words.

The timeless rhythms of life continue as they always have here at the confluence, but a dusty drive back up the Bridge River, past Camoo Creek, Antoine Creek and the Yalacom Valley leads directly to the past's violent collision with the future. It comes in the form of a wall of earth and rock that seals off the lower Bridge from its source in the icefields surrounding Mount Monmouth, 120 kilometres back in the Coast Range. BC Hydro's Terzaghi impoundment dam is only one of the eight hundred licensed dams that have already been built across the Fraser Basin for everything from flood protection to urban water supplies, electrical generation, mining and irrigation storage. When this dam was built in 1948, it was hailed as a triumph over nature. Few paid much attention to the aboriginal people who were subsequently flooded out by what became Carpenter Lake, named in honour of the American design engineer. August Alexander wasn't even notified. He came home to find the waters rising to drown the ranch where he was raising ten children. His wife Adeline died a year later—of a broken heart, he later said. Alexander was himself killed on an American highway, walking back to camp from the itinerant berry-picking job to which he'd been forced to turn. Over at the village of Shalalth, they still talk about the one dry summer when the water in Carpenter Lake was drawn down and the spokes of Alexander's abandoned hay rake emerged from the shallows where the horses had once grazed, a spectral tombstone for a way of life.

For all the economic benefits dams bestow on their builders, they bring a host of problems. They divert or relocate rivers, create new lakes and often cause fluctuations in water levels that destroy both aquatic and land-based vegetation essential for fish habitat. Heavy metals like mercury can accumulate behind them. And eventually they silt up and cease to be useful. In addition, diverting rivers from one watershed creates new vectors for the transfer of parasites, diseases and unwanted fish species into previously pristine environments. Dams constructed today must be designed to accommodate the safe passage of fish, but this was not always the case and some migratory fish stocks in BC have been extirpated or severely depressed because of failures to do so in the past. Of the thousands of distinct "races" of salmon that inhabited the Fraser River and its tributaries just a century and a half ago, more than one hundred are already extinct while others have dwindled to the point where they may not be able to recover.

One of the rips in the web of biodiversity that is sustained by the Fraser and its many tributaries can be found below the Terzaghi dam—although it's a tear that's now being repaired. The dam is one of three that create a network of reservoirs that channel water from the Bridge and Seton rivers through four generating stations with capacity to produce 3,000 gigawatts of electricity— enough power for 300,000 homes in the Lower Mainland. Built in 1948 and rebuilt in 1960, the earthfill dam severs the Bridge and, until recently, posed a major hazard to fish stocks. Although migrating salmon use only the bottom 40 kilometres of the river for spawning, sudden fluctuations in the flow would sometimes leave fish stranded without sufficient water and other times would scour away spawning channels and blow salmon preparing to lay eggs right back to the Fraser. But following public outcry and a federal investigation over several such environmental disasters in the early 1990s, BC Hydro and the federal Department of Fisheries and Oceans signed an agreement to restore and maintain adequate flows below the dam. Spawning and rearing habitat was reconstructed, the spillway was modified and in August, 2000, just as the first runs of chinook, coho, pink, sockeye and steelhead began their return journey to the Bridge, a new flow regime was initiated that may one day help restore the river to its past abundance.

Cross over the Terzaghi dam, continue up the hairpins and switchbacks to the top of Mission Ridge and you can look west to Seton Portage, the land bridge that separates Seton Lake from

Anderson Lake and was once a key crossing for the fur brigades on their way from Fort Kamloops to Yale and then on by canoe to Fort Langley. Simon Fraser's report on his descent through the upper canyon by canoe was so discouraging that the idea of the river as a commercial route to the sea was abandoned. The first pack train of 400 horses and outriders in fringed buckskins went by Seton Portage to avoid the Fraser Canyon, although that route, too, was abandoned after more than 70 horses and 25 packets of freight were lost. Instead they would take another route through the Similkameen Valley. None of them ever imagined that one day the impassable chasm in the Coast Range would become the most important transportation artery to the Interior and the rest of the continent. In its unexpected role as a commercial route, the Fraser can be said to have created modern British Columbia.

The transition came in 1857 when eight hundred ounces of gold nuggets traded at Hudson's Bay Company forts by Natives from Lytton were shipped to San Francisco to be refined and minted. On the gold's arrival, "Fraser fever" swept California. Farmers abandoned their crops in the fields, restaurants boarded up their windows between meals, houses that had just been bought for $500 went on the market for $100 and between 25,000 and 30,000 stampeders embarked north on anything that would float. "Old hulks which had long been known to be unseaworthy and rotten were refitted for the new El Dorado. Engines, rusty from years of idleness were polished up; leaky boilers were repatched—paint and putty filling gaping seams; and with names often changed, to hide their former reputations, steamer after steamer sailed from our port loaded to the guards with freight and black with the crowds who were rushing to the newly-discovered land of gold," one contemporary account wryly observes. Almost overnight, sleepy Fort Victoria's population went from 300 to 3,000 with another 6,000 transients passing through for the Fraser at any given time. The stampede picked up steam in 1858 following reports of a strike at Hill's Bar about three kilometres south of Yale. This rising tide of miners worked its way upriver gravel bar by gravel bar, clambering over the ingenious ladders and suspension bridges built by the Natives and following ancient trade and hunting trails.

The invasion was not without tension. When armed American miners began driving aboriginal prospectors off the bars and molesting their women, the original inhabitants, known as the "Couteau" or Knife Indians, struck back hard. What became known as the Fraser Canyon War began with a slaughter of Americans at China Bar. Ambushes picked off solitary parties and their headless bodies were tossed into the river to float downstream and terrorize those who hadn't yet moved beyond Yale. "Captain Snider took out of the water at Yale ten dead whites; at Deadman's Bend on the opposite shore they took out 19 and the Hudson's Bay Company at Hope took out 31...some of the corpses made their way to the ocean," wrote W.W. Walkem, who years later collected the narratives of surviving miners like Ned Stout. The Americans organized themselves into irregular military units bearing names like the Whatcom Company and the Pike Guards. When they moved upriver, led by a former Texas Ranger named Rouse, the fighting was fierce and of the scorched earth variety. "We lost a man nearly every day; Jack McLennan was one of these, and at Slaughter Bar we lost six of our comrades," Stout told Walkem. "This Slaughter Bar was between Boston Bar and Jackass Mountain. Opposite Keefers we made an attack on their caches which contained all their dried salmon and berry cakes, and burned the rancherie as well." That was enough for the new colony's governor, Sir James Douglas. He had the Royal Navy dispatch a warship with eighty-four guns and more than seven hundred seamen and marines, met with the Indians to negotiate a peace and sent Sir Matthew Baillie Begbie, undeservedly nicknamed "the Hanging Judge," to impose British law and order on the unruly Americans.

Then, to support the prospectors, came the riverboats—stern-wheelers captained by men who had learned their trade dodging snags and shoals on the Mississippi and Missouri. But even they dared not try the Fraser Canyon itself. In 1860 a mule trail was built from Yale to Spuzzum and a year later, the rush having pushed up the Fraser to the Quesnel River, construction of the Cariboo Wagon Road began. In 1862, a traveller remarked in some wonder that on one day he'd actually encountered ten loaded wagons between Yale and Lytton. What Simon Fraser described in 1808 as a place "where no human being should venture" is now a major tourist attraction. At Hope, the southern entrance to the canyon, the Chamber of Commerce recorded 70,000 tourist stops at the visitor centre in 1999. The Hell's Gate Air Tram has attracted about a million visitors since 1990 and Darwin Baerg, who operates Fraser River Raft Expeditions, estimates that in 1999 alone about 25,000 adventurers went out to ride the rapids that were once so feared and frustrating.

The real importance of the canyon, however, is as a conduit for the raw materials and finished goods upon which Vancouver's success as a merchant port is predicated.

Canada's two national railways pump coal, sulphur, lumber, grain and mixed freight through the canyon to terminals on the lower Fraser and the port of Vancouver at an average of a train every thirty minutes or so. And the Trans-Canada Highway through the Fraser Canyon still averages a motor vehicle every five minutes—many truckers prefer it because the grades offer a fuel advantage—and that's after significant volumes of traffic have been siphoned off by the Coquihalla Highway.

This torrent of raw materials, manufactured goods and consumer items leads to the great economic engine of the lower Fraser itself where the river eases out into the alluvial flood plain that has laid down some of the richest and most productive agricultural land in the world. With rich soils, a long growing season and proximity both to domestic markets and a global transportation nexus, it's not surprising that the Fraser Valley generates more than half of all the province's annual agricultural production from operations that have a production value per hectare that is fifteen times the national average.

Officially, the lower Fraser extends west of Hope to the Strait of Georgia, south to the Canada–US border and north to the heights of land where the tributaries that feed the Lillooet, Pitt and Stave rivers rise. Here conditions shift dramatically from the arid Interior to a wet, humid, temperate marine climate where annual rainfall can reach 3,500 millimetres. This region, too, has historically been an immense natural salmon factory. The federal Department of Fisheries and Oceans estimates that the small tributaries of the lower Fraser between Vancouver and Hope support 80 percent of the Fraser's chinook salmon and 90 percent of its chum, 65 percent of its coho, 80 percent of its pink and significant numbers of sockeye. Even the ditches in this environment can provide important coho habitat. But precisely what made the Fraser Valley ideal for salmon runs makes it the most valuable landscape in the province and a platform for inevitable conflicts between the demands of development and those of the environment.

The single biggest impact upon the Fraser River occurs during its final 100-kilometre journey to the sea and it comes from human population pressure. Almost 60 percent of BC's population lives in this region and growth here is double the provincial average. Municipalities discharge 50 percent of the waste water entering the lower Fraser, most of it from showers, bathtubs, kitchen sinks, washing machines, dishwashers and toilets. Even after treatment, these effluents can damage aquatic habitats by introducing excessive nutrients, suspended solids, detergents and soaps that are lethal to important micro-organisms, while sewage can introduce unwanted bacteria and other micro-organisms. So, in considering the state of fish stocks in the Fraser Basin, it's not so much an issue of distant dams and faraway landslides, as it is an issue of what must happen in Greater Vancouver's own backyard, where population growth is driving urban sprawl east of the metropolis and farther into the river's floodplain. "Replacing the natural environment with impermeable surfaces such as roads, parking lots and buildings has more permanent impact on natural hydrology [water flow patterns] than any other human activity," says one federal report on Fraser Basin sustainability. "Significant changes in hydrology occur when 10 percent or more of a watershed is developed. Considering that 50 to 75 percent of the average city lot is covered with impermeable materials, it is easy to understand the tremendous impact that urbanization has on water flow." Nowhere on the Fraser has the natural hydrology been changed so much as here in the last stretch before the sea. Watersheds surrounding the Pitt and Stave rivers have been repeatedly logged for more than a century, many of the lower tributaries have been dammed for hydroelectricity, and the massive dikes of the Fraser estuary designed to protect residential, commercial and agricultural areas from flooding are estimated to have now destroyed 75 percent of the natural wetlands, intertidal marshes and side sloughs that are vital for fish and waterfowl. The intensive nature of farming in the Fraser Valley poses yet another threat to the river's health, particularly where there are high concentrations of livestock adjacent to the small, slow-moving tributary streams that are critical to more than 65 percent of the Fraser's coho stocks. In addition, agricultural chemicals can be a pervasive problem, contaminating groundwater as well as entering surface water.

But travelling toward tidewater, it doesn't take long for the farm fields to give way to the dense complex of factories, booming grounds, shipyards, sawmills, container landings, shipping berths, chip barges, scrap heap piles and lines of shiny new vehicles awaiting transshipment that mark the boundaries of the Fraser port. Located on the main arm of the Fraser and extending 62 kilometres upriver from salt water, this is the largest single concentration of industry in the province. More than 350 businesses and industries are active here; they directly employ 6,000 people and contribute $1.4 billion to Canada's gross national product. The 22 million tonnes of cargo that pass through the Fraser mouth each year is valued at $9.2 billion and is comprised of lumber, steel, pulp, paper, automobiles, wood products, chemicals, specialty grains, construction aggregate and various industrial chemicals.

Drifting down the river from the Port Mann bridge, the observer discovers the raw industrial beauty of this landscape, as stark in its own way as the rock and ice where the river began. Everywhere one looks there seems to be an ironic metaphor. Here's the dirt-stained hull of a ferro-cement yacht shorn of its masts, a filthy tarp over the cockpit—somebody's half-finished dream moored, not behind the gleaming reef of a South Seas atoll, but in a grimy industrial backwater. There's the gleaming white, and inexpressibly tacky, splendour of the *Royal City Star*, a faux riverboat that doesn't quite ring true to the gritty past it purports to emulate. On one barge, a neat stack of crushed cars worth about $4 million to the few hundred people who bought them new—and just around the bend, a shipment of gleaming Japanese models just arrived and lined up in rows, waiting to go out to the dealerships. The shadows of jumbo jets from Sea Island bound for Asia pass over the long-vanished village site of the Musqueam. When the chiefs whose great houses lined this shore first encountered Simon Fraser almost two hundred years ago the river, not the runway, was the path to the future.

In the delta, the industrial insignia that's most evident is wood. Whole convoys of chip barges list under the weight of their pungent new-sawn cargo. Scalers skip across the rafts of floating logs on caulk-booted feet that would challenge Fred Astaire. Boom boats bustle about with that peculiar, rotund, rust-covered officiousness that only they can affect. Here and there a log salvor strains against the current. But mostly just kilometre after kilometre of log booms bob in the hiss of the current, the raw, unadulterated evidence of the almost unbelievable deluge of wood passing out into the world through the portal of the Fraser. The magnitude of the industrial event staggers the imagination. In a way, it's become a river of time. These trees, some of them 600 or 700 years old, represent a vanishing heritage that may never be seen again—certainly not for another thirty-five generations.

When the industries that seem so permanent are gone, when the laughing Gulf Island children who splash so briefly at Russell Beach, gathering their basket of memories in water that began its journey in the clouds on the Fraser Pass, when they and their children's children are long in their graves, the land and the mighty river that shapes it will still be here.

But will we? Will the salmon and the great blue heron, the Pacific shrew and the Salish sucker, the silvery clouds of eulachon and the distant speck of the bald eagle rising on the thermals, the grizzly bear and the green sturgeon, the killer whale and the Nooksack dace, the young man finding his manhood with the dip net and the old woman seeking solace for her spirit in the timeless mysteries of the smokehouse? What is to become of them? And, in an ecology where all our fates are entangled, what is to become of us?

The Last Run

The chum salmon that spawn in Jones Creek, a small tributary stream that tumbles out of mist-shrouded Coast Mountains just shy of Hope, are one of the wonders of the Fraser River system. They are the earliest migrating chum stock in the world's biggest producer of wild salmon. This specialized adaptation makes them of great interest to science and of critical importance as a genetic component in the biodiversity of Lower Mainland salmon. By helping to expand the spawning window of their species, these Jones Creek chum are part of a remarkable survival strategy. Arriving at different times, they diminish the risk of stocks being wiped out by specific natural disasters like floods or droughts. Perhaps they are also a grim harbinger of what the future holds as human technology modifies more and more of a complex and intricate natural system that it doesn't fully understand.

The Jones Creek chum are about to become extinct. Despite all the political rhetoric about saving the Pacific salmon, human beings have accomplished in a few decades what nature hadn't been able to achieve in 10,000 years.

When the chum that hatched in 1992 came home to complete the four-year cycle that makes the salmon such a dramatic Pacific Northwest metaphor for death and renewal, they returned to find the eternal circle of life broken forever by a man-made curtain of steel and concrete. And instead of a clear, cool, well-oxygenated spawning channel, the salmon found only a turbid, grit-laden torrent turned the colour of café au lait by suspended sediments that exceeded the levels necessary for survival by as much as a thousandfold. "They are at the brink of extinction right now," says Otto Langer, head of the federal government's Fraser River Action Plan. And all this despite a forty-two-year effort, despite the best scientific expertise, despite the best examples of corporate citizenship, despite the best intentions of government, despite millions of dollars and heroic efforts at habitat rehabilitation.

Jones Creek was the prevailing model for the concept of "no net loss." It symbolized the strategy by which habitat damaged or destroyed by development should be restored and replaced through corporate commitment, government science and good engineering. Big display signs proclaimed the creek a triumph of fisheries enhancement. But some time in 1996 the government quietly took them down. All that remains is a bare wooden frame. At Jones Creek, hope has now been abandoned.

So, it seems, have the steadfast efforts of biologists like Langer. His Fraser River Action Plan, set up with the precise object of protecting salmon habitat in the Lower Mainland, may be about to disappear itself. It's one the programs the scientists expect to be declared redundant—a "sunset" program in the Orwellian euphemism of federal cost-cutting guides. Carol Lamont, a biologist with BC Hydro who has been deeply involved with the enhancement project for six years, confirms that it's now up to Mother Nature to restore this ravaged watershed and the stream that flows from it. How long might that take? Gordon Hartman isn't sure. Maybe fifty, maybe one hundred years.

Hartman is a scientist contracted by the federal Department of Fisheries and Oceans to conduct an investigation into the elements that comprise this unfolding environmental nightmare. While he won't prejudge the outcome of his research, Hartman doesn't mince words about the one indisputable fact: "I am very, very concerned about the salmon's survival here. If we are at all concerned about genetics, we don't want to lose that population." To that end, fertilized eggs have been retrieved and taken to a Chilliwack hatchery in the hope that some faint genetic remnant of the unique stock might be saved. But problems with the salvaged eggs have already emerged because they hatch according to a different timetable that is unique to Jones Creek. And while a tiny tributary creek that is still running clean has had spawning gravel placed in it, it too has risks. It is adjacent to a large dairy farm and possibly threatened by runoff. In any event, nobody knows whether Jones Creek salmon will ever imprint with the new spawning beds.

Langer acknowledges that "these are all desperation measures." "It's a real shame," Lamont concurs. "But it's really tough to do anything in a watershed with such major problems. It's been so frustrating, it's a real deflation for the people in Hydro who have been involved." The deflation comes from the rediscovery of the 2,500-year-old principle that hubris begets nemesis, that the greatest human effort, expense and ingenuity may not be good enough to retrieve the mistakes made by rash meddling in a complex natural order. "It's reached a point where people are near helpless," Langer says. "All we can do now is wait for fifty or eighty years."

The Jones Creek tragedy began in 1954 during British Columbia's great dam-building binge. BC Hydro put a dam on the creek at Jones Lake, well above the natural spawning channel. Historically, the stream supported runs of about 5,000 pink salmon, about 500 chum, several hundred coho, steelhead, cutthroat trout and even a sockeye run. "The old, old records show sockeye in there up until 1941," Hartman says. "Some people are sceptical about that but they did record sockeye returning to Jones Creek in early times." After the dam altered water flows, the return of pink salmon fell by half, chum returns fell to less than 200 and coho returns fell to 60. BC Hydro undertook to stabilize these salmon returns to the lower reaches of the river by installing an artificial spawning channel that would be "better" than the existing waterway and more amenable to the survival of hatchlings. "They've made quite a heroic effort to keep the channel going," Hartman says. "A hell of a lot of effort and expense."

But logging that had begun in the Jones Creek watershed in the 1930s began to accelerate. "The logging that seemed to cause the problem was done in the late 1960s and 1970s in one particular branch of the watershed called Three Mile Creek," Hartman says. "It's a shame because they probably could have kept that spawning channel open and functioning if it hadn't been for that logging. It's a bad situation. It's a steep, steep system, poor soils, tremendous hydrologic energy." An internal Department of Fisheries and Oceans memo identifies the problem as "disastrous" road construction through a few feet of soil sitting on top of glacially polished bedrock. "Any change in drainage or sidecasting would cause the soil to slip off the mountain face." Sediment from steep clear-cut slopes began entering Jones Creek, compacting the gravel in the artificial spawning channel. Survival rates fell from 80 percent to eight percent. BC Hydro, fully engaged with the enhancement project, was now faced with extracting the spawning gravel, washing it and replacing it every second year at a cost of up to $50,000 each time. Survival rates shot back up to 67 percent.

In 1992, the crown corporation invested $250,000 in a sheet pile weir—steel plates driven into the stream bed—designed to ensure that returning salmon were diverted through a fish-counting fence and into the artificial spawning channel.

A year later, the Jones Creek catchment area was struck by two intense rainstorms that are characterized as one-in-fifty-year events. An entire mountainside began to unravel in the headwaters. Debris torrents choked the creek, suspended sediments poured into the spawning channel and once again began compacting the gravel there at a rate comparable to the stream's main stem. Department of Fisheries and Oceans habitat specialists recorded concentrations on the order of 100,000 milligrams to the litre—

"that's 10 percent solids even if we ignore the trees and huge boulders," says Langer.

BC Hydro once again moved quickly to resolve the problem. Under the umbrella of Forest Renewal BC, working with the Department of Fisheries and Oceans and International Forest Products Ltd., $100,000 was spent to construct large settling ponds above the intake to the spawning channel. Here, the engineers hoped, lethal sediments would be trapped. But in the fall of 1995, another storm system crashed into the steep mountains that ring the Jones Creek catchment basin. It had been a wet month anyway, with record rainfall all over BC and precipitation in the area that was double the long-term average. On November 7, 117 millimetres of rain fell. Environment Canada says that amount of rain is considered heavy for a one-day total anywhere in the world. The downpour saturated an existing blanket of snow.

"That's when all hell began to break loose," Langer recalls. He says that there appears to be a pattern of major landslides fifteen to twenty years after logging is completed. This, he speculates, is triggered by changes in runoff patterns and by the rotting of the dead root system that holds soil on steep bedrock slopes. Hydrologist Mike Miles, another scientist studying the Jones Creek watershed, confirms that there are now numerous large landslides and "there's no doubt that they have been exacerbated by logging." The debris flood that roared down Jones Creek blew out the new settling ponds, redirected the main channel, filled whole sections of the stream with so much gravel that it still looks like a paved road and scoured out the model spawning channel. With that flood went the fertile eggs of the already precarious salmon stocks.

Miles warns that what we're seeing at Jones Creek is not an anomaly of unusual terrain and bad weather. He says it may instead provide a window on the future for many of the salmon-bearing coastal streams of the province. He's been examining the long-term success rate for restoration of stream habitats damaged or destroyed by logging. From Oregon to Alaska, he found, the average rate of success is only 55 percent. In biological terms, it's even less. "The long term success [of habitat restoration projects like Jones Creek] is going to be very poor. It is very, very difficult to restore fisheries habitat once it has been messed up. It's really important for politicians and the public to understand how long it takes for damaged watersheds to recover."

For the Jones Creek chum, the entrance to their now dry spawning channel choked with logging debris, the rest of the river sealed off by a steel curtain of good intentions, time has run out. And more logging is planned for the Jones Creek watershed. The unspoken question that lurks in the collective despair of the scientists is whether the fate of these salmon, despite our best efforts, might not offer a frightening glimpse of our own future.

Sammy the Seal

The vast, silt-laden plume of the Fraser River has curled its warm, coffee-coloured current southward past my Gulf Island home toward Puget Sound, as it seems to do every year at this time of the summer. For my little daughter and her pals it's a carefree time for sun-dappled splashing in the shallows. They tirelessly harvest the prettiest pebbles, bits of tide-polished glass and an astonishing variety of abandoned cockle, mussel, limpet and moonsnail shells for their "collector's log"— a huge piece of drift timber that shimmers bone white in the seagrass. But behind the children's play the air is charged with a lazy tension. The powers of the great silent and unseen cycles of marine life are beginning to harmonize all along the crumpled western edge of Canada.

The mighty salmon migrations are imminent. For humans, the cycle means the age-old preparation of gear in the slips of isolated fishing villages like Oona River and Bella Bella. Along the big-city floats of Steveston and Victoria, Native and non-Native alike get ready for the traditional gillnet fishery. In the wild, the grizzly bears of the Khutzeymateen begin to drift down from the alpine meadows to the river shallows where they will take their share. Soon the eagles will begin to congregate above the sandbars of the Qualicum. And riding the tidal streams and ocean currents off the rocky coastline, whales and porpoises, seals, otters and sea lions all wait to take their bounty.

It can scarcely be by accident that the seals whelp just a few weeks before the teeming pink and sockeye runs sweep into Juan de Fuca Strait and down through the narrows of the Inside Passage toward the estuary of the Fraser River. This time of plenty is when the mothers will replenish their strength and body fat, pumping rich milk into their pups in preparation for the lean pickings that must follow. Where I live, July is the month when seals nurse their silvery little newborns. Mothers bask in the sun and the cries of roly-poly, milk-fed pups rise above the drying reefs and craggy islets that stud the lower Gulf of Georgia. About a kilometre off my beach, with the skyline from White Rock to West Vancouver cast as its glittering urban backdrop, one big reef humps up out of the water at low tide. On some days, scores of harbour seals haul out to soak up the warmth.

Behind my house, eagles bicker clumsily in the sparse tops of old-growth Douglas fir. I'm always astonished at the contrast between the thin cackle of these immense birds—a reedy kleek-kik-ik-ik-ik—and their power and grace in the air. They will lumber out of the treetops to join the ravens and red-headed turkey vultures joyriding on thermals. These currents of hot air shoot up like invisible elevators from the exposed ledges and shelves of tilted cretaceous sediment that heat and cool faster than the surrounding sea. Once aloft, their wings wider than the height of the tallest NBA basketball star, the eagles will spiral for effortless hours above the seal rocks. They watch without mercy for any signs of the weak, the sick, the wounded or the briefly abandoned.

When it comes to easy pickings, all great predators have an impeccable sense of timing. Given the regularity of the seals' reproductive cycle, it was no surprise that just before sunset a pod of killer whales cruised the necklace of reefs strung more than 100 kilometres from US waters to Nanaimo. The whales came through at high water when mothers encumbered by pups were most vulnerable and had nowhere to retreat. How many they killed, only the whales know, but the next morning there were only a few lonely pairs left on my reef. In the night, frantic mother seals had brought their babies inshore, driving the unweaned pups up above the high tide mark. Safety from the killer whales tonight would mean danger from otters, dogs and eagles tomorrow, but even in the animal world—perhaps especially there—there is a constant affirmation of the idea that sufficient unto the day are the troubles thereof.

I was mentioning all this during a visit with a bush pilot pal passing through on leave. I met Dominique Prinet when he was flying Beech 18s over the barrens of the High Arctic. He fixed those planes with wire and crazy glue; now he's fixing an African airline for the World Bank. Big Dom was telling me about elephants when the phone rang. "Better come home," my wife, Susan, said. "We have a three-day-old seal pup in the front yard. We have to talk."

I went. Just below the grassy space before the house, skin wrinkled, brown eyes big and wide as one of those make-believe waifs in a velvet painting, the seal pup was at the edge of tidewater, bawling for a mum who didn't come. "He's been here all day," Susan said. "So what do we do?" What we do is nothing, I argued, putting on my non-interventionist hat. Let nature take its course. We can't go about saving every pup orphaned by killer whales, sharks or trigger-happy fishers who prefer to blame the seals for salmon shortages caused by human greed.

"No, we can't," she said with a mother's implacable logic. "But we can save this one. We're a part of nature, too, you know. Perhaps you'd care to explain to Heledd why the baby should be left to them." Susan cocked a thumb at the ravens, gathering like a conclave of undertakers in the trees. The pup gave another mournful yawp. I looked at my four-year-old, mesmerized by Baby Seal. She was trying to cheer it up by singing verses from "The Silkie," an old folksong from the western isles of Scotland about a seal who changes shape to marry a human with woeful results. I thought of what ravens do to the helpless. I beat a retreat from Malthusian non-intervention.

"OK," I said, "We phone the aquarium. What will they say?"

"I already have," said Susan. "Sasha says if it's been alone all day, leave it one more night. If it's still here in the morning, Harbour Air will divert a float plane and fly it to them in Vancouver. We're to call Paul, the pilot, at 6:30 a.m." Where else but the Gulf Islands, I ask, do you find a pilot happy to do a mercy flight for a baby seal?

I stayed up until dark to shoo off ravens. My wife sang Kipling's seal lullaby to my own hyperventilating little one until she, too, finally fell asleep close to midnight. At 5:30 a.m., I got up. Susan was already scouring the beach. She'd been out since the first crack of dawn gleamed over Mount Baker. But there was not a sign or a sound from our noisy little visitor. "Either mum came back, or something got him," I said. Susan called the pilot to cancel. Paul seemed as glum as she was. I went back to bed, secretly glad not to have to drive the 15 km to the float plane dock and back.

But the story, of course, turned out to be far from over. Bright and early, with a big swell from the northwest booming across the beach ledges and fringing the shoreline in white lace, our phone rang.

It was Jean McLean. Jean and her husband David live in an English garden, fragrant and informal, that snuggles into a rocky, arbutus-clad headland about a ten-minute walk through the woods from my patch of salal and wild roses. Retired from teaching, Jean now puts her nurturing skills to breeding purebred golden retrievers. The prized pups of Sunshine and Goldilocks now show up like familiar summer sunbeams all across the Islands. Jean also has a run of plump, glossy chickens. They attract raccoons, eagles and anything else that thinks it might heist a free lunch. Defending her family of unusual laying hens has turned her into a hawk-eyed sentinel. This time, she was calling with news about the orphaned seal pup. It wasn't good news. Jean reported that while walking her dogs after the whales came, she'd counted five dead seal pups. "There's something in the rocks toward your place," Jean said. My heart sank. She didn't say dead. She didn't have to.

Terry Quigley, a retired logger and longshoreman who lives in the other direction, told of tiny bodies with the tell-tale row of holes—"like a machine gun"—from whale teeth. When the killer whales slash into a group of seals, he explained, they often kill or cripple as many as they can as quickly as they can, crunching them in their huge jaws before returning to dine at leisure on the crippled and the dead.

"The eagles are all up in that big fir and the ravens are down hopping on the beach," Jean said. "You know the way they hop..." Her voice trailed off. I do know the way they hop. I once watched a pair of ravens gleefully torment a chained dog, one tempting him to dash into a bone-jarring stop at the end of his tether while the other pecked the eyes out of his frozen fish. Then they did turnabout, keeping at it until the dog gave up and lay there, stunned and sullen, while the birds ate his food. The hopping Jean described meant the ravens were homing in for the kill.

I went down. The ravens retreated to bluster from a tree so laden with predators and carrion birds that it looked like a cartoonist's emblem for doom. Below the tree, wedged into a hot, dry crevice in the rock, was Susan's seal pup. Unable to retreat into the pounding surf, the four-day-old baby had now been abandoned for seventy-two hours. It was alive, but it would shortly have its eyes pecked out by ravens. So much for non-intervention. I scooped the baby out of its hiding place. The soft, silky fur was loose and difficult to grasp, but I got one hand under its front flippers and the other under its wriggling abdomen. Like any other frightened baby, it promptly widdled all over me.

Up at the house, Susan had readied Heledd's yellow plastic swimming pool. We kept it dry because the aquarium biologists said the pup didn't need to be kept in water. The pool would serve to keep the pup in one place. Meanwhile, the travel cage we use to take her two cats to the vet for annual shots and checkups was retrieved from under the house and readied.

I thought my daughter was going to burst with excitement. "Teachable moment," said Susan, and sat Heledd down for a talk about the life of pinnipeds while her daughter was able to watch a real one wriggling about in her pool. "Boy or a girl?" she wanted to know. I'm pretty good on people, but figuring out seal gender is another matter. With a child's wisdom, Heledd decided to call the baby Sam, that way it could be either a Sammy or a Samantha. She wet down the pup's open mouth with her water wand. She examined the flippers with their big, blunt nails. She looked into the liquid, unblinking gaze from eyes adapted to underwater sight. She exclaimed over the tiny milk teeth that gleamed every time the pup yawped, which was often.

The seal pup was ready to go anywhere to get away from the big, smelly humans. Sam got up over the edge of the plastic pool and headed for the crawl space. I put it in the cat cage. The seal bawled forlornly. Heledd came up with the idea of lending the seal baby her own mum to sing it a lullaby. There was no evading this offer. So Susan settled her little one on her knee and sang to the other about killer whales and summer gales not being good for baby seals. It worked, too. Sam fell asleep.

Not so dad. I scrambled to rejig schedules. An interview in Victoria was cancelled. Harbour Air was still willing to pick up the seal, but had no flights until the next day. I doubted the pup would last till then and so did the aquarium. We'd missed the direct ferry to Tsawwassen, about 40 kilometres south of Vancouver. To get Sam to the aquarium now, we'd have to add long hours travelling via Swartz Bay on Vancouver Island or wait for the evening sailing to Tsawwassen. The aquarium wanted minimum time in transit to reduce stress, so we opted to wait for the direct trip late that afternoon. Overhead, hopeful eagles waited all day. This time, they were out of luck. The back seat of the car was lowered, in went a boat tarp, the cat cage was stowed and off to catch the ferry went Dad, Heledd and a loudly protesting Sam.

In the Gulf Islands, the direct route from A to B is not always the fastest. The ferry lost an engine en route. We limped toward our connection at Village on Mayne Island about forty-five minutes late. Susan relayed a message that the biologists planning to collect Sam at Tsawwassen now could not be there. They were committed to a public address on sea lions. I made a call from the ferry's radiotelephone to report the seal pup's status: Sam appears seriously stressed, breathing shallowly and is becoming listless. My report was overheard by a kindly woman who tapped me on the shoulder. She wondered if there was anything she could do to assist me with my ailing granddad, Sam, whom I'd left down there on the car deck. She was gallant indeed, considering I'd just been complaining about how bad Sam smelled.

By now, my car was truly ripe with seal, a rich odour to which my daughter seemed oblivious but that for me conjured memories of the Inuit kamiks I once dropped in the dark at Resolute Bay. Unfortunately, they landed beside the heater. Made from the flippers of the bearded seal and hand-sewn with special overlapping seams, these Inuit boots are a miracle of engineering—supple, warm and waterproof. But my pair had been made for service in the deepfreeze of the Arctic ice floes, not the hallways of a federal government airbase. They were raw seal skin, untanned and untreated. From beside the heater, their stench quickly cleared the bunkhouse while I slept. I remained friendless for weeks. I'd just reached the conclusion that I wouldn't be welcome in the car pool for awhile, either. I wound down all the windows for the trip down the freeway from ferry terminal to downtown Vancouver. We rolled along Granville Street toward Georgia, Dad with his head stuck out the window, daughter singing merrily, hidden seal pup yawping and bellowing at the steel and glass towers of high finance. At stoplights, I noted pained looks from pedestrians hurrying to dinner and the theatre. One slightly inebriated pedestrian leaned over to offer his beer-perfumed advice: "Lord, music lessons won't help that kid!"

The aquarium was closed for the evening when we arrived. A sense of panic began to prickle at the back edge of our mercy mission. I knew Sam would not be welcome in any motel bathtub we were likely to find in Vancouver, even down on skid row. The idea of sleeping in my heavily perfumed car with a bellowing seal was bringing on an anxiety attack. My daughter tugged at my sleeve. "Dad, there are people in the gift shop." There were. A Japanese tour group was dawdling over last-minute presents. While I sought an aquarium official, Heledd enthusiastically introduced Sam to a circle of admiring Asian youngsters. Japanese, English, Seal talk—language posed no barriers among the children.

Sammy's a boy, it turns out, and he now has new digs. It's a high-sided plastic tub in the old monkey cage being phased out along with the archaic zoo facilities and now put to better use in the saving of life instead of constraining it. The Vancouver Aquarium's Marine Mammal Rescue and Rehabilitation Centre promised to fatten Sammy up on formula, wean him to fish and three months later, when he'd put on the nice thick coat of blubber mum would have provided, return him to the arms of the slow swinging sea.

We left him to the care of the biologists and raced for the last ferry. Luckily for us, it wasn't on time: arriving half an hour late, I found I was an hour early. None of this mattered to my little daughter. Happy in her day's good deed, she fell into a deep sleep and dreamed of Sammy, she tells me, all the way home. Who knows what dreams fill a sleeping child's head? But Heledd didn't stir, not when we bumped down the steep washboard of the lane that twists to tidewater among the whispering cedars, not even in the transfer to her own warm bed, where the sea beneath the window fills her slumbers with its own restless bedtime stories.

Canada Day at Yuquot

As an antidote to the tired assumptions that always seem to colonize our Canada Day weekends, I decide that for the first one of the new millennium I'll take my ten-year-old daughter Heledd to Yuquot to visit the place where modern history first collided with the West Coast's ancient and mysterious past. We first drive 266 kilometres north from Victoria to Campbell River, then another 88 kilometres through the rugged mountains west of Campbell River to Gold River, where Margarita James, director of cultural and heritage resources for the Mowachaht/Muchalaht First Nations, dispatches us for another hour by boat, dodging deadheads and crashing through glossy swells.

Yuquot is where the compelling Mowachaht Chief Maquinna confronted the European superpowers of his day just over two hundred years ago. A place of stunning beauty, it straddles a narrow isthmus connecting several rocky outcrops to Nootka Island. Think of two crescent moons lying back to back. That's both the shape and the luminous colour of the two great canoe beaches, one opening to sheltered waters, the other facing the booming green combers of the outer coast. The old village site is one of those places that resonates with energy from the moment you step ashore and notice the strange, perfectly oval pebbles that are polished as smooth as glass beads and left in heaps by the tireless sea.

It's a difficult feeling to describe, an eerie combination of history and some less tangible spiritual presence. But perhaps this feeling is merely the burden carried in by the visitor who has taken time to read about the mysterious, mystical whalers' shrine that was located on an island in a sacred lake. It was here, long before Europeans had even arrived in the New World, that Mowachaht inhabitants of E'as and Tsaxis, two ancient villages farther north on the wild, hurricane-lashed western fringe of Vancouver Island, first began hunting and harpooning gray and humpback whales, later bringing their knowledge to Yuquot. Whatever I might have felt from the weight of this history, my carefree daughter is soon wading through the sun-bronzed grass that nods over the ruins of a settlement from this culture that was already ancient when the Greeks went to sack Troy. The surf booms and seethes up the shingle, the breeze makes cat's-paws on the rippling meadow, nectar-laden bees fumble at the Indian paintbrush and blue camas and the air is rich with the sweet scent of clover. Some things never change.

We stop to chat with Ray Williams and his wife Teresa, the last continuous occupants of the site, largely abandoned in 1967 when the federal government moved the inhabitants to Gold River. "The chiefs asked us to move, too, but we said no," Ray tells us. "We stayed. We're the caretakers of Maquinna's lands. That move, that was a mistake—a really big mistake. The government moved our people right next to that pulp mill in Gold River. It was an awful place, babies were getting sick." Ray gestures to where his talented son Sanford is at work carving a new totem pole and directs us to where we might look at some ancient poles, now down, moss-covered and already rotting back into the earth as they were meant to do. "This place is our people's spiritual centre," Ray says.

I follow my daughter along the beach and into the trees. Below us glimmers Jewitt Lake, named for John Jewitt, captive of Maquinna for two years after the rest of the crew of the ship *Boston* had been killed by Mowachaht warriors in 1803. It surrounds the island where the whaling chiefs had the shrine that is also known as their Washing House, certainly the most important monument in the west coast aboriginal whaling culture. The shrine, a spectral structure of carved wooden figures and human skulls, was the focal point of the long and arduous rituals of purification and preparation that had to be undertaken by the chiefly lineages, which, like the kings of Europe with their royal deer and Indian rajahs with their tigers, reserved to themselves alone the right to hunt whales. Although the Whalers' Shrine is considered one of the most significant artifacts from that interface between the physical and supernatural worlds inhabited by both mythic and shamanic figures on the pre-contact West Coast of Canada, its power is defined as much by the absence of reference points as by anything else.

Collected by George Hunt at the instigation of anthropologist Franz Boas in 1905, the shrine was dismantled and removed to the American Museum of Natural History, where it resides to this day. Yet even stories about it obtained from First Nations informants are scattered and scarce, as though even those who knew what it signified were reluctant to talk about its origins and the way the rites practised here shaped the society around them. One thing is clear: like a dark body that's discerned by astronomers through its influence on the space surrounding it, the gravity exerted by the Whalers' Shrine upon the spiritual cosmos of the Nuu-chah-nulth who lived at Yuquot made it a pretty skookum place.

Yet there's another residual power here that affects newcomers, too. This is where, in 1778, Captain James Cook became the first European to set foot on the Northwest Coast. These days it's popular among the politically correct to sniff at the accomplishments of men like Cook, but his voyages of exploration in small wooden ships on an uncharted sea so vast it could drown all the Earth's continents is more akin to journeying to the moon than our technological hubris likes to acknowledge. Cook, in fact, was greeted with enthusiasm by Maquinna, who quickly seized the political opportunity to make himself a crucial power-broker and established Yuquot as a key base in the commercial fur trade that followed. During a visit eight years later one Mr. Strange, a passenger aboard a visiting sailing ship, gave Yuquot its English name: Friendly Cove. It proved a good name.

Britain and Spain were at the brink of war over rival claims to the Northwest Coast when the Spanish established a fort here in 1791. Maquinna invited Captain George Vancouver and Captain Juan Francisco de la Bodega y Quadra to a formal dinner, helping defuse the tension while a solution was worked out between the two great European powers. In 1795, when Spain peacefully withdrew, the British commissioner presented Maquinna with the Union Jack that had been raised when London's claims prevailed.

Today, Friendly Cove is a national historic site and these great events are commemorated with a cairn and various plaques—not one of which, my daughter observes, makes any mention of either Maquinna or the Mowachaht people who had been there for 4,300 years. But that soon changes. Up at the white glare of the abandoned church with its stained glass windows depicting the historic events that entangled these three nations forever, we find the pews pushed aside, the smell of fresh paint and a bustle of activity amid the rainbow splinters of light that spill across the age-darkened floorboards. Robin Inglis, director of the North Vancouver Museum and Bob Eberle, a theatre professor at the University of British Columbia, are frantically preparing for a remarkable event—the arrival of three crates aboard the coastal freighter *Uchuck III.* They contain a gift to the Mowachaht and Muchalaht from the Spanish government. It's a collection of high-quality artistic reproductions of the charts and drawings of Yuquot and its original inhabitants made by Tomás Suria and José Cadero, members of Quadra's crew more than two hundred years ago. "These are the images you see in all the textbooks," Robin says. "What an interesting thing for the Mowachaht to have this collection of images from the moment of first contact." Robin and Bob are helping to set up a summer-long exhibition at the site in preparation for a celebration when the Mowachaht of Gold River will hold a reunion at Yuquot. Visitors were invited to join them for a salmon feast, traditional songs and dances while the Spanish were to formally present their gift.

In the meantime, an extra set of muscles is welcome and I am pressed into service helping load the heavy crates aboard an all-terrain vehicle and then keeping them in place behind the driver as we bounce our way back up the overgrown plank road from the wharf to the church through the salmonberry canes, blackberry brambles and salal. At the church, a young woman comes down to help unload. Marsha Maquinna, daughter of the present chief, reaches in and lifts out a picture. It is Suria's imposing portrait of her own ancestor, the great chief Maquinna himself. And as my daughter observes, on this coast, you can't stuff much more Canada into a Canada Day than that.

Lock, Stock and Barrel

The wind had been picking up steadily out of the southeast all afternoon. What began as fitful gusts was now blowing at more than 100 kilometres per hour, lashing the crests of the icy swells of Hecate Strait into lacy white. Spindrift had begun to splatter against the cabin glass like bursts of liquid buckshot. It was September 28, 1972, a date that is burned indelibly into the collective memory of most Canadians. That was the afternoon that Paul Henderson banged the puck past Vladimir Tretiak to win game eight of the first Canada-Russia hockey series The date is imprinted upon the memory of Chief Joe Gosnell, too. But his recollection has nothing to do with hockey. It has to do with the day on which the course of his people's history came within a perilous hair of taking a different direction.

I had come to talk to Joe in New Aiyansh, more than 800 kilometres north of Vancouver, just before the new treaty between the Nisga'a, Canada and British Columbia came into effect. It had taken more than one hundred years of tears and tenacity to fashion this new political relationship among equals but only a nanosecond to demolish the old paternal one. At the first stroke of midnight on May 10, 2000, the Nisga'a Tribal Council, of which Joe is president, ceased to exist and the new Nisga'a Lisims Government exerted its sovereign control over 1,900 square kilometres of territory in the Nass Valley and its 6,000 citizens in four villages and three urban locals. The two hundred years of colonialism ended here with a patriotic eruption of red and white maple leaf flags to celebrate the Nisga'a nation's emotional entry into Canada.

"We got our flags up there," Mary Davis, a receptionist in what's now the new capital, told me with enthusiasm. "Three flags came out right away, as soon as the phone call came. Three is a lucky number. Gosh, it feels good to be part of Canada."

"It's slowly sinking in. We're Canadians. We're not numbers anymore," marvelled Jane Gosnell, daughter of the late James Gosnell, the Nisga'a Tribal Council president who in 1983 bluntly told a provincial government refusing to recognize aboriginal rights that Natives owned British Columbia "lock, stock and barrel." James died in 1988 at the age of sixty-four and his younger brother Joseph emerged as the president who would lead the negotiators who have now brought the treaty home. And at the end of a long and occasionally acrimonious debate that was still dogged by a couple of unresolved court challenges, the people of the Nass were holding out a giant olive branch to a country whose most powerful political leaders once described them as "bestial rather than human," outlawed their religion and cultural practices and seized their children for re-education in the ways of the dominant society.

There are still many critics of the treaty. Some, like Canadian Alliance MP Keith Martin, have likened the agreement to South African apartheid. Others say the treaty creates a third order of government, which the Nisga'a and their supporters deny. "Their critics don't accept them as a people," says University of BC political scientist Paul Tennant, who has been studying the First Nations land question in the province for decades. "They accept them as individuals but not as a collective people. The rest of us have said we do accept them as a people and welcome them into Canada on that basis. Colonialism, for the Nisga'a people, now ends. They now, on their own terms, come fully into Canada."

But there was no time for rancour among the Nisga'a when phones and cell phones began to ring all over the valley, a kind of high-tech chorus signalling that the first treaty in BC's modern history had passed through the Senate by a vote of 52 to 15 and was on its way to Governor General Adrienne Clarkson to receive Royal Assent. There were tears. There was joy. There was quiet reflection on the scores of elders who had grown old and died in the long struggle to realize the right to govern themselves—leaders like bold Chief Israel Sgat'iin, who in 1886 sent a squad of provincial government surveyors packing from the Nass with their instrument boxes unopened, perhaps the first assertion of Nisga'a sovereignty that Victoria actually understood. And there were grateful thoughts for still-living elders like Frank Calder, the 84-year-old whose own father was part of the Nisga'a Land Committee formed in 1890 to fight for aboriginal title. In 1913, the land committee sent three chiefs to London to petition the privy council. It referred the matter back to Canada for resolution. Later the committee morphed into the Nisga'a Tribal Council, which Frank revitalized while launching the bold 1968 lawsuit that forced the Liberal government of Pierre Trudeau to begin negotiations.

"I'm really happy today," says Jane Gosnell. "I guess as the day goes on I'll just feel happier and happier. When they first announced it I didn't know what to think. I stayed with my mom [Christine Gosnell], she's very emotional today. She was thinking about my dad, I guess. He was there negotiating for the first twenty years. I think there were probably tears when she was in private."

But after the remembrance of things past, it was time for fun in the here and now. Spontaneous parties broke out in all four Nisga'a villages.

The first celebration began in Kincolith, an isolated community of 377 that nestles beneath snow-capped peaks on the rugged north shore of the inlet into which the Nass River empties. "Everybody was just bubbling. They had a parade all the way from the church to the rec centre," says Mary Davis. "We didn't know how to react. It hasn't really begun to sink in yet."

In New Aiyansh almost half the town's 800 residents gathered to celebrate at the recreationand cultural centre. "We're going to have a banquet for our leaders," Mary says. "You know Ed Wright has been there for the last thirty years and we're all so happy for him. We watched them for a minute on the TV coming down the stairs. They were all talking on their cell phones, calling their wives I guess."

"I'm feeling pretty emotional, kind of excited. I've got butter-flies," says Debra Clayton, who works at the Coho Convenience Store. "There were quite a few people who put out their maple leaf flags today. They were just hanging them on the patios and off the railings, that kind of thing. This makes me feel a lot more Canadian." But Debra says she can't stay to party. "I have to go to work. Life goes on, you know."

James Gosnell would understand. While he lay dying in a Prince Rupert hospital, the Eagle chief of Gitlakdamks gave the Vancouver *Sun*'s Terry Glavin a message to convey to British Columbians. "If the BC government figures that Jimmy Gosnell is going to die, and so goes the land claim, they're badly mistaken. Badly mistaken," he said. "It's going to come. There's no question in my mind. It has to come. But maybe I will be visiting with St. Peter when that day comes." It's twelve years to the day since he made that prediction in 1988. St. Peter, no doubt, is sharing a smile over the posthumous triumph and the outburst of good will.

Meanwhile, James' little brother's task is to guide the transi-tional government as it prepares the way for its full democratic successor. And while he's serving as the first elected Nisga'a leader, Joe admits that he's tired, that after almost a decade of fighting to bring the treaty to fruition, he really wants to retire from politics and, he hopes, get a few more seasons aboard his 11-metre fish boat, the *Nisga'a Cloud*. "If I miss this year, it will be my seventh year off my boat," he says ruefully. "I told the last [Nisga'a] convention that once we've seen the passage of the treaty, that's it for me. I think I've made my contribution."

But twenty-eight years ago, out there on the storm-tossed Pacific about 750 kilometres northwest of Vancouver, when all this lay in the future and he was many hours from hope of safe harbour, the man who would inherit the name Sim'oogit Hleek and become grand chief of the Eagle Clan, the chief destined to lead the Nisga'a nation to its hour of glory, was simply trying to stay alive. "We knew there was a storm coming," he says, shaking his head. "We made the decision to try and beat it back [to the mainland] from the Queen Charlottes. Big mistake. It caught us halfway home. What should have been a ten-hour trip took eighteen hours."

There were eight boats caught by that storm in the middle of Hecate Strait, as mean a piece of water as there is on this coast when the equinoctial gales come roaring all the unobstructed way from Cape Caution to Naikoon, the sandy spit at the north end of Haida Gwaii where the tidal streams meet in a seething overfall of breakers and whirlpools. Joe was alone aboard the *Miss Marilyn*, named for his beloved first daughter. His big brother James, who would precede him as president of the Nisga'a Tribal Council, was skippering his own boat, *PE 259*. And his father Eli, whom Joe credits for whatever wisdom and personal discipline he has been able to bring to the arduous and sometimes fractious treaty negotiations, was piloting the *Lady G*. The examples set by both James and Eli, Joe says, were crucial to the development of his own formidable leadership skills—abilities that would enable him to broker a deal that was acceptable to his own people as well as to the federal and provincial governments. That he was able to do so in a climate of acrimonious opposition from both aboriginal and non-aboriginal factions is evidence of the soft-spoken but tough-minded diplomacy that characterizes his political style.

But back then, trying to keep his footing on the pitching deck, all the toughness and self-discipline he could muster was in demand for himself. Out of sight of land, combers were now breaking over the deck of the *Miss Marilyn*. Joe had already climbed into his immersion suit—the insulated flotation device that might give him a few more hours of life in the frigid waters. "Twice I almost walked off the boat," he says. "The waves were coming right over her. I took all my personal ID and I taped it to my chest so that when they found my remains, they'd know who I was."

Today, everybody knows Joe Gosnell, the man who brought home the Nisga'a canoe launched by Frank Calder when he took the federal government to court back in 1968, losing the case on a technicality but winning a stunning acknowledgement that aboriginal rights are a legal fact. The present chief's beginnings were humble and "I first screamed my protests at the world" at a salmon cannery on the Nass River on June 23, 1936, one of five sons and five daughters born to Eli Gosnell and Mary Moore. His father, a deeply religious man who prayed with the Salvation Army, insisted on a strict upbringing both in the Christian faith and in the ancient culture of his people. "He never allowed us to do anything on Sunday, even when we were teenagers," Joe recalls. "And both my mother and my father made sure we adhered to the Nisga'a customs and traditions."

His father was a legendary boat builder who produced twenty-five boats that Joe remembers, boats that were prized in the salmon fleet up and down the coast. "My mother worked in the net loft at the cannery," he says. "She was an extremely qualified person, as so many of our Nisga'a women were. She worked all her life in that profession, right up until the year she passed on."

In 1943, when he was seven, he found himself one of fifteen or twenty bewildered children standing on the dock at the Inverness cannery. His mother was weeping and saying in Nisga'a—none of them spoke English—"you are going away to learn, to learn and be educated." The journey took two days by steamer and delivered him to St. Michael's Residential School in Alert Bay near the north end of Vancouver Island. It was, he says, the beginning of a harsh period in his tender life. Although he neither experienced nor even heard rumours of the sexual abuse and physical brutality that occurred in other residential schools, it was not an easy experience, Gosnell says. "That was a rough life. The discipline was extremely hard. Oh, well do I know the taste of soap. Every night you could hear the children crying in the dormitories." Yet the experience had its virtues, Gosnell says. "I made friendships there. Whenever the tribal groups from across the province meet, I greet my friends from those days. And it taught me discipline. It put backbone in my spine. I walked away from that and I knew I could stand up to anything."

Alex Rose, who has worked for the Nisga'a Tribal Council for many years and has written a biography of Joe, points out that it was the kind of moral backbone that permitted the Nisga'a chief to become the only official delegate at the controversial 1997 APEC summit in Vancouver to draw attention to matters of human rights and the protestors outside. Asked to deliver the opening prayer at the $1,000-a-plate dinner, he found himself speaking from a dais flanked by US President Bill Clinton, China's President Jiang Zemin and Prime Minister Jean Chrétien, while the human rights protest swirled outside. "I ask you to remember those people whose views I believe must be taken into consideration," he told the most powerful leaders in the world, breaking protocol and risking offending Chrétien, on whom the Nisga'a were relying for the passage of their long-sought treaty. "It was a defining moment," Rose says. "He refused to play the insider's game and stand at the podium as the token Indian."

Maybe that sympathy for the marginalized and the courage to express it is not surprising, considering the toughness required to survive those days when he was ripped from his parents' loving embrace and sent away to residential school. Yet if they might try to take away his language and reshape him in European terms, they could never take from him what it meant to be Nisga'a. Always running through his own dreams in the prison-like building so far from home was the great, dark Nass, the silvery rustle of eulachon in the spring and the glint of the first salmon entering the river from which his people draw their very identity. "I've been to the headwaters of the Nass," he'll say, his measured, sonorous voice going a bit dreamy even today. "The water is so clear you can see 400 feet down into the lake. The Nass at its headwaters is only about four feet wide and about four inches deep, yet from it comes this!" And he sweeps his arm in a decisive arc across the gravel bars and back eddies.

On the other side of the river, lost in the alders and cotton-woods, you can see the weathered Victorian gingerbread and bird-cage fronts of the houses abandoned in Old Aiyansh after a flood carried away the lower village. "It started at about two in the morn-ing. We walked up to my father's house and the boardwalks were already floating. By then the houses nearest the river had begun to float away." He stops and points abruptly to a greying structure in the distant trees. "That house is my brother James' house. He was quite a guy, one of the main spokesmen for the Nisga'a during the constitutional debates. We learned a lot from each other. He and I fished many, many years together. You get in a confined space together and you get to know your partner very, very well. You always observe what your elder brother says and does."

It's clear that his elder brother had a profound influence on Joe. After James' death, Joe was to inherit the heavy responsibilities of the senior chief and to emerge as the last and perhaps the greatest president of the Nisga'a Tribal Council and the first elected leader of the new Nisga'a Lisims Government. He has already lectured on this process of decolonization at some of the most prestigious uni-versities in Europe and has been granted two honorary degrees, one from Simon Fraser University, the other from the University of Northern BC. "It felt good for a grade-five guy to be able to do that," he says with evident satisfaction.

Rose says Joe is both telegenic and a quick media study, a natural leader who instinctively took the high road during an often rancorous debate over the treaty. During a speaking tour of Europe two years ago, Rose says, the North Coast fish boat skipper won celebrity status among world leaders in business, politics and at the United Nations. "They treated him with respect, as an equal. He was the star at embassies in Britain, Holland and Austria," Rose says. "In essence, he was an ambassador who graciously represented not only his own people, but all of Canada." Perhaps that is why, when the treaty finally received royal assent in Ottawa, the flag that was flying over the Peace Tower was presented to the Nisga'a chief.

And none of this might have happened if he hadn't had stiffened his spine and dismissed those thoughts about stepping off the Miss *Marilyn*'s deck and into the violence of the storm on that September day so long ago.

Go Tell it
to the Blackfeet

I scudded into the ancient village of Ans'pa yaxw (Kispiox) before a wind that sounded like a high river in the cottonwoods. It was evening and sunset trailed blue and gold streamers through the clouds piling in from the northwest. Down at the curve of the Kispiox River, young men were doing what people here have done for 10,000 years. They cast their lines into the muscular brown current, fishing for the early spring salmon already ascending the watersheds. Whatever we surmise from our commercial fishing seasons, I'm told that there is not a month of the calendar in which there are not some salmon returning to spawn. These cycles of the salmon, the rivers, the land and the people are linked in mysterious ways that most of us can never fathom.

From the bank, the austere grey totems of the Gitksan and Wet'suwet'en people tilt and stagger back toward the settlement. This is no engineer's grid of efficient streets and square lots, but the organic higgledy-piggledy of real life. It is a dishevelled sprawl of muddy doglegs, dead-end lanes, houses set this way and that. And dominating everything is the Kispiox, the river that gave birth to the community, that was its highway, the talisman of its seasonal connections with the world. Past the gape-windowed, gingerbread folly of somebody's Victorian pretensions, past the school with its traditional Gitksan murals in red and black, past the cemetery filled to the aching brim by smallpox, tuberculosis, alcohol and despair, I found the community hall.

Debbie Starr, 11, little sister Edna, 7, and Jarrett Wilson, 3, perched in a line on the front steps. They greeted me with an open friendliness and curiosity that's hidden in most urban kids. Like me, they came early to get good seats at the opening of *No'Xya'*, a play about their ancestral lands and what is being done to them in the name of progress, politics and profits. I hadn't seen the play in its earlier incarnations. It first toured BC in 1987, then Canada in 1988, now—rewritten, revised and revitalized—it's going through a six-show warmup in northern communities before taking its gritty political message to the international stage. This time it's bound for a nineties' tour of traditional Maori villages in New Zealand, timed to coincide with an anniversary of the treaty that ended the bloody war between Maoris and European settlers in 1840. Playwright and director David Diamond hopes this is its final rebirth. He says the energy is dissipating. "We need a totally new play," he told me. "Times change. You can't keep doing the same thing."

I only partly agree with him. Taking *Our Footprints* to New Zealand may be a worthy exercise in aboriginal solidarity, but if the intent of political art is to galvanize political and moral action, this play deserves a tour of Europe. There it would speak powerfully to other submerged aboriginal minorities—the Welsh, Scots, Bretons spring immediately to mind. More important, it should confront the European origins of the present Gitksan dilemma and present them with an opportunity to be part of a solution—if only by denying Canadians, and particularly our federal and provincial governments, their smug sense of superiority in matters of freedom and human rights. Because that's what this play is about. It's about conquest, occupation, oppression and denial of self-determination. And all the while we mask the whole brutal process in self-congratulatory lies about the wonders of Canadian democracy.

The play is a luminous, eloquent indictment of what too many of us passively accept. It sharpens and clarifies issues that are deliberately obscured by legal pedants, political cynics, blustering bureaucrats and, worst of all, the mealy-mouthed rhetoric of grasping business interests. Those interests happily participate in cultural genocide if it means better quarterly reports and the fat earnings which will permit branch plant executives to retire in self-satisfied comfort. "Those trees out there are not a forest, they're a bank," says one of the characters, a logging show boss. "One hundred and ten truckloads a day, that's what we can get out of this place." I'd be tempted to accuse the playwright of crude stereotyping if I hadn't heard similar words myself. This place, of course, is the ancestral homeland of a whole people—elders, chiefs, traditions, beliefs and, beyond them, Debbie, Edna and little Jarrett. What benefit to them if the price of a few jobs today is eternal severance of a timeless connection with their land and the final withering of their culture, which has endured so much suffering at our hands?

In 1858, for the last time, the Kutenai crossed the southern passes of what are now called the Canadian Rockies and hunted buffalo on the Great Plains. We know this with some precision from the Winter Count of the Blackfeet, a chronicle of momentous events begun two hundred years ago by Iron Shirt. Each generation added entries and passed it down until it came to Mrs. Many Guns of the Pikuni, whom we call the North Peigan. In the spring of 1876, the I.G. Baker Company of Fort Benton, Montana, shipped 75,000 prime buffalo hides to the tanning industry of the eastern United States. The 1879 Winter Count is succinct. Its four chilling words mark the death of a culture: "When the buffalo disappeared." There's an unusual second entry that says "when they move camp." Moving camp was noteworthy because it took place in the depths of winter during mass starvation in the Pikuni lodges.

Barely thirty years before, there had been 60 million buffalo on the western plains. Then there were none. The Blackfeet, once the most feared warriors on the prairies, were reduced to beggars. "With the buffalo went the whole basis and reason of the Plains Indians' culture," wrote Lieutenant Colonel Frazier Arnold of the US Army, shocked by what he had seen. "The greedy and pre-emptive whites, in inexhaustible numbers, kept trooping in, changing and despoiling the country and desecrating the face of nature. This was the Indian point of view, as it would have been the point of view of any war-like and self-respecting race of men under similar circumstances." The disappearance of the buffalo, of course, conveniently cleared the plains for the agriculture industry and forced Native people into the concentration camps we coyly call reserves.

David Diamond's play raises the troubling argument that history could well be repeating itself in British Columbia. Kispiox already has enough problems: substance abuse, violence, kids leaving for Vancouver, the city that eats people. Poverty is visible here, in broken windows patched with sacks, peeling paint and sagging porches. But this signals only the lack of money. A community can be poor in money and in other ways remain rich beyond count. Something here transcends money. It strikes past suffering, speaks to hope and the resilience of the human spirit. It springs from the redemptive quality of people's love for one another—the very qualities, some would argue, that the dominant culture seeks to kill in its drive to exploit the wealth of Indian lands.

Salmon and trees, not buffalo, are the central issue and while the play has been criticized in some quarters for taking a superficial view of complicated and complex matters, I don't agree with that criticism. Like that four-word entry in the Winter Count, *No'Xya'* strips the discussion to its brutal essentials: the fish, the forests and their spiritual importance to the integrated core of Gitksan and Wet'suwet'en culture. It talks about the place of these things in the dreams of a people. Their power is confirmed when salmon dancers slipped through the audience. Small fidgeting children around me gasp in awe and wonder, then sit motionless as stones in the presence of something intangible, restless and immense beyond the masks.

The fate of the salmon and, beyond them, the forests, are inextricably linked, in Lieutenant Colonel Arnold's words, "to the whole basis and reason" of Gitksan and We'suwet'en cultural identity. Those links are clearly threatened by the same "greedy and preemptive" whites who demolished the Blackfeet way of life. The most massive clear-cuts in BC ocurred in lands claimed since the first chiefs marked out the clan territories and established their laws, thousands of years before Magna Carta. "They have emptied my mother's land. I will not be chief. There is nothing left," despairs the character Gyat. Later he joins a blockade, making his grief the crucible of action. It counters a logger's incantation: "If you clear-cut the forest so the trees are all down, the birds fly away, the animals are gone and the soil goes down to the river so the salmon are gone, and that makes it easier to clear-cut the forest..." Are the interests behind clear-cuts and industrialization of the salmon fishery—in lands and watersheds never surrendered by the Gitksan—compatible with the survival of aboriginal culture? Foresters, loggers and politicians all assure us so.

Go tell it to the Blackfeet.

The People in Between

Axwin_desqxw, hereditary chief of the Wolf Clan, traces the smoothly chiselled grain of a wooden outline with his fingertips and becomes suddenly introspective, squinting into the chill wind sweeping down from the dazzling snowfields of the Seven Sisters wilderness. Up at Gitanyow village just off the Cassiar Highway, 800 kilometres north of Vancouver, the distant past intrudes into the busy present with an ease that is as disarming as it is disturbing, an eerie reminder that all this modernity is an overlay as insubstantial as a coat of paint slapped on an Egyptian obelisk. In this case, the overlay consists of lines drawn on maps by colonial authorities who knew little and cared less about the traditional boundaries that defined the ancient geopolitics of clan and tribal territories.

And now, in the spring of 2000, just as the federal and provincial governments celebrate their treaty agreement with the Nisga'a, those old tribal boundaries threaten to jam a stick in the spokes. "There was war in the Meziadin around 1861," the chief says. "We had a formal treaty, the G'Awaganis, that transferred this territory around Meziadin Lake to the Gitanyow. My grandfather died at the age of 100. He had lived all his life in the Meziadin. My mother lived there all her life. There were no Nisga'a there.

"What the government does is grant the Nisga'a rights they never had. It's very worrisome for our people. This represents a major assault against our laws, against our system. It's the supreme violation of the *ayuukl* [the traditional code of law]. The punishment for that is mourning and then an outbreak of hostilities."

Behind us, the scattered houses of an ancient settlement once known as Kitwancool sprawl across the alluvial flats above the Kitwanga River. Before us, a grassy meadow bristles with more than two dozen mesmerizingly beautiful totem poles. These poles rank among the greatest expressions of monumental art in the world, somewhere on the order of the stone lions of Mycenae, the temple art of India or the painted rooms of Knossos. Each one of the poles, designed to evoke a narrative template from the collective lore of the eight great houses, costs a chief somewhere close to $70,000 to erect—this field alone represents almost $2 million—the wealth of the chiefs dispersed to perpetuate the stories by which the people define themselves and their culture.

The images on these poles are physical mnemonics for the *adaawkl*—the intricate code of songs, names, laws and epic poetry that comprise the oral history of the Gitanyow—a history once dismissed but that is now officially recognized as a result of the Supreme Court of Canada's judgment in the Delgamuukw case. It's a history the Gitanyow chiefs say began when the first ancestors of the Frog and Wolf clans moved into the uninhabited wilderness of the upper Nass and Kispiox river systems shortly after the last ice age, which ended around 12,000 years ago. The story that Axwin_desqxw— a slender, soft-spoken man of forty-two that the rest of us call Glen Williams—is retrieving from his psychic filing system was written into memory so long ago that no one can remember exactly when it happened. But every Gitanyow remembers where it took place, and remembers with great precision. "It was at the confluence of the Nangeese and the upper Kispiox rivers," Williams recalls. "It was early summer because the river was in full flood and the bears had young cubs."

His hand rests lightly upon the first of a stunning sequence of images adorning this particular totem pole. A mother grizzly and two cubs are displayed along with the scallop gashes that represent the marks made by bears sharpening their claws on the trunks of trees. "That bear was trying to cross the river and she put the two cubs on her ears," Williams says. "But one cub fell off and was drowned in the river." The Gitanyow who saw this event composed a dirge for the anguished mother bear and her drowned cub that is still sung by its owners at ceremonials. "This song is the proof that we have territory up in that area," says Williams. "It clearly identifies us as a distinct house with a crest and that relates back to our names and they, in turn, identify our lands. We have poles that pinpoint exactly where events occurred geographically that are referred to in our oral histories."

The lands to which he refers extend from the upper Kispiox to beyond Meziadin Lake, territory that is now included in the lands obtained by the Nisga'a of the Nass Valley under their treaty with the governments of Canada and British Columbia. Which helps explain why the Gitanyow villages were the gloomy reverse of the joyous Nisga'a villages when the first modern treaty in BC finally received Royal Assent on April 12, 2000. "People were crying. It was a sad day for the people, especially the women. They were concerned about the unknown." Williams says. "I was quite shocked [at the outburst of emotion]. If most of the 6,000 Nisga'a wrapped themselves in the Canadian flag and planned celebratory feasts for their chiefs, the 2,000-strong Gitanyow spoke darkly of a coming conflict both in the courts and on the disputed territories themselves."

"Some of our people are pretty pissed," Williams says, "especially the older people. They are mad at the Nisga'a and the government both. They want to knock down some bridges on roads that are on the boundary." He says the anger of the Gitanyow elders is unusual, "but then they know our system, they know the importance of our traditional names and their relationship to the land—and they know how deep is the violation of the traditional law. I've never seen my mum get mad before but she was pretty ticked off. Every time Nisga'a came on the news, she'd get up and turn it off."

At issue is a dispute over the control of 5,294 square kilometres of territory which the Gitanyow say belongs indisputably to them but that has been turned over to their neighbours. While the treaty gives the Nisga'a exclusive sovereignty over only 1,992 square kilometres in the Nass River watershed, it provides hunting, fishing and resource management rights in a much larger area known as the Nass Wildlife Area. The Gitksan who live just east and north of the Gitanyow, also complain that another 9,053 square kilometres, about 32 percent of the lands over which they claim traditional jurisdiction, have been included in these Nisga'a management zones. "About 1,500 of our people are affected by this new treaty," Williams says. "Their whole wildlife management area is basically in our territory. Those lands have the highest game and economic values. In effect, they really just creamed the best off our territory."

The Gitanyow occupy the territory west of the Kispiox River and north of the Skeena, sandwiched between the powerful Nisga'a and the equally powerful Gitksan, to whom they are culturally related but from whom they are fiercely independent. And Harry Daniels, another hereditary chief of the Wolf Clan says they have no intention of surrendering territory annexed to the Nisga'a without a fight. "We certainly aren't going to back out. We're really committed now to defend our territory. If we accept this, there's really nothing left of our territory except little parcels."

The Gitanyow will pursue a two-track strategy, Williams says. First there are the courts. He says the tribal group has already won one court declaration, sought in March of 1998, that the federal and provincial governments have an obligation to negotiate in good faith. They will argue in court that agreements signed with the Nisga'a have no effect insofar as they apply to lands claimed by the Gitanyow. Another action will seek a court declaration that the senior governments, upon entering negotiations with the Nisga'a, breached their fiduciary responsibility to negotiate in good faith and thus breached their fiduciary responsibilities to protect the interests of the Gitanyow. But Williams expects things to heat up long before the legal challenges finish grinding their way through the courts.

"I think this fight is going to be on the ground," he says. "Some of our key fishing grounds on the upper Nass have been placed in the Nisga'a core lands. So which rights play out first after conservation concerns? Is it the undefined Gitanyow right or the constitutionally protected treaty right of the Nisga'a?

"Well, the Gitanyow are very committed. They are not going to move over. That's where you are going to have some very volatile situations develop. I worry that there might be violence. People are so very angry. It's such a big assault. They are going to get out there and exercise the fishing rights that they enjoyed without the presence of the Nisga'a in the past. We will occupy our land and we will not leave."

Williams says the development appears to be part of a silent "divide and conquer" strategy in which the two senior governments hope to benefit, creating situations that cause various First Nations to squabble among themselves. But he says it's a mistaken strategy because it's going to create more problems than it resolves. "The Nisga'a might be given replacement rights, but that is going to be time-consuming now and very, very expensive."

One solution, Williams said, would be to provide some kind of interim protection for Gitanyow interests while solutions or shared jurisdictions could be negotiated with the Nisga'a. "That would be an immediate remedy. We've asked that this be done many times but we've never had any response. The only time they might get interested is if there's violence. If somebody gets shot in the territories, that's when they'll pay attention." Harry Daniels says: "We've tried for twenty years to work with the Nisga'a and met with failure. There is now nothing that would compel the Nisga'a to negotiate with us. This treaty is a political tragedy."

If there's a sense of betrayal among the Gitanyow with respect to the two governments, which have said territorial disputes should be worked out between aboriginal groups themselves, there's also a belief that they've been betrayed by non-Native opponents to the treaty. "We met with our MP and we thought he was sincere in bringing forward our amendments. It turned out later that they had their own agenda. They just generally want to attack all aboriginal people," Williams says.

Spring is breaking across this wild northern countryside and everywhere there's an atmosphere of apprehension. In six weeks the first of the big chinook salmon run will begin to enter the northern rivers and the Gitanyow say they fully intend to be at the fishing sites they've used since time immemorial, Nisga'a fisheries management or not. "This problem is not going to go away. The Gitanyow are not going to go away. And we can't be ignored," Williams says. "What's been ignored in the last two decades of trying to resolve this is the real truth of who we are, what the true traditional lands of the Gitanyow are, but some day the truth will come out."

Meanwhile, there's the pressing matter of how to respond to the Nisga'a flag waving. Axwin_desqxw runs his fingers across the bevelled edges that define the swimming grizzly bear and her cubs. This and the other amazing totem poles are a major attraction for tourists travelling the highway from Prince George to Prince Rupert. But perhaps not much longer. "As a protest, people want to cover these poles with black plastic," the chief says. "They want to show what the government has done to our history."

The Canoe People

While politicians dither and sceptics sneer at calls for aboriginal self-government, let's go and have a look at the future. We don't need a time machine to get there. Instead we'll hitch a ride with Waglisla Air, bumping and shuddering through the crosswinds and turbulence to head north by west up the Strait of Georgia to Bella Bella, about 500 kilometres as the Beaver flies from Vancouver. I enjoy flying in these light planes. They let you feel the texture of the air, remind you that it's not some ethereal idea, it has substance. I calculate that over thirty years I've flown enough kilometres jammed into cockpits over floats, skis and balloon wheels to get me to the moon and back a couple of times. Unlike some of my more worldly colleagues who get to kick back in executive class in the milk runs to Toronto and Hong Kong, I never get over the thrill of going up in something that feels like an airplane instead of a flying piano.

Under the wing tip, ragged white clouds pile up against the crumpled wall of the Coast Range, early outriders of a low-pressure system moving down from Queen Charlotte Sound. Behind us, a sulphurous pall of yellow and brown is stalled over the basin that's Howe Sound. People like me have to live in that stuff. The altimeter clicks over tirelessly as we climb to 10,000 feet. The winter sun lances into the murk and etches a gleaming line along the dark bulk of Vancouver Island, heaving like a whale back out of the ocean to the west, snowfields brilliant on Mount Arrowsmith, the Red Pillar and The Golden Hinde.

From this vantage point it's easy to imagine Martin Allerdale Grainger making his way north aboard the decrepit steamboat *Cassiar* with a crew of pale-faced hangovers, all bound for what he called Coola Inlet and a brutal handlogging show back in 1905 or thereabouts. I've brought along *Woodsmen of the West*, his remarkable account of early days on the coast. He wrote it in 1908 and dedicated it "To my Creditors, Affectionately." It reminds me that the more things change, the more they get the same. Grainger left the bush to serve as secretary to the Royal Commission on Forests in 1910. Two years later he took charge of writing BC's Forest Act, became the province's Chief Forester from 1916 to 1919 and attempted to curb the greed, waste and careless stewardship that "sacked the woods."

Here we are, almost a century later, wrestling with the same debate in the same language, not that British Columbians like the message much. *Woodsmen of the West* is largely available as a mouldering paperback put out thirty-five years ago not by the University of British Columbia Press, but by the University of Toronto.

At Port Hardy we touch down for freight, then climb again, scudding across the winds that whistle down Goletas Channel— that's "Schooner" Channel in the Spanish tongue of 1792. Below us, the irresistible edge of North America frays against the immovable mass of the Pacific Plate. The whole ragged coastline heaves and seethes with creamy lace. This storm surge telegraphs ominous weather beyond the horizon.

Conflicting forces have touched this region since George Vancouver gave a leather belt with three rows of thimbles to the Heiltsuk chief Kyete. In 1806, off the village of Kokyete on Spiller Channel, the Heiltsuk fought one of the coast's bloodiest battles with the crew of the Boston trader *Atahualpa*. Today the loudest rumblings come from seismic activity along the deep subduction faults. But temblors of change are jarring the foundations of North America's oldest continuous cultures.

The Heiltsuk have been here for at least 9,000 years—that's the earliest carbon-14 dating by archaeologists—but their oral history says ancestors arrived by sea when there were no trees, suggesting the period immediately after the last ice age, before life fully returned to the scoured landscape. They remain a sea people, taking sustenance from what remains of the rich maritime resources plundered by commercial interests. Winter herring, inshore halibut and abalone fisheries have all collapsed under the pressure of commercial exploitation. Still, the Heiltsuk are determined to endure on the homeland they have occupied since Babylon was a few huts by a muddy river and the ancestors of Canada's dominant culture were shocking the civilized folks in the Mediterranean with their own ornate blue tattoos. There are 2,000 souls at Bella Bella, the largest community between Port Hardy and Prince Rupert. They are strung along the foreshore of Campbell Island in three neat rows of houses that share a million-dollar view of Lama Passage. At this time, there's still no real BC Ferries dock here—although the *Queen of Prince Rupert* edges in once a week to take on foot passengers—and there's no land link, which makes this the largest community in the province that's so isolated.

The isolation itself is a link with historic BC, but it's the future we're here to see. I've come at the invitation of Cecil Reid, the Bella Bella band's chief councillor. He calls himself a technocrat but this intensely private man is really an architect of a remarkable example of what Indian Power means. As we bank sharply and nose into the wind, the first sign of that future gleams over the pilot's shoulder. The rain-slicked airstrip on which Wag Air is about to touch down is broad, long and paved from end to end. That's nothing to write home about from Vancouver. Here, as we'll see, it's a matter of enormous pride.

The cozy waiting room beside the landing strip is decorated with that curious combination of the practical and the impractical you still find in all the genuine BC outports. The magazines provided for passengers are the recycled subscriptions of R.R. Coutts at P.O. Box 23. Bureaucrats in jackets and ties who are here for a formal event are stumbling among informal stacks of duffle bags belonging to a crew bound for someplace even more remote. Greasy baseball hats and rumpled suits eye one another warily beneath curlicues of tinsel and ribbon. Whether these decorations overhead are leftovers from the official opening or early preparations for Christmas isn't clear. Posters on the wall promise shopping charters to Port Hardy for the festive season—$134.95 round trip—a reminder that zipping down to the mall is still a big decision in some places.

From here, the road twists away through stunted cedar, marshy ground, rocky outcrops and a vast borrow pit that cuts into a lens of glacial till for construction gravel. All the way into the streets of Bella Bella, the roadways are the rich black colour of newly laid pavement. Above these streets gleam rows of new houses. This isn't the bland, unimaginative public works architecture that curses so many Native communities with soul-destroying sameness. Cookie-cutter prefab boxes that soon deteriorate are the norm for many reserves. Here the houses come in a variety of sizes and designs. They range from the five-bedroom split-levels needed to accommodate the highest birth rate in the western hemisphere to cozy bungalows for empty nesters from an earlier generation. Except for the fact that the only road runs from the airport to the fish dock, there's a disconcerting sense that you've stumbled into a new Vancouver-area subdivision. The homes are designed to exploit spectacular sightlines and a glorious, whitecapped view across the Inside Passage. Yet, what we take for granted in West Vancouver is startling innovation when it comes to the usual reserve housing.

The identical utilitarian buildings that characterize too many reserves can be said to symbolize the dehumanizing message of oppression and contempt that represents our collective past. It's evidence of our unspoken social assumptions and a hidden agenda that sought to change native communities from vital places of cultural richness into faceless gulags. If this seems a harsh comparison, consider the nineteenth-century origins of reserves. Aboriginal communities were perceived as savages steeped in original sin and requiring centralized regulation for their own good. We banned religious rites, discredited ancient customs and sought to make the people passive for easier management by authorities. The bureaucratic mentality that reduced individuals to ciphers achieved its zenith among the Inuit, who as recently as thirty years ago had no legally recognized names and were issued only identification numbers.

In Bella Bella, these homes signal new expressions of individuality. In modern terms, they symbolize a small rebirth of the distinctiveness that marked family houses that had survived thousands of years prior to the arrival of Europeans. Small as this development seems on the surface, it is a far more important indicator of change than the alcoholism, teenage suicide and internal differences of opinion that invite attention from the media with its ever-predictable need to frame all events in the context of tragedy and political tension. The singling out of problems that are as common to Vancouver as to communities like Bella Bella is not unexpected. It affirms the mainstream stereotype of struggling Native communities and their inability to cope with the modern world. Yet Native communities have coped for two centuries with unwanted changes that most of us can barely imagine. Here, resurgent community pride marks a tide change.

Chief councillor Reid knows that pride in your community begins at home and self-determination is rooted in self-esteem. Spiritual growth needs a material platform. Cecil is one of the architects of a bold new initiative to recreate the symbolic landscape of his people, sweeping away the unmentionable gulag from which mainstream society averts its gaze, and replacing it with respect for individuals. The new houses here are about people taking back control of their lives. They are the outcome of a community housing development financed through commercial lending institutions in the open market and backed by standard Canada Mortgage and Housing Corporation guarantees. Alex Buckman is one of the people behind the program. I found Alex in the sterile glare of an idle fish shed and we raised our voices against a wind that buffeted metal sidings and whistled under the eavestroughs: that weather system pushing the swells I saw from the air is beginning to move across the coast. Alex is what they call a program officer for social housing with CMHC. He's spent the past eight years watching on-reserve housing projects transform British Columbia's Native communities. Originally, he was set on a career with the Bank of Montreal. Now, he says, he wouldn't trade his job for anything. And what is his job, precisely?

"I try to take away a lot of the bureaucracy that entangles the housing process." That means expediting from 100 to 125 private homes a year for 36 of the province's 44 Native bands, although surging aboriginal populations means the pressure is growing. In 1989—"that was the year we went crazy"—the program provided 156. Here at Bella Bella, population 2,000, the latest project involves 30 homes for one of BC's largest bands.

In the past, federal bureaucrats living in distant urban comfort dictated everything from colour of siding to shape of toilet seats, if indoor plumbing even existed, often with an eye to minimizing costs rather than meeting consumer needs or, heaven forbid, individual tastes. The consequences of this attempt at social engineering were obvious. Construction and materials were second rate. Design was devoid of imagination and often failed to consider family size. Homes deteriorated rapidly. Social conditions were eroded by brutalized self-esteem. Bella Bella was a good example of bad examples, says Alex. "There were a lot of older homes that really needed to be demolished. Now there are very few places like that."

The idea that aboriginal communities are perfectly capable of running their own affairs has never seemed such a surprising proposition in the communities themselves. After all, they maintained a stable and productive society for 10,000 years. For mainstream governments with their cultural baggage, ethnocentric stereotypes and political preconceptions, however, the idea has long been dismissed as rose-tinted radical nonsense. Today, in a major redirection of emphasis, the paternalism is diminishing and band housing developments are planned, funded and underwritten through market-driven financial institutions. Responsibility and control now reside with the band council. If more elevated concepts of self-government and cultural self-determination must first take root at this fundamental level, how well does it work? "I've never had a problem with a band yet," says Alex. "I've always been impressed with the calibre of people in the band administrations. Most are great to work with. They understand the importance of team work and they communicate well. I can't take credit for any of this. I co-ordinate things for the band and clear away red tape, then there's another team behind me at CMHC. The band has been 100 percent behind this."

He's particularly proud of the houses themselves. He should be. They receive up to six inspections during construction and they are built from high-quality materials and are intended to last. This is an important point. People living on Indian reserves don't have the option of selling and moving up in the market as their houses age. The current philosophy aims to provide buildings that people can be proud to call home for a lifetime. There's another vital s pin-off from these developments. They provide a steady supply of jobs for band-run construction companies, which keeps money circulating on the reserve and attacks the plague of endemic unemployment. "All of the projects here have been built by band members. In that sense it is a community business. Out of seventeen projects [across BC] maybe three or four will be tendered off reserve. That's the complete reversal of what it once was," Alex says. "The whole success of our project is the band itself. They are the leaders in BC. I'm just an instrument in this process. Believe me, these guys are very, very easy to work with."

Chief councillor Reid, who took his master's degree at UBC before coming home, says this is just the beginning as far as the elected council, hereditary chiefs and elders are concerned. "We can't continue to borrow from CMHC. This has to be interim while we develop our economy and get greater access to the resource base that was once ours and by rights still should be. We're trying to look one hundred years ahead. That has to be the basis of all our planning. Meanwhile, we expect to double in population over the next twenty years. That's one of our worries. We're going to have to build four hundred more houses and create that many more jobs."

Here in Bella Bella, that future is closely connected with the past. In fact, it can be argued, the past is what shapes many of the community's future troubles. Whenever Cecil feels beset by the problems that stem from the local unemployment rate, he takes a walk to the end of the fish dock, stares out into the sleet and spindrift off the Pacific and thinks of John Reid and Louisa Steve and their apocalypse. This couple, his grandparents, believed with good reason that they were among the last of their people, poised at the abyss of extinction. Epidemics had rent the cultural fabric, depopulating whole communities, tearing huge gaps in the collective knowledge held and transmitted in an oral tradition. "Every day I think about those people," Cecil says. "I try to imagine the terror and confusion. They must have believed the end of the world had come and they had somehow been overlooked." Politicians and an ignorant public seldom take into account this profound culture of bereavement in dealing with aboriginal constitutional agendas. But what's really behind First Nations' insistence upon an inherent right to self-government is easy to understand when one considers that, in the emotional aftermath of what people like Reid's grandparents have endured, it amounts to a simple request that Canada affirm their right to exist.

In 1793, when Captain George Vancouver first sailed off Bella Bella, thousands of prosperous Heiltsuk occupied 15,000 square kilometres of British Columbia's central coast. Their ocean-going canoes were marvelled at by European seamen and prized by neighbouring tribes. Bent boxes from Heiltsuk artisans were found everywhere. The Heiltsuk traded for obsidian with interior peoples. One chief at Namu was widely known for his generosity with foodstuffs when other villages ran short.

The first white person born in Bella Bella understands that tradition of hospitality. In 1910, in a desperate race for help, David Paterson rowed his pregnant wife Catherine from Sushartie Bay not south to Comox, but 160 kilometres across Queen Charlotte Strait. Their son Les, living in Vancouver, was still going strong eighty years later. But by 1929, all but one of the Heiltsuk villages were abandoned, the totem poles were rotting back into the underbrush and only a few remembered the dances, songs and legends. Having endured the Bostons, as Americans were called, the King George Men from Britain, the Hudson's Bay Company traders, the self-righteous missionaries, the deceitful federal agents, the hostile provincial governments and a malignant education system initially intent on destroying their cultural identity, a scant two hundred survivors huddled in Bella Bella. "I get so bitter and angry," Cecil says. "Then I remind myself that there are good people, even in the bureaucracy."

Our west coast holocaust arrived with a sailor named Tom Dyer. In 1780 he brought smallpox, which by 1836 had killed an estimated one third of the north coast aboriginal population. Then, in 1862, with 2,000 people from all over the coast camped outside Fort Victoria to trade, a new smallpox case arrived from the California gold camps. The Natives died in fearful numbers. In one of history's monumental public health blunders, frightened towns-folk at Fort Victoria burned the camps and drove off the survivors. The dying Natives fled for home, infecting new communities every time they stopped. "The epidemic spread like a forest fire up the coast and into the interior," wrote Wilson Duff. "The details of its progression can be followed in dispatches from Nanaimo, Fort Rupert, Bella Coola, Port Simpson, Stickeen, Lillooet." In the Chilcotin, one white trader collected infected blankets from the death camps and resold them to other Natives. They also died. Priests and doctors vaccinated Indians in a few places. In most the disease raged until no one remained alive.

Before the arrival of Yankee traders 125,000 people lived on this coast. By 1885 there were 28,000 Natives. BC's Native communities experienced more deaths in a thirty-five-year period than Canada has suffered in two world wars. The best leaders, the most talented artists, the most loving mothers, their beloved children— all perished. The calamity had decapitated entire societies.

Once populations declined, European immigrants moved swiftly to occupy territory, dispossess the traumatized remnants of aboriginal communities and seize control of the rich resources in fish, timber, minerals and agricultural land. In August 1913, when the McKenna–McBride Reserve Commission heard briefs at Bella Bella, the chiefs objected to this invasion: "We think that the money which has been received for all these fishing licences in the past should have been (and should be) paid over to us, as all the fishing privileges rightly belong to us Indians. This place is ours...The place was ours long before the cannery people ever came here and before any white people ever came into the country at all." The province responded by unilaterally reducing the size of reserves across BC. Prime agricultural land was "cut off" and replaced with marginal lands with a fraction of the value. Ottawa embarked on a policy of industrializing the fishery, systematically reducing the numbers of small fish boats. "This program hit Indian fleets hardest," observed S.L. Pattison in a 1971 regional development study. "It also caused large economic problems for isolated communities almost entirely dependent on the salmon fishery, such as Bella Bella." But there's a new generation on the rise and the Heiltsuk have begun to reclaim their heritage and their economic patrimony.

As I walk down to the fish wharf, invigorating storm gusts tasting of salt and snow whip shoreward off the water as they have since people first settled here. Wise old trouts like Mrs. Margaret Campbell linger inside over hot coffee and a buffet lunch.

Outside, weather or no weather, the docks at Bella Bella Fisheries Limited boil with shoals of excited small fry. Marni McMahan is having no trouble with the preschoolers. Samantha Humchitt and Nikki Johnson, a couple of five-year-olds, are struck dumb by the advancing spit-and-polish vision of RCMP Constable Brian Sampson in full dress scarlet. But Kaz Jones and Caroline Reid, the grade one teaching team, struggle to keep order. Francis Windsor, Cory Hunt, Brent Wilson and Kelly Dickson all crane and chatter. "It's just Brian," announces the worldly Joshua Vickers. As children mob their pet Mountie, tugging at his Sam Browne belt and rubbing small hands on the red serge, proudly posing for snapshots, it strikes me that in these days of hit men and drug contracts, kiddy porn and pimps trying to recruit grade one kids, it must feel great to be posted to a place where the kids all know the cops by their first names and like them.

When I asked Mia Bailey why she wasn't in school, her tiny face peered up from deep in the shelter of a parka hood. "We *are* in school," she said gravely. "But we're not in *the* school. We're at the fish plant."

As is often the case with children's perceptions, there is profound wisdom in the simplicity. This now-official fish plant is a laboratory for community-based economic self-determination. It is a plain, functional model—precisely the kind of strategic thinking being urged on Canada by the high-priced economic consultants from Harvard and MIT.

Bella Bella Fisheries Ltd. intends to target niche markets and get its competitive edge not by replacing people with machines, but by providing the highest possible quality in specialty items, like the traditional herring roe-on-kelp that brings premium prices in Japan.

The fish boats supplying the plant know they must meet tough standards. Fresh caught salmon, for example, must be iced down in slush within the first hour. This high-quality product serves a demanding export market in Seattle. The plant also processes traditional Native harvests of geoduck, a giant member of the clam family prized by meticulous Japanese buyers. Despite early opposition from bureaucrats and private sector interests, for ten months of the year the plant now provides fifty much-needed jobs in a community where unemployment jumped to 65 percent with the closing of the nearby Namu fish plant. Band councillor Kelly Brown, who doubles as head teacher at the local school, sees this as only the first step. A canning line and freezer compartments are part of expansion plans.

Meanwhile, Bella Bella's political leaders are preparing to renew a bitter legal and political struggle to win greater share of the fisheries resource that once sustained their whole nation and now is increasingly diminished coastwide. "Self-government is meaningless without a resource base," says Cecil. "The only source of employment we have is from the sea. We want self-government to manage that resource. They are simply not going to be able to maintain the status quo as far as allocation of resources is concerned." The band's desires are understandable.

Under fisheries regulations devised for industry, Natives have consistently been victimized. Under commercial exploitation, traditional Native fisheries have collapsed one after the other. For now, the focus is roe-on-kelp. Cecil says that from a harvest of 10,000 tonnes, Bella Bella gets about one percent and "that's just not enough." New roe-on-kelp licences would inject a million-dollar payroll into a chronically unemployed community and add a million in revenues to the band. "We have created three hundred jobs in this community," Cecil says. "We have reduced our unemployment rate from 65 percent to 25 percent. We have a rate that's worse than the worst province—and we're a success. You know, I look at these excited little children and I ask myself how are we ever going to create four hundred more jobs for them?

"We are not sensational. We are conservative, reserved people. We believe in being honest, reliable and compassionate. Well, we've now discussed this issue for twenty years. Perhaps it is time to assert our tribal rights and then excercise them. We are now considering breaking the law on roe-on-kelp."

Take note: these are not firebrands from Oka. When the moderate, patient and wise leaders discuss defying the law to obtain simple justice, we'd better heed the storm warning. If we again betray these kids' trust in their beloved Mountie, the whirlwind we sow will be ours to reap. Ed Newman is one elder who is determined that the drive for economic stability and a prosperous future for these kids won't sacrifice the customs and traditions that make his people unique in the world. I met the hereditary chief in the hall they call Wawiskas. He stood ramrod straight beneath a banner that displays his family crest. His ceremonial regalia was already packed neatly away but a few minutes earlier I'd watched him sing and dance in honour of his community's feast guests. Yet it was not just the chief who was dancing. It was all the Heiltsuk chiefs, a line reaching into time immemorial, all the way back into the last ice age, dancing through him in a choreography passed down across generations. All the hereditary chiefs had performed at the feast—one for each of the eleven vanished communities from the dreamtime before the holocaust that left people like Cecil's grandparents as its shell-shocked victims. David Gladstone introduced them with a song called "We Wait for the Great Mountain."

The rest of the big-city media had departed long before this. Having got its quick fix of sorrow and trouble for the boob tube, why stick around for a bunch of Indian dances staged partly in their honour? The chief was philosophical. "Young guys," he said, saying everything that needed to be said about the television and radio crews that couldn't think of anything worse than spending a few nights in Bella Bella.

Indeed, aboriginal elders often portray European society as a "younger brother" whose insulting behaviour is rooted less in malice than ignorance and an inability to perceive and thus respect other cultural values. It's a wise and accommodating point of view, one I always bear in mind when I listen to the Vancouver talk-show hosts rant their empty-headed nonsense about the threat posed by aboriginal rights and self-government. It's not that they are particularly mean-spirited, just that they lack the imagination to comprehend the subtle complexities of the issue.

This feast at Bella Bella, hosted by the whole community, honoured those who helped the Heiltsuk lift themselves from the ruins of political, social and economic systems demolished in that first fatal impact. Guests included former teachers, retired bureaucrats, housing corporation executives, business leaders. "This is our way of saying thank you on behalf of our people," Chief Newman said. "We appreciate everything." Splendid in their regalia of button blankets, ermine capes and embossed aprons, their headdresses shimmering with the eagle down that symbolized "the peace in our hearts," the chiefs sang. If they brought the past to life, the future was there in the form of Kelly Brown. He led traditional drummers on a hollow log while toddlers, too young to partake of the alternate kids' feast of pizza and hotdogs, chased the dancing motes of downy feathers. In his other life, Kelly is head teacher at the school. He aims to make it a crucible for cultural pride.

Like many, Kelly once went away to Vancouver. "I made a choice for myself to come back here and provide a leadership role model for the kids in my community," he says. "I had to give up a lot of things. One of them was basketball, which I love; the other was alcohol." Today, he coaches a junior team, leads the teachers at school and serves on the band council. Yet, he says, he is less teacher than student in this process. "Our leaders are a link between the past and the present in our culture. The leadership in this community is really quite phenomenal. Chief councillor [Cecil] Reid and hereditary chief Newman are the backbone of our council. They are my teachers." Kelly sees himself as talent scout, not just for the basketball team but for the generation of leaders that must be groomed today to succeed him tomorrow. "We have a lot of leadership potential in the high school. I can see it. When the kids show leadership, we try to reward them for that responsibility. They are our future. In them lies the survival of our culture."

Jennifer Carpenter, the anthropologist, came here on field research, fell in love and married her informant. She runs the Heiltsuk Cultural Centre right out of the high school. Amid the usual sports trophies, you find archaeological displays tracing the presence of Heiltsuk people on the coast. But Jennifer knows from her own life that culture doesn't reside in museum cases; it lives in the hearts of human beings.

If Bella Bella is forging ahead in rebuilding its economic infrastructure, ensuring survival of cultural traditions, the very things that define people as Heiltsuk most concern chiefs like Ed Newman. Preserving the language is a major project. "When you lose your language you don't have a culture anymore," says Chief Newman. "There are not enough of us here who now speak the language. I want it taught in our school. I was taken away from my parents at age nine and sent to residential school at Alert Bay. When I came out of school, I could not speak my language. But I was one of the lucky ones. I was able to learn it again from my grandmother."

In a language, of course, lies a whole way of seeing the world. Every one that dies represents another impoverishment of what it is to be a human being and alive among the marvellous riches of this world we have the privilege to share. Meanwhile, Ed Newman, Cecil, Kelly and Jennifer all know that like the sea surging along the coast, the tides of change cannot be resisted. And like the ocean voyagers whose ancestral chiefs left their dances to serve as talismans against the future, their obligation is to teach the people how to catch and ride that cresting wave without it swamping the canoe that finally brings them home.

Rain Language

It was the moon of Wexes, the sacred season when Sxe Anew stirs from his winter sleep and announces in his loud, insistent, myriad frog voice that once again the world has been renewed. The auditory experience that this name evokes is difficult to describe for the urban dweller who hasn't been kept awake all night by the throbbing, passionate intensity of spring peepers announcing their presence in the West Coast rain forest. Their commingled chorus, with its otherworldly polyphonies and the pitch and rhythms of a synthesizer concert, is the voice of Sxe Anew, an archetype that can only be fully realized within the language that named it and thus brought it into being.

By our Gregorian calendar, of course, it was not Wexes. It was simply Sunday, March 3, 1940. And while the world was preoccupied with the impending end of civilization in Europe, a far more ancient universe was dying in a small farming village on Vancouver Island about 120 kilometres west of Vancouver. This was the day that a man named Klokwasha, the last speaker of the Pentlatch language, took his people's unique and irreplaceable understanding of the cosmos out of this world and into the endless dark of the grave.

"When a language perishes, a whole way of looking at the world perishes, too," says James Young, a philosopher at the University of Victoria who is concerned with language and meaning. "Every language is associated with a literature, so every time we lose a language, we lose access to its literature. If we lose access to its literature, then we lose an alternative way of thinking about the world—and then we lose the beauties that are expressed in that literature, beauties that are lost forever."

From this point of view, the loss of languages means a profound diminishment of cultural diversity. And this has been going on in Canada since its inception. Pentlatch was not the first language to die. That occurred on June 6, 1829, in St. John's, Newfoundland, when a beautiful young woman named Shawnandithit died of pulmonary consumption. She was the last speaker of Beothuk. Also extinct are Huron and three of the Iroquois languages spoken by members of the Six Nations. Nor will Pentlatch be the last to vanish. With the recent death of Dominic Point, the ancient Salish dialect which greeted Simon Fraser on his descent to the sea in 1809 now teeters at the brink of extinction, too. The much-venerated old chief was one of the last two fluent speakers of Musqueam.

British Columbia, with its rich maritime resources and dense aboriginal populations, is home to 31 of the more than 50 aboriginal languages—some linguists say the number may be as high as 70—spoken in Canada. Canada-wide, five languages are already extinct, six are near extinction and six more are seriously endangered. Of the remaining 36, all but three are in profound retreat in the face of a cultural onslaught posed by the homogenizing force of television and an education system which for the most part has ignored their existence.

And this is true in the United States, as well, where linguists estimate that 80 percent of the 150 indigenous tongues there are moribund or extinct. Edna Campbell Guerero, one of only two living speakers of Pomo, a California language, died in January, 1995. And Quinault, a language in Washington State, died on April 27, 1996, with A'aliis, the last known speaker. Mandan, Osage, Abenaki-Penobscot, Cour d'Alene—the list of languages with fewer than fifty speakers is long and growing.

Nor is this solely a North American phenomenon, although the rate of extinctions is most rapid here. Ainu may already be extinct in Japan. Ubykh, the fascinating language from the Caucasus with the most consonants of any tongue—linguists have identified around eight—has only one living speaker. Across the circumpolar sweep of Europe, Asia and North America, 40 languages—90 percent of the total—are moribund. In South and Central America, it's 160 (23 percent). In Russia, it's 45 (70 percent). In Australia, it's 225 (90 percent). Worldwide, 3,000 languages are in danger while fewer than 600, about 10 percent of the total, can be considered safe.

Linguist Michael Krauss of the University of Alaska describes this accelerating trend as a cultural catastrophe of enormous proportions. "I consider it a plausible calculation that—at the rate things are going—the coming century will see either the death or the doom of 90 percent of mankind's languages," he said in a paper written for the prestigious scholarly journal *Language* in 1992. "What are we linguists doing to prepare for this or to prevent this catastrophic destruction of the linguistic world?" Why should we speakers of dominant languages care about small linguistic groups? Kathleen Berthiaulme, an anthropologist at the University of Victoria, sees it primarily as a moral and ethical problem. "I'm against might makes right," she says. "Language is a symbol of group identity throughout the world. I feel and have always felt that small groups of people [with distinctive languages] are as deserving of respect as large groups."

Leslie Saxon, a linguist who specializes in Dogrib, a Na Dene language with about 2,500 speakers in the Northwest Territories, and is involved in the practical problems of inventing education programs for previously unwritten languages, echoes both the philosopher and the anthropologist. "A language is a small entity," she says, "but it carries a universe within it. The biggest threat to indigenous languages in Canada is the overall dominance of anglophone culture and the lack of respect in the dominant culture.

"[Aboriginal] kids know right away that it's not respected, so it's not cool to speak the language of Granny. In many of the Salish communities people are just devastated by what's happening to their language. There's such a feeling of loss and sadness."

Ewa Czaykowska-Higgins, at work on a comprehensive grammar and dictionary of Nxa'amxcin, a Salish language spoken in the Columbia River area, concurs. "There's just not enough respect in general," she says. "Value just isn't accorded these languages. There's always hope [of saving a language] until the last speaker dies, but there has to be support in the general community. The most powerful communities in Canada must be much more respectful." Besides, Sxe Anew might tell us, there's a practical as well as an ethical realm to be considered. Just as biologists have come to recognize the importance of the frogs that sing the praises of renewal each spring as critical indicator species that tell us when there is a grave ecological imbalance emerging, perhaps we should see the speakers of small languages like Pentlatch, Musqueam and Straits Salish as important indicators for the state of our own cultural health.

On the melancholy day that Pentlatch died, Klokwasha told his wife that his time had come. But he told her not to worry, that he was well satisfied with his life, that it was a good day to die. And so he did, on the banks of the Tsolum River, a tawny, sun-dappled Vancouver Island stream that winds down through punch bowl falls into a series of clear, tranquil pools near Courtenay. The Tsolum River was famous, then, for its immense salmon runs, although now it's best known as a dead river, its spawning beds mined for their gravel to build an airport, its headwaters stripped by loggers, its clear waters poisoned by the acid that still leaches out of old mine tailings up there in the *hyas cultus illahie*—the "very bad place" that we call Forbidden Plateau and Mount Washington. But all that lay in the future as Klokwasha lay dying.

To his neighbours, Klokwasha was just Joe Nim-Nim and it's doubtful that many knew him as a chief, the son of Haiquotan, last in a long line of chiefs, or thought much about the once powerful nation that held sway between the warlike Euclataws to the north and the fierce Cowichans to the south. How old he was, nobody knows. He said he was forty when he met his first white man after the smallpox had destroyed his people in 1862. That would have made him well over 100, easily a contemporary of Sir James Douglas, the first governor of British Columbia. At his funeral, his coffin was draped with a Union Jack.

Klokwasha left our world just as his people's great winter ceremonials drew to a close. Around him, the spring landscape burst into green leaf, the silver shoals of herring moved in to spawn and the whole coast from the Winchelsea Islands to Kuhushan Point was suddenly alive with the clamour of diving birds and sea lions. Wexes and the voice of Sxe Anew was about to give way to Pexsisen—the moon of opening hands, the blossoming-out moon, the season of Xelxelj, the small black geese we call the Brant, the acknowledgement of which lingers on, largely unrecognized, in our contemporary Brant festivals. Yet when Klokwasha died, so did an embracing, encompassing wisdom accumulated over a span of time that reaches back beyond Abraham, that was old when Moses led his people out of Egypt. He took with him the rich and intense vocabulary by which these timeless cycles might be understood, interpreted, named and celebrated in their mysterious beauty. It was a knowledge like the invisible, unconscious information in your genes, encoded in the liquid syllables and complex rhythms of his people's now-forgotten tongue. What had the Pentlatch learned that we will never have an opportunity to learn? What knowledge did his people decipher that we cannot? What vital segments of the DNA of collective human experience were snipped out of intelligence?

Indeed, linguists around the world increasingly use the

vocabulary of geneticists, biologists and ecologists as they attempt to grapple with the accelerating phenomenon of what is known as "language death" and what it means for human culture. "Language endangerment is significantly comparable to—and related to—endangerment of biological species in the natural world," Michael Krauss argues. He points out that of 4,400 mammal species, 326 (7.4 percent) are either endangered or threatened. The next largest group is birds, with 231 (2.7 percent) of 8,600 species endangered or threatened. To battle this trend there are more than 300 environmental organizations from the Audubon Society to the World Wildlife Fund.

Ecologists concerned with the loss of biological and genetic diversity caused by animal, plant and insect extinctions, for example, have described the loss of these species as a bit like popping rivets one at a time from the fuselage of an aircraft. Lose one rivet and the implications are minimal—the plane will still fly. But sooner or later you will arrive at a rivet that holds the plane together. Pop it and the plane disintegrates. Which species, ecologists wonder, might be the one whose extinction causes the whole complicated web of life to unravel? And which language, some linguists wonder, might be the one that has encoded into it some secret essential to human survival?

Yet, beyond a scattering of university-based research institutes, the gallant initiatives of individual linguists and a few developing but usually underfunded educational programs, there is little organized resistance to the ongoing cultural extirpation of languages. "Why is there so much more concern over this relatively mild threat to the world's biological diversity than over the far worse threat to its linguistic diversity, and why are we linguists so much more quiet about it than biologists?" Krauss asks. "Surely, just as the extinction of any animal species diminishes our world, so does the extinction of any language.

"Surely we as linguists know, and the general public can sense, that any language is a supreme achievement of a uniquely human collective genius, as divine and endless a mystery as a living organism. Should we mourn the loss of Eyak or Ubykh any less than the loss of the panda or California condor?"

There are thought to be approximately 6,000 languages spoken in the world. Between now and the year 2100, increasing numbers of scholars predict, 95 percent of them may have joined Pentlatch in extinction. The reasons for language death are complex and not well understood, points out linguist Stephen Wurm in the philosophical journal *Diogenes*. Why, he wonders, were the Hungarians able to preserve their language for 5,000 years despite the repeated reinvention of their original culture and social structure on templates imported from Persia and Turkey before the present manifestation, which grafts a western one onto Slavic and German foundations? Why has Irish largely ceased to be a language of daily life despite massive attempts by its government—with strong support from the non-Irish speaking population—to resurrect it? Why is Welsh, a language no less important symbolically to its speakers as a way of differentiating their culture from the English behemoth next door, undergoing an explosive renaissance among teenagers and young adults? And why has the last two hundred years seen such a rapid acceleration in the number of indigenous languages that have either become extinct like Pentlatch, moribund like the Musqueam dialect or endangered—like most of the aboriginal languages in Canada?

One reason, suggests the Royal Commission on Aboriginal Peoples, is the success of what some argue was an overt policy of cultural genocide rooted in colonial paternalism. For several generations it was formal policy to discourage the use of aboriginal languages, particularly in the context of residential schools, to which children were relocated—removed from the community where their language had a natural life—and where they were punished for attempting to speak it among themselves. "The use of aboriginal languages was prohibited in those institutions expressly to dislodge from the children's minds the world view embodied in the languages," the commissioners found.

"With aboriginal languages an underlying reason for the decline is the rupture in language transmission from older to younger generations and the low regard many aboriginal people have had for traditional language proficiency as a result of policies devised by government and enforced by churches and the education system."

How to atone for such crimes? The commissioners urged federal, provincial and territorial governments to show respect by declaring official status for aboriginal languages within their own nations, territories and communities wherever the local people chose to do so. And they called upon Ottawa to establish an aboriginal languages foundation with a $100 million endowment that would produce annual revenues of $4 to $7 million a year to fund programs designed to save and revitalize endangered languages.

So far, the aboriginal community is still waiting, although the federal government and the Assembly of First Nations have launched a major initiative to plan and design a comprehensive aboriginal languages program that is national in scope. But teachers like John Elliott, 50, carrying on with an ambitious attempt launched by his late father Dave Elliott to resuscitate Straits Salish on the Tsartlip Reserve near Victoria, are not sure how long people can wait for help. They've got a book of creation stories encompassing the Saanich people's cultural beliefs and traditions. It's on the computer but there's no money to publish it. The same thing is true of the dictionary and grammar that he and Earle Claxton have been working on for the last twenty years. "There are many groups like ours that are just skimping along," John says. "We're struggling to get the language into a teachable form. I can't fully explain it," Earle says. "It's not like English. This language describes everything. It describes things so precisely you can almost see a picture of what you are talking about."

For him, time is of the essence. There are now only about twenty fluent speakers of Straits Salish and most of them are elders. At sixty-seven, Earle, who's spoken Straits Salish all his life, is still learning the nuance of his tongue from his ninety-year-old mother, Elsie Claxton. The moon of Wexes and the song of Sxe Anew will come again to Wsanec, the heartland of the Saanich people, as it has come again to the country of Klokwasha and his vanished Pentlatch. But if John Elliott and Earle Claxton fail in their brave attempt in the classrooms at Tsartlip's school, it may never again be celebrated in Sencoten, "the beautiful, beautiful language." And that would be to the shame and diminishment of us all.

The Spirit of the Pipes

The drones and chanter of Carol Wilkowski's bagpipes gleam against the spotless lace tablecloth, all ivory mounts and silver fittings and the deep lustre of African blackwood brought from the ends of an empire on which the sun never set. They are Hendersons and they seem vaguely out of place here in chain saw country, laid out so reverently in the dining room of this modest home that nestles in a dripping alder forest at Stories Beach, just south of Campbell River. But perhaps not. These Scottish pipes are one more mysterious thread in a curious and wonderful Remembrance Day story of loss and redemption.

I've come here to trace those threads back to their source. They extend across the electronic loom of the Internet to a fusty school display in the highlands of Scotland; from suburban Chilliwack to the World War I service files in the National Archives; from the endless rows of numbers that scroll down the computer screen when logging onto the Commonwealth War Graves Commission's global database to a faded scrap of an uncommon tartan in the museum of a famous regiment in a drafty Victoria armoury. It's a story that spans two continents and three centuries. A story that reunites the faint embers of memory in an old woman at a White Rock hospital with the bright smile of a long-lost youth, binding together families and generations with the bittersweet cords of grief and pride, connecting the rest of us in our humdrum lives to heroic sacrifices made on distant battlefields so horrific that they beggar the imagination.

Beside the bagpipes on Carol's table lies a remarkable snapshot from the beginning of the twentieth century, its black-and-white contrasts slipping into the sepia tints of age, as though even the photograph were slowly beginning to lose its memory, too. In the picture, a strikingly handsome lad strides across a field beside a stern-faced man. The boy wears a cloth hat and straight black trousers that are already a bit short for the high-cut boots of Scotland's Edwardian working class. Tucked under his arm are these very Henderson bagpipes that now rest on the table. The lad is being instructed in the complex, never-to-be-fully-mastered art of the piper—as much a psychological matrix of responsibilities, duties and ancient traditions as of the technical skill with grace notes, wind and fingering that must be acquired.

There's an unusual cast to the boy's expression, an inner light that one comes to recognize as a barely concealed joy. And if his companion appears unsmiling and constrained, the teenager seems about to burst into flight and the rest of his life. The boy's name is James Cleland Richardson and he's the first owner of the pipes that would later come to Carol in 1974 when she was fifteen—his age in the photograph—on the unwritten contract that she could have them only if she promised to play them, a vow with which she's kept faith these past twenty-six years.

It was not an easy promise to keep for a teenaged girl with high school and boys and all the other distractions of youth in small-town Nelson. Yet she kept it, struggling through a difficult eighteen months just learning the fingering on the chanter. "I used to go up the mountain behind Nelson on a little Honda 90 motorbike and try to play. But transferring from the chanter to the pipes—it's a whole different instrument. And these pipes are very temperamental," she says. "All of a sudden one day it came together. The sound of the pipes was so wonderful—a mellow, deep sound that makes other pipers stop and listen—that I started to cry. I knew then that I would always play them and I've loved playing them. There's something about the music going from piper to piper over the generations. I believe it's in the heart."

James Richardson's pipes came to Carol through her great-uncle, Robert Richardson, into whose care the pipes were given when his older brother, James, bid him and his wee sister Isabel farewell and went to enlist with the 72nd Regiment of the Seaforth Highlanders one golden day in August of 1914. He'd only been in Canada for four years and still spoke with the resonant burr of his native Lanarkshire. His father, David Richardson, had emigrated with eight children, hoping for work in Vancouver. Finding none, he took a post in Chilliwack and found himself the police chief.

James had been active as a Seaforth cadet. When he took the King's Shilling on August 10, it was to serve as piper for a regiment that had only been formed as a militia unit four years earlier but had already become entangled in British Columbia's history. Billy Bowser's Seventy-Twa, as the Seaforths were then derided, had been mobilized as an aid to the civil power in 1912. It was sent to restore order when what became known as the Big Strike swept Vancouver Island's coalfields. The miners saw the soldiers as company troops, although there was a grudging respect on both sides. When war with the Kaiser was declared, the regiment got many of its best recruits from the tough union men who laid down their pickets and enlisted with the units they'd been jeering the day before.

James Richardson was seventeen when he left for the war, travelling up through the Interior, peering out the windows when the train stopped to pick up other volunteers who had paraded in civilian clothes in the dusty streets of small towns and at unmarked crossings. Cowboys rode in from the bunch grass prairies of the Nicola Valley, gave their horses away and signed up. Loggers and hardrock miners missing fingers and even limbs would try to persuade recruiting officers to turn a blind eye and let them enlist.

There was an innocent enthusiasm about it all. Young women

in long skirts and high-collared bodices would bring baskets of fruit down to the sidings and flirt with recruits who had flocked to enlist with units bearing Kiplingesque names: the Kootenay Borderers, the Rocky Mountain Rangers, Tuxford's Dandys from Vernon and Merritt and, of course, the romantic Highlanders, the Gordons from Victoria, led by Arthur Currie, and the Seaforths from the Lower Mainland. For some the war promised a high adventure, for others an escape from the dreary and jobless recession in which the Canadian economy had been mired for two years. Few of them imagined that by the following summer they'd be eye-deep in what soldier Alex McClintock would later describe as "hell with the lid off." Forty-three thousand men, 10 percent of BC's entire population, would enlist. Five years later almost 20,000 had been killed or wounded and many who returned would never recover from the injuries to body and mind.

James Richardson sailed for Britain in October and endured a dreary bivouac at Salisbury Plain during which the troops humoured inexperienced officers. When one came up with an ingenious method for boosting morale, threatening punishment for anyone seen without a smile on his face, "the sergeants and officers suffered grievously," records one soldier's diary. "We would slop through the mud on the parade ground laughing boisterously. If put on fatigue everyone would 'ha-ha' and quack like ducks. Sergeant Dougall came into the hut for a bunch of men for a working party; immediately the whole hut commenced to roar with laughter." The high spirits took a sharper focus, however, when it came to the high command's decision to form a new battalion, the 16th Canadian Scottish, from companies drawn from the two original militia regiments—the Gordons and the Seaforths along with the Cameron Highlanders from Winnipeg and the Argyll and Sutherland Highlanders from Hamilton.

What tartan would the new battalion wear? The first scheme called for khaki kilts. It was not well received: the regimental sergeant major denounced it as an outrage; a Victoria officer said he'd lived in the Gordon tartan and would die in it; a whole company refused to wear the khaki. The scheme was quietly withdrawn and the Canadian Scottish went to France in 1915 wearing the assorted tartans of the regiments with which they'd enlisted. For James Richardson, that meant the Lennox tartan would adorn his regimental war pipes. It was the tartan of the Scottish sept (extended family) to which belonged the wife of the Seaforth's commanding officer, Lieutenant Colonel Edward Leckie. Not until 1917 would the Canadian Scottish adopt a uniform dress including the Mackenzie kilt tartan. Years after the war it adopted the Hunting Stewart tartan of the Royal Scots regiment with which it was allied, but even today ribbons of the original Lennox tartan in which it first went to war grace the instruments of its pipe bands.

The role of the piper was arduous. Pipers were expected to perform at all appropriate ceremonies behind the lines, of course, but also to play and keep playing so long as the battalion was on the march and then to lead them into battle. James Richardson's Canadian Scottish fought strictly by the code of the Highland clan system and no engagement with the enemy was without the skirl of the pipes. Five pipers, one for each company and one with the commanding officer, led the troops. Competition for the honour of piping the advance was so intense that pipers drew lots to see who'd go over the top first. After the charge, the pipers became battalion runners carrying orders through the chaos of the battlefield, bringing up rations and ammunition and serving as stretcher-bearers to get the wounded to the rear. It was among the most hazardous duties at the front. The battalion had fought at Ypres and Festubert and by 1915, seven of its pipers had already been killed or were too severely wounded to return to duty. Of the seventeen who mustered with James Richardson that year, only three would remain on November 11, 1918. Over the war, ten would be decorated for valour.

On October 8, 1916, the Canadian Scottish were in the front line facing the ruins of a village named Courcelette. They were preparing an assault in what would prove one of the last, futile gasps in the battle of the Somme. Their objective, 700 strides away, was Regina Trench where fierce German marines lay in wait. The battle had begun that summer with the worst catastrophe in the history of the British army, more than 60,000 men killed or wounded in the first eleven hours of an advance across open fields into the enemy machine guns. By the time the carnage ended, more than a million casualties had shed their blood at the Somme. A continuous rain of shells buried the dead and then disinterred them. Corpses oozed out of the sides of trenches to be eaten by rats. Flying shrapnel maimed the living with gruesome wounds. Men lost their wits in the bombardments and shook with terror by night, listening for the muffled sound of enemy sappers setting mines under their defences. James Richardson was not yet twenty and he was living through something so grisly that his little sister Isabel and brother Robert, on whom he'd bestowed his beloved personal pipes for fear they'd be destroyed in the war, could not imagine it. And yet, when lots were drawn to see who'd pipe this attack and he proved unlucky, James, with tears in his eyes, implored his pipe major for permission to go over the top, too. It was granted.

When the brain-pulverizing barrage ended just before a moon-less dawn, the 16th Battalion advanced into withering fire. They discovered to their horror that the German barbed wire was intact. Pinned down before it, most officers were soon dead and their men were being slain by the score. Which is when the youth from Chilliwack rolled over to his company sergeant major and asked: "Wull I gie'em wund?" "Yes," his sergeant replied, "Give 'em wind." He rose with his regimental pipes and, walking up and down before the wire in full view of the enemy and under constant fire, played his demoralized company back to the attack to "The Reel of

Tulloch" followed by "The Devil in the Kitchen." The Canadian boys swept Regina Trench.

"One of the great deeds of the war," wrote his commanding officer Lieutenant Colonel Cyrus Peck. "The conditions were those of indescribable peril and terror. The lad's whole soul was bound up in the glory of piping." For his courage, the teenager would earn the Victoria Cross, the British Empire's highest military decoration for bravery. But he was never to know it. Later that day, escorting his now-wounded sergeant major and several prisoners to the rear, Piper Richardson realized he'd left his pipes behind. Despite pleas to the contrary, he went back to get them. He vanished into the storm of shellfire and was never seen again.

Eighty-four years later, Pipe Major Roger McGuire of the Canadian Scottish in Victoria got an e-mail query from Tomas Christie, a 49-year-old estate manager near Elgin in the north of Scotland. The Christie children attended a school in which an unusual set of bagpipes was on display. How they came to be in the school is unclear, but a note said they'd been found on the battlefield near Courcelette in the spring of 1917. They still had the mud of the Somme on them and the tartan bag cover was faded and partly rotten from lying in the open. Curious, a piper himself with two sons following in his footsteps, Christie tried to identify to which British regiment they might have belonged. He found only dead ends. The tartan was one that no one in the military could identify—certainly it was not one ever used by a unit raised in Scotland. He wondered if the Canadian Scottish Regiment might help. When a photograph of the pipes came by post, McGuire was stunned in a way that only a piper who knew the tradition could be. The bag cover was the same Lennox tartan that was used by his own regiment, but only during those early years of World War I. "It is definitely the Lennox tartan. They are definitely 16th Battalion pipes," McGuire says.

Whether they are the same pipes James Richardson played

before Regina Trench is, like his fate, known only to God. But there was only one other Canadian Scottish piper killed on the Somme. His name was John Park and there's no mention in the battalion's official history that he was playing the advance at the fight near Courcelette.

On October 11, 1916, three days after James Richardson disappeared, the 16th Battalion was withdrawn. It had suffered 867 casualties. Of its commissioned officers at Regina Trench, only one lieutenant survived. Later, the ground for which so much blood had been spilled was abandoned as strategically unimportant and the Canadian Scottish would not pass over it again. So, McGuire reasons, on the balance of probabilities, it seems that if Piper Richardson vanished forever into the fog of battle, his war pipes at least have been redeemed from their obscurity, found through a technology unimaginable to the men in the trenches almost a century ago.

Yet, dramatic as the discovery is, perhaps the pipes that remain most important are not those in the museum, but the personal ones Piper Richardson gave into his little brother's safekeeping when he undertook his perilous duty and said his goodbyes. Isabel, in her mid-nineties, now lives in a White Rock hospital and the pipes have passed from Robert to Carol. The pipes serve as a vivid reminder that whatever it was of Piper Richardson that died on October 8, 1916, amid the mud and slaughter on the Somme, it was not his spirit. For that spirit lives on in the stirring Celtic music that rises whenever Carol plays the pipes he so loved, his first pipes, the pipes James Cleland Richardson, just 17, left behind when he went from peaceful Chilliwack to that fury on the Somme. He asked only that they be used, knowing that an instrument not played is like a life unlived and that should his be lost, the music would not.

Divine Wind

This is a story of the waste that is war. It's a reminder of how ephemeral are those great causes for which we march off to fight. And a reminder of how often, over time, the only result of human folly is the same endless echo that the poet Aneirin heard fourteen centuries ago—"the steel ringing in the heads of mothers." This story begins where it ends, on the rain-slicked sidewalk of the small Vancouver Island community of Cumberland, once renowned for its coal mines at the head of Comox Lake.

At the entrance to the Cumberland Legion stands an austere white arch. Its flanking pillars are graced by stained bronze plaques listing those who made the supreme sacrifice in the Great War, the war to end war, the war that laid foundations for the next one. In the Great War, the Japanese were allies. In the World War that followed, they were enemies. Now, they are allies again. Those names from the war of 1914 are neatly balanced, ranked in equal numbers on either side, as though this were some precise accounting of human souls. They reflect this coal town's roots in Yorkshire and the Scottish border. Yet two names stand out among the McNultys and McIntoshes, Armstrongs, Dempseys, Urquharts and Garricks. They are T. Natsumura and M. Yamada.

Two of the surviving Canadian soldiers from Cumberland bearing Japanese names were introduced to King George V for their courage under fire. But on the memorial plaque, the Japanese spellings merely intrude into the neat alphabetical order. Each name appears last in its column, as though added by afterthought. Their memorial is a testament to more than glory.

They gave their lives for Cumberland and Canada, at a time when people of Japanese descent often found themselves liked as individuals while despised collectively. The two men on the cenotaph hailed from Japtown, which was out beyond Chinatown, beyond even Coontown where "Nigger" Brown the prospector lived, where police would once raid a household when a white woman was seen there. It was assumed she must be a victim of the white slave trade. She proved to be a black labourer's wife, which raised an ignorant clamour of another kind.

The Japanese came to Cumberland in 1892 to fill a Tokyo syndicate's contract to cut mine timbers and railway ties for the booming collieries. By the end of World War I, Nakanishi's Hardware was a fixture, so was Shiozaki's Jewellery. Sensjiro Hayashi ran a thriving photographic studio and left us a record of the period. The Japanese community had founded its own school in 1918, when Mr. Aoki came from Japan on a three-year contract. He stayed for sixteen years and his school achieved the highest standards of Japanese education in North America. But some Japanese students attended the public high school to acquire the language and cultural skills their parents knew they would need for success in the wider world.

Long-retired schoolteacher Margaret Egger remembered those days with the bittersweet fondness we all reserve for worlds lost with our distant youth. "During the summer months the Japanese ladies opened a traditional tea garden for people spending the day at Comox Lake. It was all very elegant. They had shrubs and ponds and running water. You could take your lunch with you and just get tea, or you could buy little Japanese cookies and sit on the benches. It was very refined and pleasant." Mrs. Egger went to high school with two of the boys from Japtown. Ton Abe was a tousled, slightly rebellious boy, typical, she says, of Cumberland teenagers.

In the formal class photo from 1923, he's the only boy who has dared to unbutton his starched collar and loosen his tie. Ton Abe wasn't much of a scholar. He was in high school, perhaps, only because his parents saw schoolbooks as an escape from the dirt and danger of the mines. Like so many in Cumberland, one of his family had already died in an explosion down Number Four pit.

Toshio was another kind of boy, a mysterious figure even today. He was born into a traditional family among the immaculate cottages and tea gardens of No. 1 Japtown out by Comox Lake. Yet half a century later, even the spelling of his family name remains uncertain. At the Cumberland Museum, Toshio's surname is recorded as Kajiyama, the recollection of a visiting old-timer who saw his photograph. In mine records, it's Kajiyani. But Mrs. Egger remembers it as Kojimata. She is also certain that Toshio was very refined; he had lovely manners. He had special qualities: "Toshio was not quite so ordinary-looking as the other Japanese boys. His hair was always carefully parted. Not a hair was out of place. He had beautiful wavy hair, I remember that. And his manners were impeccable. He was very much the Japanese gentleman, even as a lad. He was quiet, gentlemanly, prim almost. He was a stocky lad. He came to school in his collar and tie. He wasn't rambunctious like a lot of the Japanese boys. I couldn't imagine Toshio roughing it up. He was a very studious boy. He was like a little bit of old Japan.

"I met him as a schoolmate at Cumberland High School in 1923. He was in grade ten and I was in grade eleven. He sat not many desks from me. He asked me to help him with his algebra. Then his geometry. Then his French. He was very determined to do well and he was an apt learner. He planned to go to university and become a doctor and help his people. 'There are so many good deeds that you can do,' he said." Toshio graduated from Cumberland High School in 1925, Mrs. Egger says, and went to university, one of the very few to do so. "He studied medicine and graduated somewhere in the east around 1931 or 1932—I believe it was McGill, because McGill had a connection with the West Coast."

Mrs. Egger went on to become a teacher at Fanny Bay School, where most of her pupils were the children of Japanese workers in the sawmills and lumber camps. She loved those kids, and her feeling shines through when she looks at the photo albums and names them. Some of those students, now grandparents themselves, still write to her in spite of all the suffering that's intervened.

"The cleverest boy I ever taught was a Japanese boy at Fanny Bay. His parents managed to put him through one year of high school, then he had to go to work in the logging camps. Then the war came and he was sent away. We knew that Japan was getting ready for war because Japanese ships began coming to Union Bay to collect our scrap metal. I knew what was coming. I took my school class down to visit one of those ships. I asked the crewmen what they wanted with all this scrap—they just laughed."

The children's parents sensed the gathering storm, too. "A number of my pupils at Fanny Bay made sudden trips to Japan before Pearl Harbor. Many of them wrote me farewell letters. They all said they were going to visit their grandparents or to pray at the shrines of their ancestors." Perhaps they knew, after fifty years of exclusion from the mainstream, what would happen to them if they stayed, how their community would become a lightning rod when war fears discharged old racial hatreds.

On December 7, 1941, the Japanese attacked Pearl Harbor. On December 11, Cumberland's Japanese sent a message to the local newspaper with the minister of the Japanese United Church:

We the Japanese residents of this district wish to reaffirm our loyalty to Canada and we will continue to the utmost to support this country's war effort.

Nearly all of the Japanese population here are Canadian-born or are the parents of children born in Canada. This is our home and our future lies with the welfare of this country.

We do appreciate the sympathy and the understanding shown by the authorities and by the public. Only the maintenance of this attitude will make it possible for us to continue our normal daily life, so we will be allowed to do our share for Canada in this time of emergency.

But in Cumberland, the Japanese cemetery was desecrated. The gravestones of the men who had died in the mines over the previous seventy-five years, the markers over their wives and children—all were defaced, broken and scattered. The Japanese were uprooted, transported, interned and almost erased from Cumberland's consciousness. Their houses were taken, the tea gardens left to the rank undergrowth, the glass plates of Sensjiro Hayashi's brilliant photographs used as panes in local greenhouses. Minto School reverted from a three-room to a one-room school when it lost its Japanese students in the relocations. "Mr. Wilton Dalby was the principal. He was one of these men who was interested in and good at everything—music, art, science, literature," Mrs. Egger says. "He had a tremendous amount to offer the teaching profession. He joined the army. He never taught again."

There are no Japanese in Cumberland today, except for those two names on the cenotaph and the dead who lie in a beautiful cemetery later restored by a community with the courage to be ashamed of what it had done. And, of course, the fading memory of Ton Abe and his classmate Toshio, the brilliant student who became a doctor so he could gain honour by doing good deeds. They were both in Japan when war was declared.

"Toshio, Toshio." An 85-year-old hand rests a moment on the sepia photograph of that eternally youthful player, so proud in his Cumberland Nisei baseball uniform, standing in 1922 beside the older brother who was to be killed with sixteen others in a mine disaster before the season was out. "Such a fine, fine mind. Such fine lads. What a waste. What a terrible waste," Mrs. Egger says.

Fun-loving Ton Abe and Toshio, the doctor who dedicated

himself to the saving of life, both plunged to fiery deaths as Kamikaze pilots. It was as though they were determined not to survive what war, that eternal waster of lives, compelled them to do in the name of honour.

Going Wild

Mid-summer. Across the northern third of Canada, the midnight sun circles the sky. Vistas of pink granite sweep to the far edge of the earth. In every fold of rock, icy lakes pool their reflections. The sky above roils in a curious blue, swirling across the Canadian Shield like some royal cape. Most Canadians will never have an opportunity to experience the vastness of a northern landscape and the great forces that make our voices seem insubstantial and humble experiments in a timeless place. But most of us yearn for it. As the first weekend of July arrives, families and individuals everywhere across the country break out the raincoats and hiking boots, camping gear and canoe paddles and set out to renew their acquaintance with Canada's wilderness.

But nowhere is this annual rite practised with greater fervency than here in the West. From Riding Mountain in Manitoba to remotest Gwaii Haanas in the Queen Charlotte Islands, national parks across western Canada can expect to generate more than 10 million visits, the majority of them occurring over the summer holiday season. And from Atlin to Yahk, British Columbia's provincial parks will experience almost 20 million visits. Factor in visits to provincial parks in Alberta, Saskatchewan and Manitoba and a pattern of seasonal transhumance of astonishing proportions emerges, something equivalent to the entire population of Canada picking up and heading for the bush.

It's a reminder of the attitude toward wild places that historian William Morton identified as crucial in differentiating Canada's identity from that of the United States. The distinction begins with language itself. The *American Heritage Dictionary* defines wilderness as unsettled or uncultivated land. In other words, if human beings are not using it for something, it's "waste" land. But the *Canadian Dictionary* emphasizes wilderness as a region "without tracks or trails, such as forests." To us, wilderness is defined less by the degree of exploitation than by the absence of human impact, creating a kind of corollary to the American axiom. One definition is rooted in expansionism, the other in a kind of acceptance and adaptation. Perhaps this difference arose because while the Americans pursued a policy of ethnic cleansing from the outset, Canada's fur trade required co-operation between newcomers and the people already here. Americans passed laws banning interracial marriage; Canada gave birth to a whole interracial people, the Metis. In the process did we absorb some of the values aboriginal people associated with the landscape to which they had adapted and that sustained them? Did this shape an appreciation for wild places that endured long after demographic change had shifted the balance of power to marginalize the aboriginal peoples who were initially economic partners and political allies? Whatever the source, "the line which marks off the frontier and the farmstead, the wilderness from the baseline, the hinterland from the metropolis, runs through every Canadian psyche," Morton said when he wrote *The Canadian Identity* almost forty years ago. Fred Bodsworth, the nature writer who's best known for a poignant lament for the passing of traditional Inuit life, saw more tangible evidence. "There are more paintings of wilderness lakes, spruce bogs and pine trees on more Canadian living room walls than in any other nation on earth," he observed. "We may scoff, we may deny, but the wilderness mystique is still a strong element of the Canadian ethos."

And the farther west one goes, the more deeply etched that mythology of wildness appears to be. BC is the greenest province in Canada and not without reason. Look at a map and the relative paucity of large parks east of the Manitoba border and south of the 49th parallel compared to BC is striking. Part of our fascination with wilderness clearly springs from the risks that give an edge to our otherwise humdrum urban lives. The bush introduces a natural disorder into lives that are managed to the minute. In the bush, you can step beyond the road's edge or cross the border of suburban domesticity for a morning walk in the North Shore woods and simply vanish forever. "In the wilderness you seem to realize the omnipresence of danger to a far greater extent than do those who move forward through life bumped by the elbows of their fellow men," wrote Eric Collier, whose *Three Against the Wilderness* became a classic of Canadian literature. Yet there's more to this than the piquancy that comes of taking a calculated chance. Susanna Moodie wrote from the frontier that her most eloquent thoughts flowed out of the deep silence and "sublime solitude" of the country's pathless forests, that this experience put her in the presence of God. Ever since, Canadians as dissimilar as Margaret Atwood and Mordecai Richler, John Diefenbaker and Pierre Trudeau have all recognized a kind of spiritual solace, renewal and even national redemption in the vast wilderness regions of the country.

To be cruelly honest, in our pursuit of this myth most of us will settle for a reasonable facsimile. We will go to a campsite with a pull-in for the car, a gravel pad for the tent, a picnic table, a metal firepit with a grill and dry wood split by the park maintenance staff and, preferably, a nice swimming beach for the kids or some manicured walking trails. We will tolerate the way governments have turned wilderness into a commodity, meekly accepting a $70 family access fee to national parks, or paying $42 for the privilege of camping in the backcountry where there are no services, or reserving a muddy campsite for $24 a night—about the rent on a cheap motel room.

Some of us, usually younger, will venture farther off the beaten path, hiking 10 or 15 kilometres down some trail or paddling down the lake, where we'll devoutly hope we won't run into somebody else whose idea of a sojourn in the wilds means taking along a boom box and tapes of the Barenaked Ladies. Once upon a time, hiking the West Coast Trail from Bamfield to Port Renfrew, or hauling a pack over the Chilkoot Pass was considered going really remote. Now the hikes are rationed and those in search of solitude are sent off in flights, like runners at a middle school cross-country meet, and the giant spruce in the Carmanah have to be shielded from those who seek solitude in their presence. Fewer yet will venture into the true wilderness, kayaking down the Brooks Peninsula on northern Vancouver Island's windswept outer coast of storms and sea surge, or among the remote, labyrinthine island passages of Gwaii Haanas National Park Reserve. More than a million of us visited Kootenay National Park last year, for example, but only 1,798 ventured into Gwaii Haanas and fewer than fifty went to Avlavik. Fewest of all will take the opportunity to drop alone into the remotest possible country and experience what the Great Lone Land really is.

Once flying out of Nahanni Butte, a tiny trapping settlement of eighty-five about 1,500 kilometres straight north of Vancouver, we passed over a lake with a lovely white sand beach at one end. This kind of opportunity comes only once, so, on the spur of the moment, I asked the bush pilot to drop me off and pick me up on his return leg a couple of days later. When the sound of that Cessna 185 dwindled into nothing, it suddenly sank in that I was at least 200 kilometres from the next human being and that if the plane failed to come back I was not going to be walking out. At first the sense of loneliness was overpowering, crowding in upon almost every thought the way wild nature presses into every garden. But then the clutter of human busyness began to fall away. Before me was a huge, dishevelled landscape where not much of anything was happening. Time slowed. The details of what at first seemed empty began to emerge—the varying sounds the wind makes passing over different kinds of leaves, the iridescence of damsel flies. What seemed desolate was rich and full.

And that's one of the wonders you discover in wilderness: everything operates on a scale that makes your own life appear frenzied and even foolish. It's an illusion, of course, much like the illusion of wilderness itself, which is partly a construct we use to frame our own desires, but it helps create a sense of proper perspective. That night as I lay gazing into a black sky with more stars than I'd ever seen, I found myself counting the bronze specks of satellites. In reality there is now no part of the planet into which human industry has not intruded. And I was glad and relieved when my plane showed up.

Coming back from a small community in the bush to the urban sprawl where 80 percent of us live reminds us of a curious reversal in relationships. To us, the wilderness seems to be an enclave. It is something we fight to protect from industry, from too many thoughtless people. We define it with fences, prohibitions, regulations, boundary lines on maps. We provide it with its own jailers, though we call them rangers. The animals are in protective custody. In our national parks, when the bears get rowdy, we catch them, cage them, ship them out to the backcountry to cool their heels in isolation. In places like Nahanni Butte and Lower Post and Kispiox, the settlement is the enclave, its presence defined by a wilderness that presses always inward. Here the wild is not a tourist promotion but something primeval, restless, dangerous and unpredictable. In these communities, the fences are there to keep the wildness out, not keep it in.

Our view of Canada from the urban belt along the US border

often seems limited by the politics of latitude. The roads and air routes and rail lines all run from east to west, fixing our national perspective in a narrow corridor of linearities. But in its longitudes, Canada is greater from north to south than it is from east to west. The geographic centre of Canada is Baker Lake. North of it there are only thirty-one settlements and a total population of just over 16,000. Most of Canada is still wilderness by any definition. "The Canadian north, with its vast expanses of primeval country, can restore to modern man a semblance of balance and completeness," wrote American naturalist Sigurd Olson with more than a little envy. "In the long run, these last wild regions of the continent might be worth far more to North Americans from a recreational and spiritual standpoint than through industrial exploitation."

Perhaps we should try to visualize our country not as knots along the tense cord that connects east and west, French and English, Atlantic and Pacific. Perhaps we should adopt, instead, the imaginary attitude of the snow geese, sharing their southbound prospect down the 125th degree of longitude, sweeping down from the Arctic across the abstract of nationhood. In this vertical Canada are the ageless patterns that predate the visitations of mankind, a sense of the country that existed before Europeans came. From the stiff calyx of the polar ice, all lines diverge, lead to transitions that glide from stark asceticism to richness and rank profusion. Beyond the icebound coast, the antediluvian power of the Barren Lands. Surreal chromatics of ochre and rust. A blue tincture of shadows etches the undersides of spilled boulders, a boundless litter of bits and pieces sprung loose by permafrost and shattering weather. Strange outcrops, the crazy erratics of lateral and terminal moraines, the debris of eons jumbled under escarpments that resemble the exposed vertebrae of deposed Titans, avatars from a time before life—and perhaps after it. Caribou herds that cover 50 square kilometres. Then, along the ridgetops, the first lonely sign of human beings: Inuksuks—stone cairns set down the skylines by Inuit hunters who range across the empty land, and survived in it carrying little more than the genius inside their heads. The word Inuksuk means "something like a man." Suddenly, the softer shimmer of moss and lichen, green traceries smoothed by altitude, a frosting of ground willow. A multitudinous scattering of lakes, glinting like scales in the sun. The thin scar of the treeline hurtles past, a neat instant laid straight as a razor's edge against the soft swell of the tundra. Next, the brooding sea of the boreal forest, quaking muskeg, tea-brown seeps in the peat bogs, a seamless rolling from horizon to horizon, until suddenly it breaks against the newer dimension of Canada. Dark drifts of spruce and tamarack streak the rough pasture of homestead and stump ranch, yielding in turn to the manicured fields of cropland. One by one, the farms fall into the draftsman's grid of section roads, clear-cuts and the whole vast net sweeps everything into the ragged embrace of sprawling cities. Fort St. John. Prince George. Vancouver.

And through it all—unconscious of the precise imperatives of cartographers and politicians, oblivious to the lines on maps, the graphs of economists and the profit and loss statements of corporations—the great, silvered ribbons of lakes and rivers. Carving through the mountain walls that form the backbone of our continent are the Peace, the Stikine, Skeena, Thompson, Fraser and Columbia. Relentless as time itself, those rivers remind us that our Canada of politics and regionalism is an illusion, all our dreams of a grandiose posterity rendered ephemeral by the wild landscape.

What integrates us, as aboriginal people have always known, is the land itself. This is the true power of wilderness, one that defines our place and spiritual purpose in the world. It is what shapes our national being as it shapes the being of all those strange and wondrous creatures that have become our moral charges.

"Standing alone on the mountaintop," wrote American naturalist John Muir just over a hundred years ago, "it is easy to realize that whatever special nests we make—leaves and moss like the marmots and birds, or tents or piled stone—we all dwell in a house of one room—the world with the firmament for its roof—and are sailing the celestial spaces without leaving any track."

Narrow Road from the Deep North

You are coming up from Down North. Arctic Red River is a dream that dwindles behind you. It recedes with the Fort McPherson of the lost patrol, the bone-white grave markers peeping from the earth tones, lonesome as spring snowdrops among the dog pounds and peeled logs. Francis Fitzgerald and his men never made it home from Dawson with the mail that winter of 1911. Inspector Dempster of the North West Mounted mushed his dogs 640 kilometres to find them and bury them in permafrost. The dead became artifacts for the tourists of the future; Dempster becomes only a name on this narrow ribbon of gravel and hardpan. Last winter, when you hitched a ride to Tuktoyaktuk, you were amazed to be in a Suburban, hissing down the smooth expanse of an ice highway. Now it's all ruts and stiff Jeep springs and flying rocks that star the windshield.

Eagle Plains is behind. And the Bonnetplume. And that stretch of barrens where the gravel road serves as the emergency airstrip. Some bush pilot left his Cessna on the shoulder but you note that he yanked out all the avionics before chancing a ride to the Outside. The Blackstone dwindles under a whirlwind of dust. Ahead lies North Fork Pass where you will encounter a solitary Japanese student. He wears enduro leathers and trudges beside his dirt bike. He bows. No English encounters No Japanese in the tundra 3,000 kilometres north of Vancouver. Sign language and pidgin work as they have since the Russian explorers first came into this country, skirting north around the self-sealed fortress of the Shoguns, crossing the Bering Strait, founding Wrangell, St. Petersburg, and trading up the Yukon River. He's out of gas. You siphon enough to get him through.

Ahead lie Dawson and Dog Island. The Klondike, Bonanza, Bonanza Pup, the Pelly. Even then, you will still be 2,500 kilometres from the steel and glass of Granville and Georgia. To get home you have to go beyond the black jet of the Stikine. The Iskut, the Skeena, the lava flows of the Spatzizi. You're travelling light and you're travelling fast.

Along the way, imperceptibly, your pack begins to change. When you left it was so neat: socks here, notebooks stashed on the end, space made for a dog-eared little translation of the *Oku-no-hosomichi*—Basho's *Narrow Road to the Deep North*. But now things are being squeezed out. Notebooks overflow. The sage wallows in the trash under the jump seat, more like Li Po, the boozy, carnal Chinese poet whom legend says was drowned trying to embrace the moon's reflection in some rich patron's goldfish pond. At first, your smelly socks were wrapped in a dirty shirt. Now the soiled laundry is stuffed into a plastic bag and tied off so the earthy, pungent odour of sweat and body oils can't contaminate the dwindling supply of what's clean. Across the centuries you share a fate with Basho.

Born Matsuo Munefusa near Kyoto in 1644, he was already famous as a master of the haiku when he took for himself the name of an unassuming tree near his house, abandoned comfort and set out despite age and ill health to take his journey to the interior, a journey into his country and his self. High in the mountains known as the Shirakawa Barrier, a line of demarcation between civilized Japan and the wild, dangerous marches of bandits, beasts and menacing spirits, he took refuge in a sentry's hut for three days of rain and buffeting wind. He wrote in his notebook the seventeen syllables of misery tempered with humour that are so adeptly translated by American poet Sam Hamill:

Eaten alive by lice and fleas
now the horse
beside my pillow pees

Contemplating the vileness of your own laundry, you muster no verse, but harbour a guilty knowledge of what your wife would say about this burden: "Oh, sure, shove it in a bag. Pretend it's not there. Very elegant."

Women don't grow dirty laundry the way men do. Males will lug swollen, festering packs from watershed to watershed. Women carry more stuff, yet it never seems to accumulate. You are reminded of Ashley Montagu's book *The Natural Superiority of Women*, an anthropologist's notation of the small ways in which women everywhere accomplish the impossible every day. Women organize their laundry into small tasks. They drape it to dry over huckleberry bushes or chipped motel bathtubs. They actually carry little retractable clotheslines for this purpose. Women travel in clothes made of fast-drying synthetics. They can wash stockings in a tiny sink. Somehow this never works for your soggy wool trail socks and fleece liners.

Men always try to squeeze just one more day of travel—one day too many—from their gear. So you turn your last pair of undershorts inside out, douse yourself with the cheap aftershave in the blue bottle you picked up for a couple of bucks—just something to convince yourself you aren't getting too ripe. Then you push for a few extra klicks.

Maybe it's from Bella Coola to Cork screw Creek to One Eye Lake to Chilanko Forks. Or Keno Hill to Yukon Crossing to Five Finger Rapids. Or Prelude to Prosperous to Fort Providence. Most of it is gravel and the dust is into everything. Between your teeth, under your nails. The grit bites into your neck, ankles, crotch. Your snot goes black. The sun's at a bad angle and your eyes ache from squinting. Then you stop. Abruptly. Some place you never planned. It's just that you know you have to do that laundry. And if it's some place you never expected to be, somehow it always seems to be the same place.

You scout for the laundromat down somnolent streets. All is awash with the burnished hues of just-before-sunset. That tawny light always conjures another sense: the tactile, slightly grainy texture of a woman's skin against a calloused hand. Find the laundromat, as you always do, and the linoleum is green, or beige, or yellow. The paint on the walls is yellow, or green, or beige. The coin-op washers are the same colour. The stainless steel doors of dryers gape. You park under a light where you can watch your truck. It's a small town, quiet, but you never know these days. The RCMP report crime waves from Aklavik to Zeballos. Small-town punks get big ideas from satellite TV. Your truck is caked with back country crud but that aluminum case protecting your camera gear is a shiny invitation to passing magpies.

Inside, there's a tough woman who makes change. She's always wearing tight GWGs and smoking plain cuts. You ask the woman where the washroom is and emerge barefoot, clad in your old Ottawa Beavers rugby shorts and a mangy purple T-shirt with singing coyotes. That chorus line hangs around from the time you blew the transmission in Cheyenne, Wyoming, where the public playground is graced by the totems of our new age—models of intercontinental ballistic missiles—and the mechanic loaned you his own dinged-in pickup for three days while he fixed yours. The woman stares.

You succumb to a powerful adolescent need to explain, gesture with the stained shirt and grease-streaked jeans, careful under that withering look not to spill the unspeakables bundled inside: "Gotta wash all this stuff, too."

She skates a cold, appraising eye from naked toes to crown. "Well, I can see you ain't Superman."

"No," you say. "He uses phone booths. I'm working my way up."

"Son, I hate to mention this, but you got quite a ways to go."

The dime-eating dryer turns over in its mindless cycle. Basho is abandoned again while you idle through tabloid wowsers about Elvis being seen in West Virginia, the murky "nude" pictures of the jet-set couple, Cindy Lauper's gross dancing, how Princess somebody-or-other popped her buttons at a dinner party and Prince so-and-so gaped into her cleavage. Public adulteries. Cruel divorces. What would Basho make of this? What appetites do these vicious fantasies feed? They seem uglier, in their way, than real pornography—less honest, more mean-spirited.

In the motel, you hit the shower. The soap is the size of a Chiclet and the dust won't seem to wash off. Afterward, the grit is still in your teeth, pernicious as the fake revelations of those supermarket tabloids and their cult of soiled celebrity. Later, you lie staring at the plaster ceiling where the cracks make a face you can't quite recognize. Maybe it's Jesus, maybe it's Marx. You listen to all the indistinct voices murmuring behind thin walls, the faint noises of lovemaking upstairs, a distant quarrel, the throaty slam of a car door.

You think about how this rich spindrift of voices condenses like frost patterns upon your own passing spirit, how the imprints will later warm into life, glowing from the pages of grimy notebooks. The voices will resonate like that of the high country cowboy with one leg shorter than the other, the old horseman who told you he was "born of this earth, put here to ride the wind," who told you so lovingly about his first wife. And when you offered some platitude of sympathy, he looked sharply across the small duplicity introduced from a lazier world, branded it with a penetrating gaze that was level, blue, crushing as the sky over Anarchist Mountain: "Yeah, well I guess we ain't gonna get into that."

You think about that Burns Lake woman you walked with by the Stellako River as it sang, the one who told you in a flat, cried-out voice how she left a brutal husband, looking, she said, "for just one man who'll treat you like a person." You think again about the clean laundry you didn't fold, just stuffed into the black plastic garbage bag to wait for morning. You think about Basho writing in his own notebook so long ago, coming into himself at last, alone among the silent rocks at Ryushaku Temple, already 800 years old when he got there, 300 years before you found Basho. You think about that small encounter on the dusty highway, how goodwill reaches across the gulf of language. And of the troubled American poet chiselling free from the constraints of a difficult and particular tongue the universal wisdom in those ancient words by a weary old Japanese traveller.

Lonely silence
a single cicada's cry
sinking into stone
And when at last you sleep, you don't dream anything at all.

Look Long
Down the Valley

From the village of Shalalth, 250 kilometres by road from Vancouver, the route to the top of Mission Ridge is an exhilarating climb through muddy switchbacks and hairpin turns. With sheer drops just beyond the soft shoulder and a white-knuckle grade that leaves the best brakes smoking, the descent is not so much fun. Up here, the snowpack is sometimes deeper than a two-storey house and they park a couple of tracked vehicles in a pull-out for days when even four-by-fours and snowplows can't make the grade. But from this vantage point, Ida Joseph can look down on the long valley of her people's whole life. Far below are the two great lakes. Seton, to the left, has a strange, plastic, turquoise colour. It's opaque with suspended silt that comes down penstocks that punch through the mountain from the next valley. Anderson, to the right, is a limpid, lucent reflection of sky and forest. People have lived here for at least 7,000 years. That's the radiocarbon dating for bones found just above the ancient slide that subsequently pinched the valley into two lakes. One stunning ceremonial bowl found here has been dated at 4,700 years before present. It's sensuously carved from green Fraser River jade. The smooth frog shape is as old as treasures found in the tombs of Babylonian emperors and the great Egyptian pharaohs. Yet when Ida Joseph looks down on her valley, she sees less of the rich past than a troubling and uncertain future.

A shimmering spiderweb of high-tension power lines now

covers the valley floor. They hum with the energy of more than 1.5 million volts on the way to Vancouver and the US export market. There's no question that the BC Hydro complex at Seton Portage is an amazing technical achievement. It took thirty-three years to complete and now generates almost half a million kilowatts of electricity. The river flowing through deep canyons north of Mission Ridge is 365 metres higher than Seton Lake. Dams created reservoirs holding almost 1.5 million acre-feet of water. Then a tunnel was driven through the mountain wall to supply the eight huge turbines in two powerhouses half a kilometre below.

BC Hydro's literature tells the story as a narrative of visionary founders, brilliant engineers and valiant workers diving into murky torrents, dangling from precipices and blasting through bedrock. Lofty masculine stereotypes salt the narrative. The men are always battling the elements, taming the rivers, conquering the mountains and—here's an evocative image for the feminist handbook—"harnessing" Mother Nature to make her a "forceful servant of man." Nowhere in this ebullient stuff, from the preliminary engineering report of 1922 to the self-congratulation of post-project propaganda, did I find a single word about the people who acutally occupied the place before the ingenious and helpful engineers arrived. First Nations, it seems, did not impinge upon the awareness of the newcomers and their schemes. In the consciousness of those who pray to the idols of progress at any cost, Natives and their simple rights of use and occupation appear to be beneath notice.

Yet their presence is tangible and hard to overlook. It's most immediate in the cemetery above the old fur brigade portage at the top of Seton Lake where the prospect is one to still any tongue. Wind whispers through the tall pines that tower overhead and prickly Oregon grape takes purchase in the poor, rocky soil and the bunch grass rustles among wooden grave markers that indicate the changing tastes of generations are no less present here than in

Vancouver's Mount Pleasant. Cluada Kinabah and the others buried seventy-five years ago share white-washed wooden crosses. Before that, the vogue was flat headboards with curved tops and black enamel lettering. Earliest of all are the curious, hand-carved wooden obelisks. Lucy, who died in 1904, rests under one. As with many of the earliest markers, there's no surname on her marker. Why would one be necessary in a small and tightly knit community where everyone knows well enough who you are? On the front of Lucy's marker, in bas relief, a hand and forearm hold a branch that bursts into flower under a radiant sun. The sun is enclosed in a cloud. From its centre, an eye casts an unblinking gaze on the living and the dead alike. In one side of each of these turn-of-the-century pillars is a small round hole. Is this to let out the departing soul? Or is it to encourage the birds that nest there? Does it reflect a belief that the souls of the dead might enter birds? Or is it simply a reluctance to let go of life, dying in the knowledge that birds will be singing over the grave long after friends are gone and nobody else remembers your name? When I asked, nobody knew what the holes might signify.

What strikes me, standing among these graves, is that all these people had such long lives. Often, the earliest markers have no birthdates, a reminder that those buried here were born before the niceties of such record-keeping. Others date back to the early arrival of Europeans with the fur trade and the gold rush. In the community of Shalalth, William Oleman was more than 100 when he died. He had been born at the same time as British Columbia. Dan Alexander's life reached back to the Riel rebellion. So did Sam Paul's. Angel Link was a living bridge to the days when Chief Joseph, White Bird and the Nez Perce fought the US Army.

At the new cemetery, the tombstones write a different story. Since progress came to Shalalth in the form of a huge BC Hydro project, BC Rail's main line and road links to the rich ski resort at Whistler, a kind of holocaust has descended. Perhaps it began when the dams destroyed traditional food fisheries (I'm told a localized famine occurred), drove people from the land and carved up ancient communities to provide rights-of-way for generating stations and power transmission lines. Melanie Alexander remembers how it was before the dams. "When the fish came in the salmon were so thick you could walk across on their backs. Now you don't even see a salmon. We used to spear fish over there at the creek. We used to make our spear points out of deer antler and goat horn. You can't do that any more. Very few fish go by now, but I remember when this lake was clear and you could walk across on their backs."

Federal salmon-enhancement programs had painstakingly rebuilt the run. It was only a fraction of its former splendour, but in 1991 the biggest return since the dam ravaged the Bridge River stocks was eagerly anticipated. About 1,000 coho and spring salmon were coming back to spawn and it was hoped they might lay the foundations for future runs. But in late July, just as the egg-laden salmon moved into the river and onto artificially enhanced gravel spawning beds, the spill gates on the Terzaghi dam were opened and without warning, water was dumped into the riverbed at the rate of 3,000 cubic metres per second. "One muddy roar," was the way an eyewitness described it for me. "You could hear the whole riverbed moving—boulders, trees falling over, gravel bars. All the fish got blown out." Then, to compound the travesty, the engineers reduced the water flow by 97 percent—from 3,000 cubic metres per second to 100 cubic metres per second—which left any fish surviving the flash flood to die in isolated, evaporating puddles. The biggest spawning run in thirty years, itself a pathetic shadow of the teeming resource that once inhabited the river, was virtually wiped out. At final count, 150 salmon had returned. They came back to a habitat changed beyond recognition.

I walked the Bridge River below the dam and the evidence of damage remained vivid and appalling. The entire riparian zone—

trees, shrubs and banks that provide shelter and food for fish—had vanished as though D-9 Cats had been walked down the river. Entire groves of trees have been laid flat by the force of the water. The carefully built spawning beds are gone. The river, even in late winter, is a dry desert of silt-covered boulders. "Controlled" spills like this happened three times that year, "a direct result of weather conditions in the watershed that were beyond our control," said BC Hydro. "In 1991 we had a very heavy rainfall while in 1992 prolonged hot weather led to unprecedented glacier melt in the mountains." In fairness, it is worth noting here that the high country watersheds of tributaries flowing into the Carpenter Reservoir were stripped by loggers in the early 1990s. Too much rain, too heavy a snowpack, too much sun and a fast melt and the runoff now comes swooshing down in unprecedented volumes, scouring the feeder creeks and filling the reservoirs.

It's a process that, in this community as in others, renders our promises of prosperity empty. What we called progress ruined the salmon runs and dismembered the landscape for those who occupied it. And while the power plants earn $100 million a year, only four Seton Lake Indians had won jobs there, Chief Rod Louie pointed out. Meanwhile, across the fence in the new cemetery, he said, the graves were filling not with elders departing in wisdom and grace, but with children, teenagers and young adults laid waste in the prime of their lives.

Death records researched at the band office shocked even the chief and council: at least 44 recent deaths of people under the age of 50 in a community of 223. Translate that toll to metropolitan Vancouver and to experience the same impact you'd have to bury 250,000 children and young adults. After alcohol-related accidents, the leading cause of death for young people here is suicide, the chief says. Unnatural deaths outnumber natural deaths by a ratio of more than four to one. "A lot of it comes from a sense of hopelessness," says Rod. "Sometimes I think 'what's the use of negotiating a land claim if the people have lost their souls?'" He and other leaders are now convinced that spiritual healing is as high a priority as political and economic redress for a community that must regain its self-esteem and learn to direct its anger outward instead of against itself.

What's happening here is far more destructive than the natural grief that devastates individual families. It represents something worse, a terrible rent in the social fabric. A whole people is being dispossessed of its rich cultural past. "We don't have any elders," Rod says. "We are missing a whole generation. It's the most serious thing to us because it means the loss of our people's way of life. How do you look at compensation for something like this? How do you put a value on it?"

When these people had the temerity to barricade the BC Rail through Seton Portage in the early 1990s to protest the vast wealth removed from the heart of their tribal lands while their children suffered in poverty, unemployment and despair, we had a ready response: our police set the dogs on mothers and babies in strollers. Then our government sat down to negotiate a solution. All, of course, in good faith.

Moneyfish

Every summer, when the wind, tide and currents co-operate, the muddy freshwater plume of the Fraser River will sometimes extend 20 kilometres or more into the Strait of Georgia. For the luminous schools of Early Stuarts, outriders of the summer sockeye runs ghosting eastward toward the continent from the Alaskan abyssal plain, the plume represents one more in an array of mysterious signals that will guide them to the hazardous last leg of a 16,000-kilometre journey home.

Compressed into a muscular, streamlined perfection, capable of swimming 100 hours without rest and travelling 50 kilometres a day, each of these Early Stuart sockeye represents both an intense manifestation of the present and an intricately coded message to the far future. Take too many today and we strip mine the species' genetic destiny, which is why the Early Stuarts have been the object of the most sustained rebuilding efforts in the history of the federal Department of Fisheries and Oceans. They are as much symbol as they are the object of the plundering resource economy from which the brash, often bellicose political culture of BC extracts much of its self-image.

Mature female sockeye come packed with 2,000 eggs—the most of any Pacific salmon—and are programmed to deliver them to spawning grounds that in some cases seem almost unbelievably remote. The Fraser is one of the longest river systems in North America. The Early Stuarts are among the first of the sockeye to return to it for the simple reason that they have the farthest to go. From that first whiff of home where the plume of the Fraser licks south past Boiling Reef and the tide rips of East Point into American waters, the Early Stuarts will make a beeline for the estuary and then buck the mighty river's powerful current for close to 1,000 kilometres. Riffle by riffle, battered by rocks and whitewater, the salmon will struggle up the river. "Up" is not a figure of speech. In the river, the salmon will climb almost half a vertical kilometre from sea level to the high country where the Fraser and its immense network of tributaries are born. On hatching, their fry will winter in the adjacent lakes, gathering size and strength for a journey that will take them 8,000 kilometres from BC's remote Interior across the ocean deeps to the far side of the Pacific Ocean, returning from four to six years later.

Unique among Pacific salmon species for their fecundity, coloured a deep, glossy green on the back with a metallic green head, their sides a brilliant, shimmering silver, the Early Stuart sockeye serve as a living metaphor for evolutionary efficiency. Their genetic adaptation to the trying conditions of this astonishing marathon is what makes them the most highly prized of all the Pacific salmon by commercial and aboriginal fishers alike. Sockeye stop feeding once they enter fresh water. Because they have so long to spend in the river, these Early Stuarts return laden with much higher levels of the fat and oil that must sustain them on the last, desperate run to the spawning grounds. The Fraser, their 1,370-kilometre highway to the gravel where they will set their redds, lay and fertilize their eggs and die to provide nutrients in the river and food for bears and eagles, drains a watershed eight times the size of Belgium. The crumpled, convoluted topography of British Columbia funnels all the runoff from that vast region to a single deafening point.

We call it Hell's Gate. Every minute, on average, 850,000 cubic metres of water—enough to fill almost 350 Olympic-sized swimming pools—blasts through this keyhole in the Coast Range that's barely the width of a city street. Under dank, mossy canyon walls, where aboriginal families still gather every summer to fish for salmon in the traditional way, you can still see the remnants of great stone fortifications built in long-forgotten times by First Nations seeking to control and manage access to the river's riches. And not surprisingly, it is here, in the thunder and spindrift that surrounds the meeting of irresistable force and immovable object, amid the ruins of ancient resource politics, that one finds the tangled roots of all the present conflicts over what share of "our" fish American and Canadian, commercial and recreational, aboriginal and non-aboriginal deserve to catch.

Sockeye salmon are the real moneyfish, worth on average up to $10, sometimes $20 each—compared to the $2 or $3 that the average pink salmon brings—which is why they are the object of such fierce political wrangling over which interest group gets what proportion of the catch. Vary a sockeye allocation by 100,000 fish and it can mean a difference in margins of $1 million or more. Because of this, British Columbians are fated to endure another acrimonious cacophony of arguments and counter-arguments on the issue every summer. The rhetoric is predictable. Americans will be accused of overfishing Canadian-bound salmon stocks. Aboriginal bands will be accused of poaching. Affluent sports anglers serviced by luxurious salmon resorts will be accused of barging in at the front of the fishing queue when constitutionally they're supposed to be at the end. Commercial interests will be accused of a rapacious pillage of the resource.

Least heard in this din will be the aboriginal bands on the upper Fraser who rely on salmon runs for local subsistence. But they will accuse everybody below the Fraser Canyon of succumbing to a greed that ignores the ancient rights of those who live where the salmon actually spawn. In the furious debate over aboriginal fishing rights that erupts every summer, it's almost always overlooked that this abundance on the Fraser exists today largely in spite of the non-aboriginal interests and in large part because aboriginal people once carried the sockeye, fish by gasping fish, past the fury of Hell's Gate that had been blocked by the stupidity and careless greed of the European newcomers who now squabble over how much of the resource they deserve.

The Early Stuarts—themselves a bundle of loosely related stocks from roughly the same region of BC's distant Interior—are significant because they mark the beginning of a sequence of mixed stock salmon runs into the Fraser that are generally known as the Early Summers. How they fare is often an indication of what to expect later in the season. Normally the Early Stuarts migrate to the Fraser through Juan de Fuca Strait. Only a few times in more than thirty years have significant numbers taken the "all-Canadian route" between northern Vancouver Island and the mainland. Sweeping down the west coast of the Island, they tend to seek deeper, colder channels, crossing toward the American side of the strait somewhere off Port Renfrew, then turning around the south end of the San Juan islands for the final run home.

But whichever route they take, before they get their chance to undertake their race against time and death in the Fraser, the Early Stuarts must run a formidable human gauntlet of killing technology. First the trollers will take their toll, fishing with multiple lines and fluorescent "hoochies," a synthetic rubber squid imitation. The trollers take their catch in deep, cold salt water and their skippers claim the best-quality fish. Next come the purse seiners, the most efficient form of industrialized fishing technology, scooping up their catch by the tens of thousands where they can trap them schooling along the shore or in the narrows. Then come the gill-netters, the small in-shore independent and aboriginal operators who try to target specific stocks either close to or already in the river mouth. Finally comes the traditional aboriginal food fishery in the Fraser itself, as families gather for the timeless ritual of harvesting with dip nets, gaffs and gillnets set along the riverbank and in the back eddies.

If the Early Stuarts take their normal migration route, American boats have opportunities to fish the run all the way down the Olympic Peninsula and in the narrow passages through the American Gulf Islands. Then they get another chance on the final killing grounds: the tight triangle of American waters that juts toward the north end of Galiano Island just off White Rock. But all these scenarios are plagued by uncertainty. On occasion the Early Stuarts have been known to suddenly turn north in Haro Strait, running instead through the Canadian Gulf Islands, taking Active Pass between Mayne and Galiano islands on the way to the Fraser. Nobody knows why this happens, but some suggest that a combination of the right flood tide and a stiff southeasterly wind will push the plume of the Fraser north, away from American waters. In an El Niño year, with warmer water pushing northward from the south Pacific, the Early Stuart migration might turn east at the north end of Vancouver Island, heading instead into Queen Charlotte Strait, funnelling down the Inside Passage and confounding all the carefully laid American fishing plans.

To some extent, the Early Stuarts' fate, and that of those who rely on them, always hinges on the whims of wind and weather. And these perils continue into fresh water itself. Swollen by alpine snowpacks melting across a vast watershed thundering through the narrow slit of Hell's Gate with a noise that shakes the canyon walls, the silt-laden Fraser River in recent years has been spilling far in excess of its usual peak flow into the sea. Even in a normal year, twice the runoff of the entire state of California passes through Hell's Gate. In 1997 and again in 1999, the runoff pouring out of the vast watershed was the highest in half a century, certainly the highest since the Pacific Salmon Commission began recording. High water in the river means higher mortalities for salmon in transit. So does high water temperature. If mountain snowpacks are heavy and melt quickly at the wrong time, the velocity and volume of the current will batter many salmon to pieces on the jagged rocks and exhaust all but the strongest few. If snowpacks and river levels are low and temperatures shoot up, many will perish because the water is too warm. High water can scour out spawning beds or bury them in silt. Low water can expose them or prevent passage through shallows.

Still, if water conditions are not too onerous, most spawners will make it past Hell's Gate, through the Scuzzy Rapids and the Bridge River Rapids and Farwell Canyon. They will do so by swimming up a sequence of ingenious artificial ladders that permit them to edge around the brutal force of the river in spate. The ladder consists of eleven concrete fishways designed in Seattle and built for a $24-million cost shared equally by Canada and the US. That project, begun more than fifty years ago, represents a profound model of international collaboration in attempting to rehabilitate the Fraser's historic wealth of sockeye and pink salmon runs. These runs, once the most abundant in the world, were nearly extinguished in an ecological catastrophe that was caused entirely by Canadian carelessness, incompetence and greed.

The late Ed Sparrow, a former elected chief of the Musqueam band who was born while Queen Victoria still reigned, was one of those who was fishing for salmon on the Fraser that languid summer of 1913. It was a year of unbelievable bounty. The catch that year was the richest ever recorded. A silver torrent of Fraser River sockeye—more than 32 million—poured into BC's canneries. By comparison, the catch was more than three times the Canadian catch of 10 million projected for 1997, the year of the most recent "biggest run" anticipated since then. Despite the frenzied fishing of 1913, an estimated nine million sockeye escaped up the Fraser to spawn during that summer almost a century ago. Sparrow, still alert and aware of the current controversies when I talked to him about it—despite the infirmities that come of surviving ninety-eight years—remembered how the sinister whispers began to swirl along the Vancouver waterfront where he worked. A huge rock slide was rumoured to have blocked the Fraser at Hell's Gate. The rumours were true. And the slide was man-made.

Construction of the Canadian Northern Railway, later to become the Canadian National Railway, had proceeded at a feverish pace in 1912. BC was then in the grip of a tremendous boom. The railway would give Vancouver a second transcontinental link to compete with the four already terminating at arch-rival Seattle. Contractors were desperate to meet the 1915 deadline for driving the last spike. The last great physical obstacle was the precipitous Fraser Canyon. The Canadian Pacific Railway had already drilled and blasted a route down the opposite bank. Talus slopes marked the places where debris slid into the torrent below. Now, high-balling construction crews for what would become the Canadian National Railway were simply ignoring federal law governing waterways. To save time, they were dumping thousands of cubic metres of rock into the canyon just above Hell's Gate.

Geoff Meggs, a former editor of the United Fishermen and Allied Worker's Union trade publication *The Fisherman*, documents part of the story in his meticulously researched history *Salmon: The Decline of the British Columbia Fishery*. In 1913, just as the largest sockeye run in the history of industrial fishing was moving into the mouth of the Fraser, the rubble, debris and slides had narrowed Hell's Gate substantially. The laws of physics determined the consequences. The velocity and turbulence of the current had already been increased enormously, perhaps beyond the strength of many salmon to endure. Meanwhile, crews pressed ahead with rock cuts that seriously destabilized the entire canyon face. In addition to rubble deliberately tipped into the river in 1912 and 1913, a mountainside of granite dynamited loose during tunnel building was now teetering above the rail bed. It, too, would fall into the narrow canyon during February rains a few months later.

To fully comprehend the nature of the 1913 catastrophe in which the salmon wars of the last decade have their roots, one must try to understand the complicated nature of the Fraser's ecology. Since the last ice age retreated 10,000 years ago, Fraser River salmon had successfully navigated the kilometre-deep canyon between Lytton and Hope by developing some remarkable strategies. Their bodies were perfectly shaped to reduce friction in the fast current and the heavy load of fat and oil—the adaptation that made them essential to the winter diet of aboriginal peoples in BC's harsh, cold Interior—enabled them to expend more energy and hold longer for opportune conditions. The sockeye had also evolved remarkable behavioural adaptations to the rigours of the passage. To get through Hell's Gate, the salmon would string out in a long narrow column, sometimes travelling single file, hugging the canyon sides. This enabled them to find spots behind bulges in the sheer walls where they could take respite from the relentless current. The sockeye would hold in a pool below Hell's Gate, expend themselves in a brief, intense fight through the rapids, then rest up again once through, taking refuge in a large, slow back eddy above the fast water. And this strategy was highly successful. In its pristine state, the Fraser produced salmon in mind-boggling abundance. Some experts now believe that prior to European industrialization of the fishery and the destruction of spawning habitats by dams and development, sockeye runs to the Fraser averaged up to 50 million in dominant years of their spawning cycle. One paper published in the *Canadian Journal of Fisheries and Aquatic Sciences* speculates that under optimum conditions the pre-European Fraser produced 100 million sockeye salmon.

The first hints that the golden goose was being strangled came from worried aboriginal bands upriver. They relied on the salmon for winter survival. Late in the 1913 season, no fish were showing up. They sent scouts downriver to find out why. Meanwhile, BC's deputy fisheries commissioner, J.P. Babcock, was sent to investigate the rumours now sweeping like wildfire down the Steveston docks. Babcock's first sense of the appalling magnitude of the disaster came when he climbed down to the river below Hell's Gate. There he found a school of sockeye milling below the narrows. It extended 16 kilometres downstream and it was growing by the hour as more fish arrived. Soon it was joined by millions of pinks. Babcock quickly determined the cause. "Immense masses of rock from the railroad cut above had slid into the channel, constituting a great wing-dam. The rapid currents striking those two rock projections were deflected violently towards the centre of the stream," he reported. "Upon attempting to pass around these two points, the sockeye were obliged to jump at right angles to the current and were swept away from the shore out to the channel, where the major portion disappeared from view beneath the chocolate coloured water."

Now the sockeye's strategies devised over millennia were proving useless. Only the strongest, luckiest few were able to navigate this suddenly transformed riverscape. But to make things far worse, railway crews had systematically filled the large pool above the rapids with construction debris, which meant that even those fish making it through the rapids found the back eddy where their ancestors had rested for thousands of years had vanished. They now had nowhere to recover their strength. Most would be swept back down the river by the current. What took place next laid the foundations for the sense of anger and alienation from an insensitive central Canada that still characterizes politics in the western-most province.

Provincial fisheries minister William Bowser, who would later become premier, telegraphed Ottawa for immediate help. But it took two months for a federal inspector to make the journey from Victoria to Hell's Gate—only one day's travel by boat and train. A difficult passage was belatedly blasted through the blockage in the fall of 1913, but it was too late. The salmon had been holding in the river too long to continue their arduous journey. Their relentless biological clocks had run out. Unspawned salmon died by the millions. The stench hung like a vast miasma over Hell's Gate and the lower canyon. It was estimated that 90 percent of the salmon run that year was prevented from reaching 80 percent of the watershed.

In 1909, the Anstey River on Shuswap Lake was described as having been red from bank to bank with spawning sockeye. In 1913 an old settler rowed 140 kilometres to the river to salt down his winter food supply but he reported finding only eight fish on the spawning grounds. In north central BC, hunger stalked remote aboriginal settlements. Women and children driven off by famine perished in the attempt to reach places where they could obtain relief. There was worse to come. Early in 1914, after a tunnel was blasted through an unstable outcrop, another 100,000 cubic metres of rock, gravel and debris crashed into Hell's Gate, blocking the river to returning salmon once again.

While Ottawa dithered and the railways made excuses, desperate aboriginals from BC's Interior and from the Lower Fraser came down to the site to try to physically transport fish across the blockage. They were faced with a social catastrophe if the salmon were wiped out. For scores of Native bands from Steveston to Fort St. James, 930 kilometres northwest of Vancouver, the sockeye are more than simply a food source. They are a profound cultural icon, celebrated each year with First Salmon ceremonies that mark the ancient relationship between human beings and a once limitless abundance of nature. Even today, the Supreme Court of Canada has ruled, the salmon are so important to the spiritual survival of aboriginal culture that the right to fish for social and ceremonial purposes takes precedence over all other rights save conservation.

And so, almost a century ago, a rickety wooden flume the length of a football field was built around the partially blocked chute at Hell's Gate. Dip netting salmon below the whitewater, Chief Sparrow and the other aboriginal volunteers carried sockeye in baskets to the flume and a safe passage up the river. Later, another makeshift route was blasted through the debris and once again a pathetic trickle from the once vast runs made its way upstream to spawn. But catches on the BC coast soon collapsed from the abundance of 1913, never to recover.

And then, in what now seems like an orgy of insane greed, Canadians fished the dwindling survivors of that 1913 disaster to the brink of extinction. Some years the rate of harvest on returning sockeye reached 94 percent. In 1917, 7.8 million sockeye—the run spawned by the survivors of 1913 and a testament to the species' fertility and resilience—returned to the Fraser. Canada's commercial fishing industry caught and canned 7.2 million, 92 percent of the run. Four years later, the run was less than two million fish, virtually non-existent by standards of sockeye abundance. The fishing industry shifted its sights to other species, sequentially fishing down their abundance, too, until we arrived at the present crisis with coho, chinook and steelhead, a predicament for which almost every interest group—sports anglers, the commercial sector, federal fish managers and provincial authorities with jurisdiction over salmon-spawning habitats—seeks to evade responsibility.

In 1945, federal experts calculated the cost of the Hell's Gate disaster at $300 million—$2.9 billion in 1997 dollars—in foregone revenue. "For the Fraser," Meggs writes, "the golden age of salmon canning was over. Sockeye were scarce. Someone would have to be sacrificed to make ends meet.

"The Hell's Gate blockade initiated an era of expulsions from the salmon fishery, the forced exile first of native people and then of Japanese. The native people were driven out of the fishery because whites wanted their fish; the Japanese because whites wanted their jobs."

Chief Sparrow was one of those driven from his livelihood. Eighty-four years later, the taste was still bitter as ashes in his mouth. "If our people up the country didn't pack sockeyes over the slide there'd be no fish," he told me, shaking not with frailty but with anger. "They packed those fish over that slide by hand, one by one. Now if you put a net in the water you get arrested."

Chief Sparrow's last summer fishing on the Fraser in the aftermath of 1913, he said, he caught only 150 fish. Later he found work in a sawmill, and then, in 1924, began making the arduous, dangerous journey upcoast to fish the rich sockeye runs of the Skeena. He would not return to fishing the Fraser River runs for almost half a century. When he did, it was largely thanks to an accord negotiated with the United States in 1930. The International Pacific Salmon Commission was created to manage what was left of the Fraser River sockeye runs in an orderly manner. That treaty, the forerunner of today's coastwide Pacific Salmon Treaty, was ratified in 1937. Under it the commission began construction of fishways at Hell's Gate, specially designed at the University of Washington using a meticulously detailed scale model that recreated the complex river currents at Hell's Gate.

Like large concrete stairways about six metres wide and up to 140 metres long, the six fishways now at Hell's Gate divert part of the current and then break its velocity with a series of baffles that create resting pools for the migrating fish. Begun in 1944, the first two fishways were completed in 1946. Thirty-two years after the 1913 catastrophe, returning salmon were able to pass through Hell's Gate almost as easily as they had before human meddling had come within a few metres of sending them to oblivion. The long, painful task of rebuilding Fraser River stocks began and the fruits of that labour are what we are now calling "the biggest run since 1913"—a run, it is worth noting, that is still less than half of what it was before non-aboriginals got involved.

"The Hell's Gate Slide" is how Canadians prefer to speak of the disaster that rendered the Fraser virtually impassable for salmon returning to spawn, Meggs points out. This choice of language is revealing. It implies one more evasion of responsibility, suggesting that some arbitrary act of God—and not stupidity and greed—brought down the rock that choked the Fraser Canyon. "In fact, the disaster resulted from deliberate and illegal construction techniques of the [Canadian Northern] railway and should really be called a blockade," Meggs writes. "The magnitude of the disaster was covered up by officials who allowed fishing to continue even when they knew every spawner was required for survival of the runs. When the tremendous losses became obvious, these same officials attempted to eliminate aboriginal fishing above the slide rather than ameliorate the slide's effects or crimp the profits of the canners.

"The price of building the [CNR] was the destruction of the largest sockeye run the world has ever known."

Part of the price of attempting to restore that run has been to provide a share of the harvest to the Americans and aboriginals who helped to make it possible, an obligation that rankles with some commercial and recreational interests.

Meanwhile, the miracle of the salmon continues. The Early Stuarts ride the long plume of the Fraser in from the shadowy Pacific. It carries them through the maelstrom of Hell's Gate and on, oblivious to history and the arguments of human beings, past Williams Lake and Quesnel. Battered by rapids and waterfalls, resting in the back eddies behind submerged boulders, avoiding the current by hugging the shoreline where they are vulnerable to bears and human predators, these sockeye make the race against their own biological clocks. Already, the salmon have begun to die, their tissues decomposing even as they swim. If conditions in the river hold them up too long, time will run out and they won't make their rendezvous with the future. At Prince George, those that remain will turn west on what's left of the Nechako River, much of which has been diverted to feed an aluminum smelter at Kitimat, and then, 50 kilometres shy of Vanderhoof, they'll turn again, this time north on the Stuart River.

The last survivors will follow the Stuart past Fort St. James and the nets of the aboriginal people who have relied on them from time out of mind. Then on, through Stuart Lake, into the Tachie River, through Trembleur Lake and the Middle River, up the 100 kilometres of Takla Lake to the Driftwood River, due east of Ketchikan, Alaska. There, their backs and sides turning the bright crimson that marks the final stages of their life cycle, the Early Stuarts will begin the nine-day courtship rituals that culminate in spawning and then a sudden acceleration in the aging process and death. The fertilized eggs they leave behind will sleep beneath the ice until the following spring, when the fry emerge from the gravel, move to the lakes and prepare to begin the long, fateful journey of life's renewal and regeneration that will take them all the way to the outer Aleutians until they turn again, homing with unerring grace to the muddy plume of the mighty Fraser.

Great Tyee River

Braided between bars of glacial gravel, the swift ribbon of jade-green that is the Phillips River twists its way seaward through a landscape that still seems virgin and primeval, although in one form or another environmental pillage and plunder have been going on here for more than a century. I am 200 kilometres north-west of Vancouver. Up beyond Campbell River, past Seymour Narrows and the ghosts of Ripple Rock, past Separation Head, past Kanish and Okisollo and Hole-in-the-Wall with its killer tides. Past the Cinque Islands. Past the old lava flows changed to greenstone by heat and pressure. Past the pink granite at Otter Cove. Past Menace Rock. Then maybe an hour's run by fast boat down Nodales Channel toward the mainland, around the fat rump of East Thurlow Island and then into the inlets, those shadowy million-year-old clefts in the Coast Range made famous by Martin Allerdale Grainger in *Woodsmen of the West*, his brilliant evocation of life in the rough and tumble A-frame camps here in rain country in 1908.

Dripping stands of Douglas fir, cedar, spruce and hemlock cloak the shoulders of the fjords, their reflections dark on the slick, black surfaces below. Along the shore are the rusty eyebolts of booming grounds and the frayed ropes from old seiner tie-ups—the most dangerous job on the coast, setting loose from those, some say. In the tight alluvial fans of the river estuaries, sedges and seagrass give way to dense thickets of salmonberry, thimbleberry, blackberry, then willow and alder, all crowding greedily toward the light at the gloomier edge of the rain forest. Even now, with new snow on the mountains, this rich biotic zone teems with life. Sea and shorebirds bustle and chatter, gregarious river otters patrol the shallows, deft-footed mountain goats gleam against cliff faces above. The bears, gorging on salmon a few short months ago, now dream in their winter dens and, higher up in the headwaters, the river also sleeps under its own blanket of ice. Yet deep in the January gravel the first of a new generation of salmon already begins to emerge. Federal fisheries staff and a motley collection of community volunteers are waiting anxiously for this hatch. Through the Indian summer and into late fall, they collaborated long hours to reverse chinook runs, which have dwindled to the brink of extinction, into the Phillips River.

Once, more than fifty years ago, records show a run of chinook coming into the river in which more than half the salmon weighed 20 kilograms or more, every second fish a great tyee. No wonder this was still home to the Kwaikah long after many other bands had moved from their mainland villages to Campbell River. One of them, Johnny Macamoose, told loggers who arrived in the 1920s that as a seventeen-year-old he had participated in the burning and sinking of a sloop named the *Seabird* off Port Neville, and that following the shelling of the village by a Royal Navy gunboat he'd been one of the four "guilty" surrendered by the chief and had served twenty years in prison. The only reference I find in the formal historic record is to the looting of a vessel named *Sea Bird* after it runs aground on an island in the Fraser River during the 1858 gold rush, although there is another incident involving the shelling of Fort Rupert by HMS *Clio* in 1865, so perhaps rather than being apocryphal, the story is a conflation of two momentous events appropriated and lodged in an old storyteller's memory.

In any event, if the human history here fuses into uncertainty, the ecological importance of the region remains absolutely clear.

"Each of these inlets and the rivers that feed them are like fingers that reach into the biological heart of British Columbia," points out Rob Bell-Irving, a writer, thinker and conservationist who holds down a day job as a technician at the federal government's Quinsam River Hatchery on Vancouver Island. "They put the heart of the Chilcotin right on the coast. Imagine that."

Phillips River takes its characteristic sheen from silt carried into its watersheds by meltwater from the glaciers that still cap the high country. And this country is high. Mist-draped mountains soar an almost vertical five kilometres on all sides. Mount Osmington, Mount Pratt, Mount Jones, Granite Peak and the Pembroke Range all jam the sky. Runoff from close to 1,000 square kilometres of this broken, tilted ground channels into the mainstem of the Phillips, broadens suddenly into a long narrow lake where the valley opens out, then drops steeply to tidewater several kilometres downstream to the west. Some of this meltwater from the undersides of icefields may have first fallen as snow before human beings—or even salmon—came to populate the landscape that we call BC. Never dammed, unencumbered by log-jams, carrying a deep glacial chill even in high summer, the glossy, muscular current of the Phillips is unusually free of turbulence. With its gravel bars still intact and dense riparian cover, it provides ideal salmon-rearing habitat. This cold water is crucial for salmon survival, perhaps even more so as other rivers experience a steadily rising trend in summer temperatures.

Never famous like the Atnarko or the Nahmint, the Phillips is nonetheless a vitally important piece of BC's biodiversity puzzle, the home river for a race of slab-sided, deep-shouldered chinook salmon that can weigh up to 30 kilograms. It's home, too, to chunky coho so big they might pass for chinook in other rivers, oversized pinks, silvery chum, sockeye, cutthroat trout and both summer and winter runs of steelhead. Indeed, every species of native anadromous fish spawns in this one river and there isn't a month of the year when fish aren't moving into its lower reaches. The salmon are the loom on which a vast and complex web of life is woven. Eagles gather to gorge on the remains. And in the fall, fresh scat from enormous grizzlies gathered for their annual pre-hibernation glut steams in the willow thickets. Bell-Irving and Dave Ewart, manager of the Quinsam hatchery in Campbell River, came in the fall to assist with a remarkable community-based effort to bring the runs of these distinctive fish back to the abundance they knew before loggers, commercial fishing fleets and hordes of recreational anglers arrived to upset the delicate ecological balance.

Harry Assu, an elder and chief at the Cape Mudge village on Quadra Island who spent fifty-nine years fishing for the Quathiaski Cannery near Campbell River, remembered one season in the mid-1920s when his seiner took perhaps three million pinks in Phillips Arm. One sockeye set was so heavy with fish that it took the crew five frantic hours to land the catch. Originally, loggers were required to leave a strip of timber 800 metres wide along the river banks, but the enduring legacy of BC's last Conservative government, which came to power under Simon Fraser Tolmie in 1928, was to remove the regulation. The loggers quickly stripped the prime timber in the riparian zones and within a decade the once-abundant runs had begun their steep decline. Assu, who was born in 1905, remembered 1938 as the last big catch in Phillips Arm.

Today, fisheries scientists hope that with forbearance and hard work the runs may be restored to their former splendour. "All these mainland inlets are a long way from industry and urban blight. In the past they suffered extreme damage from logging and overfishing but, because of their remoteness, they represent perhaps the greatest hope for salmon recovery on the entire south central coast," Bell-Irving says. The community effort at Phillips River is unusual in itself because to the urban eye it's almost invisible, a network of dispersed fishing lodges, the isolated homes of people who prefer the silence of the bush to the bustle of downtown, loggers from small camps and even visitors to the occasional spiritual retreat.

There are no roads, no airports, no ferries. The sea is the highway, mostly accommodating, sometimes dismaying, always unpredictable. High pressure systems build in the Interior and then vent through fjords where the walls rise a full kilometre out of the sea. Velocity increases sharply because of the venturi effect in narrow mountain passes. In the winter, Arctic outflows pouring down the fjords can introduce chill factors that cause usually mild coastal temperatures to plummet to minus 20 degrees in less than an hour. Waterspouts, sudden squalls, sleet, freezing winds—Wally Parker of the Stuart Island Community Association (numbering no more than twenty-five people in winter) says the conditions come with the lifestyle. "Nobody's experienced life until they've experienced a Bute Inlet wind," he grins. Bute is the next big inlet to the south and cuts even deeper into the mountains than Phillips Arm. "You're really out in the bush here. It's a whole different story just trying to get simple things done," he says. "City people generally think money can buy anything. Sometimes out here it can't buy very much."

The simple thing they're trying to accomplish is to capture mature chinook, put them into in-river holding pens to ripen and then strip them of milt and eggs they hope will produce 120,000 fry in a small hatchery that's enjoying survival rates "in the high 90s." The math is straightforward. Rivers like the Phillips once produced vast quantities of trophy-sized salmon, "fabulous, huge chinook and coho of twenty pounds or more," Bell-Irving says. At the turn of the century, the river supported its own cannery, mostly targeting sockeye, pinks and chum. Since 1945 the chinook and coho runs in many watersheds have declined by close to 90 percent. On some rivers the chinook returns are down to a few hundred fish. "We had 400 pairs [of chinook] in here in 1981. In

1997 we only found four," says Greg Barlow of the Gillard Pass Fisheries Association. "We flew the river. Didn't see any coho. Four chinook. This river was dead. There are times when I've spent twenty-one days in here to get twelve fish. I think that when they had that Johnstone Strait opening to hit the Americans [during the so-called salmon war] they basically cleaned out this river."

The commercial fishing industry blames loggers for habitat loss, loggers point to ocean survival conditions, sports anglers blame the commercial fleet—or seals when the commercials aren't fishing—and everybody loves to scapegoat federal fish managers. Draconian closures imposed the previous season by Ottawa in a move to preserve endangered coho runs were widely criticized. But not here. "We haven't seen this many coho return to spawn for seventy years," Parker says. He tells me the returns prove Ottawa's cautions were right on the money. "Now, it would be really nice to see them keep that up for two or three full cycles."

Whatever the cause of chinook declines, the Phillips River fish are clearly in a precarious position. One accident of nature, or human miscalculation, and they might wink out of existence. Which is why the dispersed community scattered across these remote islands comes together each year to raise the $25,000 it takes to run their little hatchery operation. Dances, bingos, an auction, it all resembles the homespun efforts of many a small rural community—until you remember that here there are no phones or roads, that people have to travel to events by boat and hope the weather stays good.

Survival rates for naturally spawned eggs are about five percent and of those only one percent will survive to spawn themselves on the next cycle. But incubating eggs in the community hatchery and releasing fry when they weigh around a gram means survival rates increase to 90 percent or better. To harvest the eggs, volunteers run a seine from the beach into a deep pool. Bell-Irving, armoured against the cold in a neoprene wetsuit, uses a banger—a long metal rod with a cup on the end that resembles a bathroom plunger—to frighten salmon into the purse formed by the net. Pink salmon, coho, steelhead and cutthroat trout are all carefully released. The big springs are isolated.

Some of these fish defy the imagination, specimens so large they won't even fit into the oversized plastic tubes used to transport them to sturdy steel holding pens located in a steady flow of cold, oxygen-rich water. Originally, the big fish were simply kept in PVC tubes right out in the spawning channel. Unfortunately, grizzlies ripped the industrial grade plastic apart and ate the chinook. There are human vandals, too. Some misguided or malicious souls once released a whole season's hard work.

Sam Anderson, the twenty-year-old university student hired to keep an eye on things during the critical late fall season, says he loves his lonely post. He's a rarity, though. One of his stories about a nervous predecessor explains. One night the caretaker's trailer began to rock. A curious grizzly was trying to turn it over. It ran off when he opened the door and yelled. But later, while the watchman sat reading in his bunk, the bear suddenly stuck its head through the flimsy window above his shoulder to have a look around. Presumably it didn't like the reading matter because it then threw a tantrum and bashed in the end of the trailer. That was one caretaker who didn't sign on for a second tour of duty. "Actually, the bears have been pretty good considering we're in here on their territory," Anderson snickers. Mind you, his trailer today is a sturdier model—the old one, crumpled by the angry bear, still lies in the bush nearby—and when the volunteer crews go down to the river to capture chinook there's always a loaded 12-gauge shotgun within reach.

Meanwhile, the great Phillips River chinook—females averaging 14 kilograms, males close to 20—fin and swirl in the indestructible steel holding pen just below. They are a vital part of the bigger and more complicated puzzle at the heart of which is a simple question with profound implications. Can human beings and salmon find a way to live together on this coast? Or will we condemn the salmon, and possibly ourselves, to the same fate as the dodo, the buffalo and the passenger pigeon? And if, for all our wealth and knowledge, we can't save the big winter springs of the Phillips River, what can we save?

Burning the Boats

I came to fish but the weather turned on me. The sun grew fat as a blood-blister over the brassy Strait of Georgia. Day rolled into day without a feather of air, slack water moving up Stories Beach only to the pull of listless tides, even then without a wave or swell, just a slow crawl of flotsam up and down clam flats that stank of mud and decay. Behind the ragged horizon of the Coast Range, dirty columns of smoke from half a dozen distant forest fires boiled skyward. Their plumes reached into the jet stream, flattened out into long, sinister anvil shapes on the invisible wind. The fall-out added a raw quality to the light. At night the moon seemed bruised and by day everything was tainted with a bitter aftertaste of ashes.

Each morning, infused with the misplaced optimism that rises in fishermen faced with diminishing returns, I borrowed Susan's little wooden pram, greased the oarlocks and rowed a mile off shore, watching her parents' home dwindle to a dirty green thumbnail against the burnt umber of Bob Hart's meadow on the far side of the Island Highway. The foreground of the Hart place was occupied by a strange, half-finished structure: an ambitious split-level house, framed and roofed, then abandoned, doors and windows gaping to the weather. Fall southeasters roamed through its empty halls at will, slanting in behind walls of spindrift. On their heels came the eternal winter drizzle, seeping into everything, leaving its trail of punky wood and shields of gleaming fungus. In summer, the blaze of solar noon scorched the grass until it crackled underfoot like beetle carapaces, followed in turn by glittering wedges of autumn frost. How many hard seasons had burnished that exposed wood into the lustrous, silvery sheen only the Islands' western red cedar can acquire?

Bob was a prospector, face craggy as a rock bluff, berry-brown arms cabled with tendons and sinews. He found a lot of little stuff, gold pockets here and there in the elbows of a chain of crater lakes. Built himself a little hovercraft before anyone ever thought of the idea and used the clear, swift streams as secret highways into a wild backcountry that most people shunned. Once he took me up Mount Washington, showed me the old ore laced with arsenic, spread his greasy topographical map in the poisonous dust and pointed off down the knuckled spine of Vancouver Island, calloused finger stabbing the air. It waved like a symphony conductor's, sketching the way the rock buckles down the fault lines, reminding me that we live in a broken country where the underwater Juan de Fuca plate slides relentlessly beneath the piece of North America that geologists call the Insular belt, heaving up mountains in a topography sudden with earth tremors and scarred by old lava flows.

"Perfect pattern," he said. "Repeats itself like a math model. See how the lakes crater out at the base of those folded mountains? That's where the vein is exposed. If mineral shows there"—the finger descended like God's authority on the map—"you're gonna find it there. And there. And there.

"Stake it?" He hooted. "Put a claim on that and Mr. Socialist Government is just going to take it away. But yeah, I staked it." His eyes glittered with a mercurial cunning. "I rotated my charts when I filed them. The compass headings are all screwy. Try to find those claims from what I filed and you're gonna be looking up Kingcome Inlet." He cackled.

I contemplated the prospector's sharp little punji stick, set to booby-trap the unwary bureaucrat. The country behind Kingcome, far to the north and on the mainland, offers brutal terrain under dense tangles of devil's club and impenetrable brush, a fitting place in his eyes for the taxman's drones and parasites. Bob needed no money. Cared little for it. He had finally hit it somewhere—on a copper creek according to local legend—and started out to build Peggy a proper house. When her health broke he walked away from it and moved her into a mobile home on the back forty, surrounding it with white drifts of yarrow, yellow tansy, pink sea blush and the delicate spread of stonecrop—all the natural flowers of the biotic zone. Easier for her to keep wildflowers than tame ones, he said. He always turned a stranger toward the lesson told by the decaying husk of her unfinished house: "A vanity, eh."

Peggy was an Island girl, born and bred up on one of the northern bays where her dad kept the post office for the Finnish handliners, strutting the floats with their horsehead pukka knives in tasselled sheaths, jostling the rigging slingers and boom dancers—tame apes, Susan's dad called them, permitting himself the indulgence of a logger gone civilized. The trees were big then, cathedrals of fir and cedar soaring out of moss so deep you didn't need a bedroll. Nothing there now, the hotel burned and the high riggers and whistlepunks mostly gone, following the gyppo logging outfits as the prime timber played out. All across the north Island the big trees are gone, the trees that stood when Drake sailed north after sacking the cities of the Spanish Main—trees the like of which we'll never see again. You see the rotting stumps everywhere, some as wide across as a man—some twice as wide—colonized by huckleberry and fungus, standing in the spindly second growth like mute witnesses, the springboard slots, notched high up the sides for the axeman's cutting platform.

One slow afternoon, Peggy told us how to find wild honey in the ruins of the forest. "You take a bowl of fine flour, see. And you go sit up in the slash, right up in the fireweed. Sit there real quiet. Then when the bees come to the flower, you dust 'em with your flour. Then watch real sharp like. Those white-coated bees will make a beeline to their nest. Not too far. Never a mile. Then you know where the honey is. Mark that place for the fall. Keep a weather eye, might get a bear, too." Fireweed honey is the Island itself. A tawny amber with deep glints like flecks of gold leaf, though when you come to put it in your tea it's clear as water, something you see that isn't there—or something you can't quite seem to see when you think you ought to.

I'd pack sandwiches made with fireweed honey from Brown's and slide Susan's pram into the sea. Gently, though. Her beloved *Seal* was old and frail. The boat was made in the basement by a father who knew what things are important, what things you have to get right, but even the finest work starts to go after thirty years of hard use. The seams of Susan's childhood were sprung and in some places even the lamination in the plywood was separating. That was my only knowledge of the boat, except for her stories of how it had set her free as a little salt-bronzed girl on the beach at Arbutus Cove. The summer she let me borrow her boat to go fishing, Susan's father sanded her pram almost down to the glue and then laid on five coats of gooey green marine paint. Then her dad filled the pram up with water and left it to soak for a week while I dug the ditch and laid the pipe to his new septic field. *Seal* floated fine and reasonably dry after that, though the bottom was thin enough in some spots that her dad circled them with chalk so I wouldn't accidentally put a foot through the hull some morning when I was out there a mile into the straits and a tide change set to carry me off.

There are plenty of accidents looking for a place to happen in these waters. The summer before, fishing off Shelter Point, I watched a big cutter-rigged boat out of Vancouver come boring down the inshore like they were racing the Swiftsure. All these tanned Howe Street-types in their fifty-dollar Aussie deck shorts were hanging over the rail and waving back at the friendly Island yokels who stood up in their battered 14-foot tinnies and frantically tried to semaphore a warning. They piled that yacht right into the house-sized rock that sits at the end of the spit barely submerged at high tide. It was sad rather than funny, watching the beautiful hull shudder and that big mast whipsaw. Somehow she wasn't holed, but they dragged into Campbell River like a kicked dog.

This particular morning I packed my honey sandwiches, a paperback book, a transistor radio and a couple of interesting spoons that Susan's dad had made out of tin can lids when he was a kid. The spoons were killers, I can attest to that. I eased Susan's boat across the drift logs in the front garden. The house had originally been a boom shack, floating from logging camp to logging camp, bolted to a couple of skid logs and winched up the beach into the sword grass by the old steam-driven donkey engines. Somehow it came into the possession of Cougar Smith, a legendary slayer of the big cats, and stayed on Stories Beach until his widow approved the buyers and sold it to Susan's parents. Those drift logs had been in the front yard for almost a century and Susan's dad swore to me they did a better job of keeping the southeasters out of his living room than all the fancy concrete breakwaters put up by the big-city lawyers who figured they knew more than Mother Nature and bulldozed the foreshore to improve things. Pushed by a good gale, the big tides would find a way to come around the ends of their seawalls and swamp their carports and Bill would laugh like hell and deliver little homilies about the perils of disturbing the foreshore—although he wasn't above bolstering his own logs, especially after the winter night he woke up to find the surf breaking under his living room window. For myself, I didn't care if the big Buicks of the dumb were drowned. We'd been years in the prairies and I just wanted to get out onto the saltchuck and catch salmon. I'd slide the borrowed boat gingerly over the logs, then hump her across the flats and out into the slack tide, wading among the sculpins and crabs until I could board without putting too much strain on the paper-thin bottom that was mostly paint.

I started by working the sea side of the inshore kelp, fishing the tide change by running the homemade spoons at different levels. You do this by rigging different weights, two ounces and twenty pulls of line runs you closer to the surface than four ounces and forty pulls. Rigging two rods and fishing them alternately saves having to change weights and gear. It sounds silly to talk about this, but in these days of downriggers, fish finders and hand-held global positioning systems, setting trip weights seems to be a dying art. I would change the weights and work the same route until I found the depth where the salmon were feeding, a progression as mathematical as Bob Hart's prospecting, drilling through the strata and looking for the seam where it sandwiches through. Fishing this way is not so bad trolling behind a kicker, but for me it was all sweat and cramps when towing the tackle with a set of oars. Rowing has its own pleasures and benefits, though. The slightly uneven pull of the oar blades sets a spoon wobbling and fluttering with the ideal action of a crippled herring. No mechanical motion can match it, which is why it's still the prescribed method in Campbell River's world-famous Tyee Pool.

Still, after hours of this, shoulders aching and sweat caking above my eyes, I let the tide take *Seal* and eased myself down to the bottom planks. I settled back with a Lucky Lager and my book, *Zen and the Art of Motorcycle Maintenance*, nestled the radio against the transom and switched to CBC. It was playing Mozart's *Concerto for Two Pianos* in E flat major. The rhythmic nature of the music might have been a metaphor for the sea itself: muscular surges punctuated by gentle troughs, bright trills sparkling like light on the wave tops. Tackle stowed under the seats and the oars inboard,

Seal bobbed, and I, drowsy with beer and the warm sun, drifted in and out of fragmentary daydreams.

In my dream, somebody sighed. And sighed again. I woke with a start. It came again, a long sigh. I was a long way out and the hair crawled up over my scalp and stood on end. Again, the long, slow sigh. When I eased myself up for a look over the gunwales, I found *Seal* surrounded by porpoises, a whole pod of them, purple eggplant skins gleaming where they rolled to blow, white markings shining like wings along sides and bellies. They slid down the hull, brushing it, corkscrewed and came back under the keel, fleeting shadows against the deeper green of the sea. This was not exactly play, yet there was a sensuous air of pleasure about it. It was then I realized the porpoises were an audience: they were listening to Mozart as the sound waves resonated through *Seal's* hull and into the water. For a whole wondrous hour they stayed, then sank away and vanished as silently as they had come.

Three more days I rowed out and shared the CBC with the cetaceans. Brahms, Haydn, strange compositions I failed to recognize—the porpoises were of like mind. The fourth day there was no classical to be found, just some of that flabby rock and roll CBC announcers will play in their bizarre attempts to win young listeners with the music of their parents. The porpoises never came. I took it as a portent and stopped my fishing, too. In a week I hadn't even hooked a dogfish, it was that slow.

When I mentioned how slow it was to Susan's father, he looked a long spell toward Mittlenatch on the other side of the straits, a strange little island that always looks closer than it is—optical illusions and mirages make it seem to recede as you approach. In summer it rises like a scorched ghost wrapped in a pale mantle of gulls. The birds nest on its bare crown and the island shines in a hard, beautiful light. Binoculars reveal the truth of the white glare: a torrent of bird shit cascading down its crags. Bill squinted at the island. At seventy-five, he had the faded wrinkles of a well-used road map in his face, a lot of rough miles tracked across country none of us will ever see again. "It used to be you could hear the salmon come in," he said. "I was a boy and we'd listen for them. A long silver rustle up and down the whole coast." Once you couldn't look on this water without seeing a fish in the air, great shimmering arcs as they jumped—for what? He didn't know. To knock off the sea lice? For sheer joy at the first taste of fresh water along the shore? He told me how he'd take the dugout canoe he got from the Cowichans and catch springs with spoons made from tin can lids. I fear he saw the best of it. It's ourselves we're killing too, I think. What kind of world will it be without salmon in it?

There was not a mention of porpoises, as if they'd spoken for themselves already. Bill turned his attention back to the neat squares of garden carved out of the seagrass in sheltered spots along the foreshore. His and Hers plots: pods of snow peas, the sweet succulence of tomatoes and strawberries in Win's; a prickly brawl of squash and potatoes in Bill's. "The Harts have gone," he said, almost sharp in his abruptness, the tines of his fork plunging into the poor, sandy soil made rich and dark with his treasured compost. "To Nanaimo. Bob has Alzheimer's or whatever they call it. He's almost all gone. He recognizes Peggy sometimes. I hear he sits still until people forget he's there, then he tries to get away. Where's he going? Up the river and into the bush?"

The next time we came to visit, *Seal* was in bad shape. Fifty coats of paint can't keep the dry rot out forever. The seams gaped and the plywood bottom had worn through. The usual fate for old rowboats is a couple wheelbarrows of dirt and a cargo of pansies and petunias. Susan is tougher about these things. She wasn't having any of that for the boat she took handlining that last summer of high school and before she went to work in the cannery, cutting fish to pay for the study of Horace and Sextus Propertius. Instead she came home with a bottle of whiskey and a decision to burn her boat. She did it on the beach on a falling tide. She said it had to be done at Lammas, the first of August, with the tide ebbing south into the soft summer gulf. I had to look the name up in the dictionary. Oxford's says Lammas was formerly observed as the harvest festival, but in the unabridged there was also a reference to a later-Lammas which was celebrated as the non-existent date; the day that will never come.

I helped skid *Seal* down the rocks, a clumsy exercise as we tried to avoid banging the frail hull. Susan slipped on a slick stone and fell on the keel, a blow above the heart that showed for weeks afterward in big livid welts along her breastbone, as though one had to mark the other before parting. At the waterline, she filled her boat to the gunwales with driftwood and set her alight. The first curlicues flickered through gaps in the hull, the fire probing for weak spots just as the sea would have done, then she filled to the brim with flame that shimmered like water. The beloved boat burned to ash and the ash blew away on the sea breeze and the tide turned and came to a full flood, silver and still under the moon and the high river of the Milky Way.

The next day, when we went down the shingle, *Seal's* bronze hardware had spilled together, an offering at the tide line that Susan recovered for a place of honour in her next boat. Further out, just into the shallows, I made out a shadow in the water. It was the boat's perfect shape, printed into the rocks themselves by the heat of her burning. The shadow was purple, with pale wings, and it seemed to move, although that was only the undulation of the waves. The next day even the shadow was gone—to join the porpoises, maybe.

Like I say, I'd come to fish that summer but the weather turned. The creeks dried to a trickle, some even going underground at the estuaries, leaving a dry pan that filled with brackish sea water at high tide then evaporated off. No oxygen and a gummy soup of salt and algae. The salmon seemed to sense it, holding off as though they knew there was not a hell of a lot of use in coming in to stooge around in the creek mouths waiting for rain. They need the rain: first a freshet to get them over the bar: then a rill sufficient for the ominous dash past the shallows where nature makes its killing ground; finally, up through the blue bedrock chutes to the spawning beds. A sudden downpour is a mercy to them. They can hold in the pools for so long, but they need that current to sprint past the bears and the fish hawks and the thick, heavy-shouldered cutthroat trout, hanging like sleek bandits in the willow roots and ripping into the bellies of females as they come by, gorging on the eggs they jar loose.

I used to wade out into my own river as a kid and stand in the swift, clean current until I went blue, feeling the lithe power of the salmon sliding through my legs. Pinks came first, booming through in high summer, then the chrome-sided springs, the bullet-shaped coho, the big-scaled chum, prized for Indian smokehouses—great hook-nosed males with dog teeth snaggled out of twisted jaws. Their deep shoulders would roll out of the shallows and ravens and gulls would swoop and tear strips of the ripe flesh loose, the purpling skin streaming back like ribbons pinned to the shoulder of an old bull. They'd hold station over their section of bottom, trailing ghostly clouds of milt, holding, holding in the current while the soft pink eggs settled into the cold gravel. Spent fish would roll their pale bellies skyward and drift silently away from their downstream positions, leaving the last males to guard something no longer there, twisted jaws swaying back and forth in the current. The neurons would start to break down, messages firing blind through damaged synapses and the salmon blundering in deranged circles, swimming out of the water and up the gravel bars to the waiting crows and gulls and hordes of insects.

The big runs have gone from the river of my own youth now, as they dwindle in all the watersheds, scoured out by runoffs from the merciless clear-cut logging and poisoned by the toxic runoff from industry and the tireless spread of the suburbs. Thirty years ago, just as Bill had listened to his silver rustle thirty years before me, I would walk to the foot of my father's apple orchard above the Nanaimo River, climb down the rock face and sit alone on a ledge above the shallows, a small acolyte learning the mystery of death.

I watched one big spring work his way out of the water and up a sandbar long enough for a raven to flash in and take both eyes before he muscled his way back into the river, sightless and aimless. He went back into the main current, sank like a stone, rested motionless on the bottom until everything seemed to have forgotten he was there, and then suddenly he burst forward, picking up his blind momentum, moving strong and true across the river to the other side, driving up the gravel bank and scattering the scavengers, driving right up, over the bar and out of sight into the wild scrub. I went down and got him later. That fish was as big as I was. And my father dug him into the garden where I once lived and where the white blossoms of the apple trees still scent the air each spring.

The Saddler's Tale

Donald Horsfield never wanted to be a saddler. In fact, he went to the ends of the earth trying to avoid it. Still, I found him behind a littered work bench just about where you'd find the living room coffee table in most homes. Visible through the window behind him, a few strides across the puddled stretch of dirt called Riverside Road, the muddy freshet of the Bulkley River slithers past the little village of Telkwa. Unseasonably heavy rains and the melting snowpack on the glacier-clad ranges 50 kilometres to the west have combined to bring the river dangerously high. Now, lethal and smooth as the skin of a boa constrictor, the river's passage creates its own wind. It roars through the silver-bellied canopies of the cottonwoods that fringe the channels and flood plains.

Don is not perturbed. He tucks the awl he's been using into his leather apron, sets aside the round knife bequeathed to him by a Boer War cavalry saddler and straightens the templates for a rifle scabbard and saddle boot that occupy his work bench. "It crowned the other day," he says. "I'd say she's gone down eighteen inches overnight. Pretty high for this time of year, though. You should come back in October. That river will be still and clear as gin—best steelhead fishing in the world up here."

Telkwa, about 10 kilometres south of Smithers, in the heart of the Bulkley Valley, was founded in 1906 and grew up around Joe Bourgeon's sawmill and Jack McNeill's hotel and general store. There were seventy-four settlers scattered from the landing to

Hungry Hill. It was a rough settlement. Nan Bourgeon, who died at the age of ninety-six, was in the valley before the Great War. Bound in-country to a chambermaid's job at the Telkwa Hotel, she wrote a fascinating memoir. She tells of chatting with a homesteader's wife returning from her yearly shopping trip to Prince Rupert.

"Do you know how to fire a gun?" asked the prim young Englishwoman.

"Whatever for?" Nan asked.

"Oh," said the rancher's wife, "I keep one loaded just inside the door when I'm alone. The bears are a worry but the men are worse."

Until Nan met and married Joe, she'd retreat to her room at night and wedge a chair under the doorknob. A good thing, too. She said she never forgot the squeak of caulk boots in the corridors and her doorknob being turned stealthily by the muleskinners, trappers and loggers passing through.

Today, Telkwa is a dispersed community of 863. Lilacs spill from the hedges along unpaved lanes, their scent whipped away on the river's breeze, and the air trembles with the roar from a wall of whitewater where the tributary for which the village is named crashes into the Bulkley from the southwest. Once these rivers were highways to the Interior. Now they are prized as sport fishing water. Don tells me how he took four steelhead on his final day of fishing at the end of October. "One had 100 yards of backing out," he says. "But it were damn cold, I'll tell you that!"

The dialect is pure Lancashire, although it has twenty-five years of Bulkley Valley lacquer on it. I came to talk to him because I'd heard it kicked around on the sport fishermen's grapevine that Don Horsfield makes the best fly rod cases anywhere—and makes a living at it. He laughs. "I'm a saddler and harness-maker by trade. I specialize in pack saddles and harnesses. But, yes, I make cases for fly rods. And rifles. And cartridge bags. And lawyers' briefcases."

Born in Clitheroe, a rural midlands village, he was indentured as a saddler's apprentice at the age of fourteen. He hated it. At seventeen, he fled to the army hoping for adventure. The army had other plans. It was in desperate need of saddlers. Posted to Hong Kong, he spent six years as a corporal making saddles for the pack mules essential in mountainous country before the advent of helicopters. Don returned from the Far East with just two things in mind. First: a young man's fancy to go dancing with a nice English girl. Second: never to look at another saddle. He found his dance in a small Lancashire village and met his English girl. She took him home to meet her dad, who worked out of his front parlor much as Don does today. He made saddles.

"Life is the strangest thing, isn't it? All saddlers in my family—it goes a way back," says Pam Horsfield. "It's the strangest thing for me to marry one and bring him into a family of saddlers. Anyway, my dad really liked him." So, it turns out, did Pam.

When Don returned to England from six years of making pack saddles and mule harnesses for the British army, it wasn't exactly in his mind to make a career of it. But he had just married Pam and, to his vast surprise, her whole extended family of saddle-making, leatherworking in-laws. If you can't beat 'em, you'd better join 'em. So he buckled down and signed on with the famous old saddlery firm of James Edwin Cook, making harnesses for the British gentry.

One day he received an unusual commission. A great country house near Preston wanted him to repair and replace a collection of centuries-old leather bottles burned during the blitz. It was a daunting prospect. He had to teach himself rarified skills largely forgotten since the Bottelars Guild ran head-on into technological change and dissolved itself in 1476, joining the Horners Guild, which made horn drinking cups. Working from ancient pictures to determine the appearance and size of the drinking bottles, he taught himself how to shape them, handstitch them with flax thread, line them with pine pitch, carve and fit the polished hard-wood stoppers, stain them with natural pigment and bring them to the proper lustre. It was interesting work, but there was always that looming fact of technological change: in an age of aluminum cans and screw-top bottles, what was the future for a chap who special-ized in making leather bottles of the sort they used in the Crusades?

Like a lot of people right after the war, Don and Pam came to Canada looking for a better place to live. They found it in northern BC, where the rivers belong to the people, not the aristocracy. How did he choose the Bulkley Valley? "I was working at a copper mine and living in a trailer. One year we decided to drive west instead of east to Burns Lake. We came over that rise and I said to Pam, "This is it. This is the place.""

The place is one of the oldest in Telkwa, a rambling false-front building on Riverside Road. It was built in 1911 and served vari-ously as Chinese laundry, notary public's office with walk-in safe, and counterculture haven. Finally, in a kind of return to its pioneer roots, it became Horsfield's saddlery, purveyor of matchless rifle scabbards and working gear to the demanding outfitters and picky cowboys of our last frontier.

"Where I came from, who the hell could actually live on the river and fish for steelhead in it?" In England, some wealthy landowners rent out stretches of riverbank at so many pounds a foot. When someone asks if you'd like poached salmon for dinner you have to think carefully before you answer. It may be grilled *and* poached. He gestures toward the brown surge of the Bulkley through his workshop window. "Anything below high water here is mine—to be shared with all the other people in BC, to be sure, but still mine and not some titled lord's."

Don came from the Black Country. Cradle of the Industrial Revolution, it took its name from the soot of endless smokestacks that coloured the very rain as it fell. He believed he'd escaped all that when he abandoned saddle-making and came to the north-west to work construction sites. Now he worries that the forces that blackened the English countryside will ruin his stretch of paradise. Rich seams of bituminous coal lie just west of Telkwa. A massive strip mine is proposed, and glossy government brochures promise "a great impact on Telkwa when it goes into production." Don doesn't doubt the impact, but he wonders what it means.

"First there was talk of a coal mine. I'm scared to death of acid leach killing the rivers. Now they're talking about a steel mill, too. Maybe it's all linked. That would be ironic for a chap who escaped from the Black Country.

"It's just horrendous what they're doing up here. They're just raping the country," he says. "It's coming. The end is coming. I can see it. They can see it, too. That's why they're highgrading the timber."

"If they ruin the Telkwa, then they ruin the Bulkley. If they kill the Bulkley, they will kill the Skeena..." His voice trails off as he stirs his tea. The spacious kitchen is rich with the mingled scent of Pam's freshly baked gingerbread and the buttery odour of freshly tanned hide. Light pours in from the garden and Simba, their golden retriever, dozes like a sunbeam at our feet. Behind us, the great river sings through the trees. "I love that river. That's the thing that always held me."

The closing chapter of Don's story proves those proverbs about how every cloud has a silver lining and all things come to those who wait. The recession of 1982, the worst since the Dirty Thirties, didn't really arrive in the farthest reaches of the northwest for another eighteen months. You'd pick up the day-old papers and read the scary stories from the nickel belt and the oil patch, but somehow it seemed a long way away. When it arrived, the recession ripped through the small operators and independents like a tornado, littering the landscape with the debris of dreams. Don watched it happen like a slow-motion nightmare. "I had lots of friends who lost everything. They lost their homes, their trucks, their boats—they just lost everything. It was pretty grim."

When he arrived in Canada, he came determined to leave the old ways of Europe behind—his trade as a leatherworker, the assumptions of class. He got himself a heavy equipment operator's ticket and set about making a new life for himself, his wife Pam and three daughters. He was labouring on Hastings Street making deck tarpaulins when a pal told him there was big money at a mining camp on the Queen Charlotte Islands. The big money came from shifts that ran ten hours a day, seven days a week. "There were always four crews in camp," he recalled. "One crew coming. Two crews working. One crew leaving. God, the turnover was awful." But for a boy from the closed-in skies of England's Black Country, the huge panoramas of BC's wilderness set the hook deep.

Alice Arm, Granisle Copper, Rigby Island, the Stewart–Cassiar highway—for eighteen years he was in demand as a grade mechanic. Then the recession arrived and he was out of work. But not out of ideas. He dug out the keepsake he'd been given by Tommy Bracewell as an apprentice. The old man was eighty-four and a scarred campaigner who made saddles for cavalry troops in the wars of the nineteenth century. "He used to send me for a pint at dinnertime. I'd bring it back in a little billycan. Mr. Bracewell gave me this." He pulled out a leather-cutter's round knife, the blade worn to a fragile, glittering crescent by a lifetime's work. That blade connected him, somehow, with his distant youth. He got out the hand tools he'd inherited from Pam's father, got himself a hundred-year-old, treadle-driven British United No. 6 harness stitcher, set up shop in the front room and in 1985 fell joyfully back into the trade he'd deserted for most of his life.

He began by thinking small and marketing locally—saddle panniers for outfitters, pack saddles, harness repairs for working cowpunchers. There were, it was clear, certain limitations to this market. "Up here, who's going to put a $2,000 saddle on a $200 horse?" he shrugs. In business, the ability to recognize a niche market is often the difference between success and failure. One day he got a request from a New York executive who had seen his work—could he build a replica of a leather suitcase that had been a treasured family heirloom? He could. His $1,500 fee was paid without a blink. "That's when the lights went on. I decided to shift to the high end of the market." Word of mouth in the right circles is the most powerful of advertising media. One Vancouver client spent six months tracking him down to Telkwa. "And the world gets pretty small when you have a fax machine."

A fisherman himself, it struck him that many of the people who flew in for steelhead were sporting types with the money to buy top quality merchandise. He started making fine leather cases for fly rods, reel cases, cartridge bags for bird hunters, rifle scabbards and traditional leg o' mutton gun cases. Today, he's selling $350 fly rod cases to a Japanese marketing consortium and filling an order from Holland and Holland, one of the world's premier gunsmiths, for three rifle cases at $1,000 each and a dozen $300-plus cartridge bags.

The sign on his front door says "No Harness Repairs Until Further Notice," but when the phone rang with a strictly local request for one plain saddle bag, he took it. Selling in New York, Tokyo and Vancouver is great, but out on the edge of the bush, you always take care of your own first. And you sleep well, knowing they'll take care of you.

Greater Love
Hath No Man Than This

Up behind Nanaimo's Old Quarter, a few blocks north of Jingle Pot Road, a carefully groomed lawn descends toward an achingly beautiful view of the city harbour where square-riggers once anchored while waiting to load coal. Beyond a string of jewel-like islands, the blue cloak of Georgia Strait is embroidered with whitecaps all the way to the distant mountains of the Coast Range and the snowfields above Vancouver fade into a soft, late-afternoon flush of peach and fuschia. On Newcastle Island, dry-belt Douglas firs give way to arbutus and Garry oaks. Amber meadows sweep down to a sea-carved shoreline of honey-coloured sandstone that is punctuated by silver drift logs and white shell beaches where lovers dawdle and kids swim.

The last long weekend of summer is usually a tranquil one here on the sunny east side of Vancouver Island and in an informal tradition that goes back even farther than that first Labour Day in 1894, many mid-Island folk will take the short ferry trip across their harbour to the provincial park that now graces Newcastle Island. They'll stroll up to the shadowy dance pavilion built sixty years ago, or along the meandering sun-splashed beach paths, celebrating Labour Day with the simple pleasures of an ice cream cone and, if the weather co-operates, an end-of-holidays splash for the kids in sun-warmed shallows. Most will just relax and cherish one last lazy respite before the rains come. Maybe some will remember that this holiday helps commemorate legislation setting the standard work day for British Columbians at eight hours. Some might even ponder the fact that in the 1990s BC workers suffered more casualties on the job than all the Canadian soldiers, sailors and air crew did in the First and Second World Wars combined. A few might even think a bit more deeply about exactly what it is we are supposed to celebrate on this holiday.

What indeed? The good life, certainly: we enjoy a level of prosperity neither attained nor distributed so broadly by any other civilization in history. Relatively secure incomes, even in periods of recession and contracting markets. Holidays and holiday pay. The time to actually have a family life. A high quality of education for kids who must deal with the increasingly intellectual workplace of the future. The knowledge that if those kids ever need a doctor, their treatment will be affordable, undeniable and among the world's best.

Conservatives will claim all this as a gift of the marketplace. Yet on this Nanaimo hillside with its beautiful prospect of the sea, the grass is studded with time-worn reminders of how recent those blessings are—that they were no gift—and how easily today's beneficiaries forget the painful sacrifices with which they were bought. For none were bestowed by a benevolent market. They were created, not by individuals but by the collective efforts of working men and women who wrested them from a brutal system that oppressed individuals and exacted a cruel price in flesh and blood. And it is not in history books or academic papers, but here in the grass of humble, unadorned cemeteries like this one, that the narrative of that effort is most vividly written.

If the coal mines are mostly gone from Vancouver Island, the legacy of the miners who toiled and died in them is with us yet. Those gritty, self-educated miners, not the mine owners, helped trigger the ethical upheaval in the first twenty-five years of the twentieth century that reconfigured a brutish capitalism into the more humane shape that many of us have come to assume it has always had. BC's coal miners were among the first to organize and to negotiate contracts despite bitter opposition from industry and government. They were the first to recruit Asian workers into their union. They led the fight for fair wages and better working conditions. So it's the tough, militant, often radical miners and their brave wives who lie on this hillside that working British Columbians should thank for their eight-hour day, their two-day weekends, their mandatory vacations, their sick benefits and disability pensions and, perhaps most important, the fact that their kids go to school every morning instead of disappearing down some hellhole from which they might never return.

"Take care of my children," one Nanaimo gravestone pleads, a pathetic cry from the era before group life insurance, widows' benefits, or welfare. Others are simply stoic acknowledgements of family-destroying catastrophes.

"Henry Edwards, Killed by a Fall of Rock at Nanaimo, Aug. 30, 1884."

"My beloved husband John Williams, killed in the last Wellington Mine, May 20, 1885."

"John Abernethy, killed by a fall of coal in the Nanaimo Mines, Dec. 28, 1886."

"Thomas Harris, killed by a fall of coal in No. 1 shaft, April 19, 1887."

"George S. Bertram, A native of Yorkshire, killed in the explosion, May 3, 1887."

"Erected by his brethren in memory of Samuel Hudson, aged 37 years, who died 3 May 1887 in a brave attempt to rescue coal miners after the dreadful explosion in No. 1 shaft Nanaimo."

That "dreadful explosion"—one of the near annual disasters that killed miners across BC by the hundreds at a time—occurred at 5:55 p.m. and the blast was so powerful it rocked Nanaimo to its foundations. Bricks flew from chimneys and witnesses were still traumatized seventy years later by the vision of "women and children, some of the women pregnant, streaming down toward the mine...The women in most cases were tugging little children, with tears rolling down their faces." The starched white aprons many of the women wore remained incandescent in fading memories. The aprons meant they had just dressed for a dinner at which their husbands would never arrive.

Of the 155 men down No. 1 shaft, 148 died, not all of them in the blast: survivors were deliberately entombed in an attempt to stop the fire from spreading into merchantable coal seams. The doomed men scratched farewell messages to their wives in the dirt on their shovels. The following year, 77 men were killed in a blast at Wellington. In 1901, the entire 64-man shift was killed in a methane inferno at Cumberland. In 1902, 125 men were killed at Coal Creek near Fernie. In 1903, 19 died at Cumberland and in 1904, 13 more. In 1914 an explosion at Hillcrest blew the rope-riders out of the shaft to the height of a six-storey building and killed 189 men. In 1915, 20 men drowned when a mine flooded at Ladysmith. In 1917, 34 men at Coal Creek were crushed when the mine "bumped" with such force the steel wheels of ore cars were flattened. In 1922, 17 miners were killed at Cumberland and the following year, another 33, most of them sons and brothers of the men just buried. The fatal blast in Nanaimo, still ranked as one of the country's most gruesome industrial disasters, occurred in a mine whose silhouette once dominated the exterior landscape of the town in the same way that it dominated the inner lives of the people who worked and dwelt in the long, grim shadow of the pit-head.

Looking out from our air-conditioned offices or the fitness centres where we retreat after work to pursue the exercise that wore our grandfathers and grandmothers into early graves over a life-time of 12-hour days and 72-hour weeks, it's difficult to visualize what labour historian Jack Scott describes as "the murderous conditions, low wages, long hours and semi-feudal rule" that once prevailed in BC's workplace. While nobody would admit to wanting to see those conditions return, there are those who now argue philosophically against the state interventions that prevent them. Minimum wage laws, for example, are seen as a drag on business; collective bargaining as an unnecessary anachronism; prohibitions against child labour as interfering with individual freedoms; universal health care as coddling the lazy and irresponsible; while unions themselves, which now represent a declining minority of the workforce, are claimed to be too powerful. And yet, surprising as it might be, there are still people alive who can remember what it was like when there was no sick leave, no medicare, no maternity leave, no time off when a child, or wife, or husband died, no overtime pay, no pause in work when a man was killed on the job, no rules governing child labour.

A Royal Commission in 1889 found that it was not uncommon in Canada for boys and girls of eight to be set to hard physical labour and to be disciplined by employers with savage beatings that frequently knocked them senseless. Some mines used "tool-boys" or "nippers" to collect gear needing repairs. In one horrifying incident, ten boys were riding to surface in a cage carrying drills and steel bars that somehow came loose. When the protruding bars snagged on the shaft walls during the ascent, the cage was torn apart and eight "nippers" were ground to pieces; the two boys who survived were horribly mutilated. One Nanaimo "winch boy" never forgot his starting day. His first lift was a mule killed at the face. His second was a man whose head had been crushed by a block of falling coal. Another remembered arriving at the Extension mine to apply for a job just as a coal car came out of the mine with his best friend's dead father draped on top. And yet it would be another twenty years of fierce labour agitation before the law would stop mine operators in BC from sending boys and girls younger than fourteen underground. That was in 1910. The Americans wouldn't ban child labour until 1916 and it wouldn't become a universal standard in Canada until 1929.

All these young men beneath the plain stone tablets that look down on the Labour Day visitors to Newcastle Island once lived and worked in the conditions that spawned such carnage. Among the inscriptions on these gravestones, for example, you'll find the name Mottishaw. Oscar Mottishaw was blacklisted by the mine owners after his safety committee reported gas in the explosion-prone Nanaimo workings. He sought work in Cumberland. Three days later, when the company found out, he was fired there, too. This small injustice was the straw that broke the camel's back. In September of 1912, every coal miner on Vancouver Island walked off the job in what's still remembered in Nanaimo as The Big Strike. It was a transformative event. One of the Cumberland miners who downed tools to support Mottishaw and the gas committee was an eloquent young mule-driver from Yorkshire named Albert Goodwin. He was deeply affected by the experience and later went to organize smelter workers in Trail.

The Nanaimo miners spent their daylight hours cutting coal from more than 11 kilometres of dank drifts that snaked out beneath the seabed. Down there in dripping tunnels bearing names like the Kileen Incline, Puywallop and the Ha Ha, they'd sometimes uncover the perfect fossilized imprints of 65-million-year-old swamp fronds. Eating lunch in silence and listening to the click and ticker of falling coal, they would hear the eerie throb of steamer screws passing through the deep water overhead. Above ground, a fine rain of soot from the tipple sifted out of the sky, leaving a patina of grime on everything it touched, including the washing hung out on the line by women haunted by the constant threat of sudden widowhood in a world where they and their children would be left to the charity of other impoverished mine families.

Island mines were the most dangerous in the world. They were wet and filled with explosive gas. At first, miners were expected to work by the light of open lamps burning fish oil. Down pit boys learned quickly to carry their lamp chest-high: too low and it winked out, smothered by the asphyxiating gas called black damp; too high and the methane known as firedamp would flare along the ceiling with a roar. "If a man got killed or that, there weren't much said about it. There weren't compensation like we got now," one unidentified old-timer told interviewers for the Coal Tyee Society's award-winning chronicle, *Boss Whistle*, written by historian Lynne Bowen after its tireless organizer Myrtle Bergen was killed in a car accident. "But at the same time, if a horse or a mule got killed down there, somebody got fired for it. They were more important than the men because they cost more. They could get men for nothing." "In them days a man was worth nothing," another recalled. "They never even lost a car of coal. They just put him on top of the load and took him out."

Miners were paid by the tonne. Theoretically, the more coal they cut, the more they got paid. But then it was found that the mine owners had rigged the whole weigh-scale system so that a fixed maximum was recorded—and every extra tonne not tallied was pure profit in the operator's pocket. The mine owners, of course, did not intend to let that profit go without a fight. And so, just as the nineteenth century bled into the twentieth, the owners of mines, mills and factories were anxious to crush a labour movement in its infancy. Nowhere was this conflict more evident than across the West, where the stakes were vast, the owners ruthless and the miners tough and not easily intimidated. Disputes often turned violent as strikers battled company goons and the mining towns from Montana to Vancouver Island seethed with secret union meetings, company spies and paid police informers.

We get some inkling of this shadowy, dangerous contest not from the official records, but from the fiction of mystery writer Dashiell Hammett, whose dystopian vision of a culture tainted by corruption sprang from his own experience in the Western crucible of labour versus capital. In 1915 he had answered a vaguely worded ad in a Baltimore newspaper and found himself working as a secret Pinkerton agent for people he later described as gentle, polite, distinguished-looking and "with no more warmth in [them] than a hangman's rope." The Pinkertons had been active in Nanaimo, Ladysmith, Cumberland and the Interior during the strikes there but Hammett's target was the Industrial Workers of the World, which had been organizing both hardrock and coal miners in Washington, Montana, Idaho and in BC's Kootenays and the Crowsnest coalfields.

Two years later in 1917, Hammett was offered $5,000 to murder Frank Little, a one-time leader of the Western Federation of Miners who's said to have introduced Trail smelter organizer and BC Federation of Labour vice-president Albert Goodwin to miners at a meeting in Fernie. Hammett refused. Shortly afterward, in Butte, Montana, Little, a small, partially-blind man who was laid up with a broken leg, was pulled from his bed by five well-dressed men in the middle of the night, dragged on a rope behind their car to a bridge and then lynched. No one was ever charged—but then, the establishment didn't like radical labour. "Good work. Let them continue to hang every I.W.W. in the state," one newspaper responded. "His death is no loss to the world," said another. A few months later, Goodwin himself fled Trail and was hiding at Cumberland on Vancouver Island, where he was hunted down and then shot dead by a seedy sharpshooter-for-hire who'd been cashiered from the Victoria police force for extortion a few years earlier. Goodwin, like the fellow miners for whom he fought, lies in an Island grave marked by a large granite boulder. It says, simply, "Ginger Goodwin, Shot July 26, 1918, A worker's friend."

"Greater love hath no man than this," the Bible tells us, "that he lays down his life for his friends."

And maybe that is what Labour Day is really all about, love and sacrifice as an antidote to greed and self-interest. Maybe that's at the heart of what Islanders are trying to remember when they pile the kids into the car and head for Newcastle Island, spending the last, lingering holiday of summer strolling among sunny meadows and shade-dappled glades, savouring the moments of peace and pleasure bought at such a price by the legions of the blasted, burned and gassed who lie in the long silence of their graves on the hillside high above.

The Spirit Pole
of G'psgoalux

This is a story of betrayal and redemption that reaches across continents, generations and cultures, linking a time constructed from memory to the virtual realities forged in cyberspace. It's a story of ignorance and enlightenment, of philanthropists and philosophers. It's a story that connects the Eagle chief of the Haisla nation to the king of Sweden. It's even a detective story. But mostly it's the story of a profoundly spiritual journey of forgiveness, hope and renewal in a world that sometimes seems trapped in vengefulness, cynicism and materialism. Everything revolves around the voluntary return by Sweden of one of British Columbia's most important cultural artifacts—an ancient totem pole—from the Stockholm museum where it has resided for more than half a century to the north coast village of Kitamaat. And it revolves around the corresponding goodwill gift from the Haisla people of a new pole, carved from a giant red cedar that was taking root on this coast about the time the modern Swedish state was being shaped by the Vasa monarchs of the sixteenth century.

This story begins with an apocalypse, a time when the world seemed to be ending for those who inhabited the remote fjords and rich river valleys on the North Coast. In 1862, smallpox once again stalked the Haida and the Tsimshian, the Kwakwaka'wakw and Haisla. It came on the heels of what were called "the immigrant diseases" of the 1840s. Before that there had been "the intermittent fever" of the 1830s. And before that "the mortality" of 1824. And before that, the first visits of the smallpox in 1775 and 1801. Wherever the smallpox walked, it left empty cradles, cold hearths and echoing houses. Shell-shocked survivors huddled together and tried to make sense of what had laid their villages to waste, reducing coastal aboriginal populations in the hundreds of thousands to a few scattered handfuls.

"My grandfather told me that four villages in the Kitlope numbered 3,500 people," says Ken Hall, a hereditary Eagle chief who is also the 700-member Kitamaat band's elected chief councillor. "But the people living in the Kitlope fell to 57 people. If you go into the graveyard you see names that no longer exist, families that have been extinguished." Gerald Amos, who preceded Hall as chief councillor and is now the band's lead treaty negotiator, says the memory is still disturbingly strong in his own family. "My grandmother was one of three unmarried women of child-bearing age in all the villages," he says. "A lot of our history died with the influenza, died with the tuberculosis, died with the smallpox."

At the Haisla village of Misk'usa, the entrance to the vast and beautiful Kitlope wilderness about 600 kilometres northwest of Vancouver, the great Eagle chief G'psgoalux had lost his little children, his beloved wife, his house and all the members of his tribe. In this void of grief, the chief went alone into the forest. A spirit revealed itself to him. When the chief explained his desolation, the spirit gave him a transparent rock and told him to go back to where his loved ones were laid out on their mortuary platforms and bite the crystal. He did and to his awe and amazement, he saw his people, accompanied by the spirit, walking toward him out of the trees. To commemorate his visionary encounter with the supernatural, G'psgoalux commissioned Humdzeed and Wakas, two powerful chiefs of the Raven clan at Kemano, to carve him a nine-metre memorial pole, which was erected at Misk'usa with great ceremony in 1872. The pole depicted the spirit rising above two mythical grizzly bears, one of them from beneath the sea, which are symbols of great spiritual power. Even today, it is forbidden for the Haisla to kill a grizzly except in self-defence. "What makes that pole so important is that it acts as a portal between the three worlds, the world of water, the world of the earth and the world of the air," says Haisla elder Louisa Smith, whose brother, Dan Paul, now holds the name G'psgoalux and is the Misk'usa pole's owner.

For fifty-seven years the pole stood, both a witness to the sorrow and the suffering and a sentinel at the mountain gates to the pristine 323,000-hectare homeland of the Haisla. But while the Misk'usa pole could withstand the storms and summer sun, it could not withstand an institutional mania for collecting things that ravaged northwest coast cultures much the same way disease had destroyed populations. At the turn of the century, triggered by Christian missionaries who saw the oral history evoked by masks, totems and other regalia as works of the devil, and abetted by the desire of museums to collect the artifacts of what they thought was a vanishing culture, a period of what is now seen as the sustained looting of northwest coast art and ceremonial beliefs took place. "My grandmother told me about the masks being burned down there on the beach," Amos says. "We were told that if we kept the masks we would be separating ourselves from God." Missionaries often sold such regalia to anthropologists to raise funds.

In the context of the times, it's not surprising that Olof Hansson, a minor diplomatic official from Sweden who was posted to Prince Rupert in the 1920s, lusted after a totem pole that he could present as a gift to the prestigious Ethnographic Museum back in Stockholm. Hansson went on the hunt for eight years. In 1927, he struck pay dirt. Iver Fougner, the Indian agent at Bella Coola, interceded on his behalf with a request that he be permitted to obtain the pole at Misk'usa, which was "uninhabited and very remote."

"I think it was the accessibility that led him to take that pole," Amos says. "There was nobody there when he got the pole. They were all away." Louisa Smith agrees: "They said this pole was at a place that was abandoned. Just because that place had nobody there doesn't mean it was abandoned. Our people would move with the seasons to where the food was, but we were always here."

And so, in 1929, the pole was quietly removed and shipped by boat to Sweden, where it was first erected and left exposed to the elements for six months and then taken down again and deposited in a storeroom where it remained hidden from view for the next forty-six years. Back in Canada, the Misk'usa pole had been erased from the map of Haisla memory. They knew the great pole was gone, but they had no idea where. A search proved fruitless. Then, sixty-one years later, a photograph of the long-lost pole turned up in an obscure anthropology text. The knowledge was electrifying.

In 1991, a delegation went to Stockholm to request the return of what belonged to them. "I went there thinking I'm a pretty tough guy," Amos says. "When I saw the pole, I cried. It was such an emotional experience seeing something from our ancestors there." "It's not just the marks of the carvers' hands that are left on a pole," Louisa Smith says. "Their breath is left on the pole, too— their spirit is in that pole." To Ken Hall, the pole was naked. In Misk'usa it would be wrapped in the rich stories and legends that reach back to the beginning of time. Every Haisla would have a personal relationship to it. The pole and what it symbolized would trigger a whole series of interactions with everyone who looked at it. In Sweden it was just another interesting object. "To them a totem pole was just a decoration," he says.

By now, recognizing the value of what it had, the museum had built a new humidity-controlled facility, sent the totem pole to its specialists to repair dry rot and insect damage and put it on display as a centrepiece exhibit. The Haisla arrived to ask that it be surrendered and the first meeting was tense. "They were more than taken aback," Amos says. "'Who are you?' they asked. 'How do we know who you are?' So we put on our blankets and we said, 'This is who we are.' It was a shock. The man from the museum said, 'I need something more than that—do you have something like a letter-head?' But there was a lot of support for our position among the Swedish people."

The Haisla said they understood the museum's position and offered to commission their leading carvers to prepare an identical replica. The museum wanted to know why the Haisla didn't carve themselves a replica and leave the original where it was.

A breakthrough in the negotiations came, Amos says, when museum officials took them to see another prized exhibit, the restoration of the *Vasa*, a warship that sank in 1628. In fact, it was the technical skill developed in restoring this ancient wooden ship that the museum had applied to the old totem pole's restoration.

"They were so proud of their *Vasa* ship and rightly so," Amos says. "So I asked them, how do you think the Swedish people would feel if we took this ship home and said, 'Just make a replica and keep that in Sweden, we want to keep the original in Kitamaat.'" There was a moment of enlightenment. The negotiations began in earnest.

In 1993, newly elected Premier Mike Harcourt wrote to Brigit Friggebo, Sweden's culture minister, to formally support the Haisla request for the return of their pole. Three months later, the Swedish government authorized the museum to return the Misk'usa pole to the Kitamaat village council. But there was an unexpected hitch. The museum said it would only return the pole if there was a state-of-the-art climate-controlled facility to house an artifact it considered a world treasure. This was beyond the financial means of the Haisla. Enter Ian Gill, president of Ecotrust Canada, an environmental organization that had been involved in a successful campaign by the Haisla to protect the Kitlope, the largest unlogged coastal rainforest ecosystem. "This pole stood at the mouth of the Kitlope River," Gill says. "It stood guard over the entire watershed. To have the pole back—well, we've come to realize that this is not just about protecting the land, it's about protecting the culture." Brokering arrangements between the Haisla, the David Suzuki Foundation, the Rockefeller Brothers Fund, the Endswell Foundation and the Swedish museum, Gill has launched an ambitious program to raise more than $500,000 to build a cultural centre that will house the repatriated Misk'usa pole, to provide curatorial training for Haisla staff at UBC's Museum of Anthropology, to commission the carving of two replicas and to pay staff like Louisa Smith who will co-ordinate the project in Sweden and in Canada.

In June of 2000, working from drawings and photographs, master carver Henry Robertson, assisted by Barry Wilson, Derek Wilson and his own granddaughter Patricia Robertson—at seventeen she'd taken a year off school to apprentice as a carver on this historic project—began work on the new poles. The first was to be erected in a ceremony that brought the far flung Haisla and their honoured guests back to the Misk'usa village site about 150 kilometres south of Kitamaat in late August the same year. "This is a major, major event in our community," Smith says. "We're going to get a pole that has the breath of our ancestors on it. Bringing back this pole is taking back our power." The other pole will be roughed out in Canada and then the four carvers will travel to Sweden to complete it at the museum there. As for the original Misk'usa pole, the Haisla have invited the king of Sweden to come to their village for the ceremonies that will see it raised again.

Meanwhile, says Amos, all this is part of an unforeseen destiny launched by the grief of G'psgoalux so long ago. "If that pole had not been taken, it would now be back to Mother Earth as it was supposed to be. But it was taken and now we have this connection with Sweden that is really, really neat."

All These Things
that are True

The hell with it. The politicians, pundits and pollsters can keep each other company. I'm off to reassure myself that a sunnier world goes on behind the lurid poster fronts concocted by spin merchants who promise either ruin or riches. I'm bound instead to search for all those things that are true and yet may be found at the small-town fall fair. For this is the season of the 4-H Club and the quilters' guild, the blackberry jam maker and the apple pie baker, the perfect potato and the prize pumpkin, sheep dog trials and cattle auctions—all those unadorned things that provide the genuine glue of a community. When the golden light of autumn lengthens on the fields and the harvest comes rolling in across the more than two hundred islands that comprise British Columbia's southwestern archipelago, even city dwellers may for a moment shift their attention from the media's dreary daily pageant of doom and miracles to remind themselves that the world is still made up of real things. And when the little fairs are over for another year, they linger on the memory like the scent of wild roses and new-mown hay.

At this time of year, with the sunbleached fields going a peroxide blonde and a hint of copper edging the broad-leafed maple, the lumbering RVs have departed for Victoria, Vancouver and points south while traffic is pleasantly sparse on the Island Highway north to Black Creek near Miracle Beach. This is a leisurely quest, so I'll pause at the big hill outside Courtenay to pay my respects at the gleaming white spire of beautifully restored Saint Andrew's Anglican Church. Just past the Oddfellows Hall, I'll stop another minute at Tsolum School to admire its big, sassy mural of the Land of Plenty unfolding beneath Forbidden Plateau and the glacier. I'm bound past places where plain-spoken people make an honest living instead of spinning illusions and prefabricated fantasies. Places like Fyfe's Well Digging operation, or the emerald fields of Ponderosa Sod Farm and its competition at Devonshire Sod Farm, or the high corn rustling between Beaver Creek Farm and Grantham Farm.

Finally, just beyond Mennonite farmsteads offering fresh eggs, fresh fruit, fresh pies and a fresh zest for life itself, I'll encounter directions to the fair. They are scrawled on a sheet of brown paper that looks like the inside of a recycled grocery bag, hand-lettered and tacked to a sandwich board propped up on the highway shoulder. Along the dead-end road that ends outside the community hall, the lawns are edged with No Parking signs along the roadside, and the visitors have respected every request. It's what I'd expect from a place that welcomes newcomers with a brochure offering not the usual tacky boosterism about shopping malls and theme restaurants but a simple promise that Black Creek's biggest asset is the fact that its distinct flavour "seldom ceases to intrigue."

The craft fair consists of tables under canvas awnings, the community hall having been commandeered for a sophisticated model railway display. Old-timers and train buffs like me are chortling over faithful reproductions, right down to the garish yellow of a perfectly rendered boxcar from the Toronto, Hamilton and Buffalo line.

Outdoors I run into Black Creek mechanic Tom Morton and his lovingly restored display of half a dozen IEL ("that's Industrial Engineering Ltd.") Pioneer chain saws. "They made 'em right in Vancouver, how do you like that!" He collected the saws over a career felling timber for Waldie Logging in Nakusp: "A very fine man, Bill Waldie. Very fine man. He owed a lot of money during the thirties, you know, but when things picked up he paid back every nickel—not like a lot of these operators we got today." Tom tells me that he and a pal are getting together an Old Machinery Restorers' Club. "I'm partial to chain saws myself, since I made so much of my living with them."

Tom left the woods after getting crunched in 1962. Nostalgia brought him back to Nakusp long after and there was his old 1949 Pioneer, waiting in the junk shop like he'd just gone for coffee. He bought that saw in the first place from Carl Stach up in Arrow Park "before they turned it into fish pasture." Carl had the highest Pioneer chain saw sales in BC at the time, he says. "You could go down to Carl's at three in the morning and say, 'I need a part for my chain saw.' He'd get up and if he didn't have that part, he'd toss you a new saw and say, 'I'll call you when that part comes in.' That was service!"

Then I admire the industry of the seven-member 2nd Mt. Washington Girl Guides. Jennah Vhay Fox, 9, Lisa Fordham, 9, and Alexia Bryson, 10, are the cupcake troop. Each brought four dozen, baked themselves. Two hours later, only the three Guides remain. I check out Elsie Doersam's handmade porcelain dolls, visit Shirley Green and her pungent strings of garlic and dried chili peppers, look over Patty Bronson's personally designed stationery and Wendy Helme's beautiful stitchery. Rainbow the Clown, a.k.a. Louise Lucieer, is using an old silk parachute and teaching a circle of kids how to do a cloud dance. Jenna Folk, 5, is pink with pride after winning ribbons for fuzziest pet and fastest corn shucking. In the sunshine, as the cloud dance transforms itself into a vanishing act under the parachute, I spy Comox Valley MLA Stan Hagen slipping incognito through the crowd. No one can blame him for wanting to savour a moment in the real world that's found beyond the smoke and mirrors, fuming and fakery that characterize so much of contemporary politics.

Frankly, it wouldn't be right to talk up the pleasures of the Black Creek fair and forget its amiable alter ego on Washer Creek which tumbles into the sea just north of Union Bay where, at long-vanished wharves, schooners and square-riggers used to take on cargo bound from Vancouver Island to Australia and points west. It's a curious historical footnote that the waters of Washer Creek once ran blacker than Black Creek. That was back when coal from Robert Dunsmuir's collieries was cleaned here. Today the creek runs clear and clean. Coal is king only in the memory of folks like community association president Hank Hatch. He came to work in a tool shop in Union Bay in 1943 when mines were still operating in the district.

I'm told Black Creek and Union Bay used to run their summer-ending fairs head-to-head, but reason prevailed and now they run them back-to-back so folks can catch both. It's a good thing, too. They're both worth catching. The fairs are as different from one another as oysters and eggs. Black Creek is a farming community first settled by forty Mennonite refugee families. Union Bay was the rough industrial tidewater for six coal mines. Black Creek is famous for fresh brown eggs, Union Bay for succulent oysters from Baynes Sound. Both are vital and throbbing with life. For example, when Lei Trobak took a dislike to open sewer ditches, she got the Union Bay Beautification Committee rolling. The ditches were soon filled and bake sales, pancake breakfasts and a quilting bee raised $4,000 a year to put flowers where sludge used to gurgle unpleasantly.

To find the Union Bay Fall Fair, I head south from Courtenay through Royston with a side trip into Union Bay proper—but just to look over the post office with its high oak writing table, brass-fronted mail boxes and wooden wickets. This is one of the best examples of an old country post office still in use. If Canada Post can't find some way to make sure it survives, I'm switching permanently to electronic mail. The fall fair takes place at the rambling

Union Bay Community Hall, another architectural wonder from the past. It stands in a field next to Washer Creek, flanked by towering old maples and banks of salmonberry and morning glory. Inside, the hardwood dance floor is marked out for basketball, volleyball and badminton courts. The walls and ceiling are panelled with age-darkened knotty pine.

I stop first to look over the ingenious wooden toys made by Mark Jackson and Derek Davies, a couple of young fellows with a new business in Royston called Typical Toys. There is a little log cabin for youngsters to assemble, a bear that climbs up a string, a walking duck that clacks as it quacks, a park-style picnic table for children. The boys are nervous on their first day of retail sales. They needn't worry. My wife and daughter like the rocking horse so much they sneak back and buy it while I talk to Greg Ladret. It is Greg's first fair, too. He's wearing a button that says World's Worst Magician but he's really a Comox native who spent ten years touring the world as a professional figure skater, first for Disney, later for the Ice Follies. Then he blew his knees out and retreated to Nanaimo to think about another profession. Along the way he got interested in masks and in Venice learned how to make striking, powerful pieces from form-fitting glove leather which he later paints. "I was broke and looked in my room and saw my masks. I thought, hey, why not finish 'em off and take them to the fair?"

Across the aisle I chat with Joanne Graham, selling wool weather forecasters for the Union Bay Elementary School Advisory Council. You hang the forecaster outside. If it's wet, it's raining; white, it's snowing; stiff, it's freezing; moving, it's windy; gone, it's been ripped off by a passing city slicker. Gerry Gavel shows me his customized caulk boots, Tom and Myrtle Hembrough have hand-painted weather vanes, artist Brenda Chalifoux-Luscombe has compiled her community scenes as a calendar and the community association is raffling a quilt. The quilt consists of twenty-four magnificent embroidered panels, each signed by the individual artist, featuring local wildflowers and butterflies. Tickets $1 and odds better than any provincial lottery scam.

No fall fair would be complete without a tour of the vegetable exhibits. Stan McKay walks off with honours for biggest pumpkin (30 kilos), best turnip, best squash, best spuds and best rhubarb. Colleen Lloyd has the best carrots and Trish Campbell the biggest zucchini. Bob Darling's eggplant isn't huge, but he deserves a ribbon just for growing one here. The prize veggies, cakes, preserves and blackberry wine are to be auctioned off later. I want to stay for the dinner at $5 a plate but Hank Hatch told me I can't. Nothing personal. "A hundred and fifty dinner tickets went on sale at one o'clock. I went up at 1:30 and they were all standing around glum as can be. I said, 'What's the problem, ticket sales?' 'Yeah,' they said. 'A big problem. They're all sold!'"

What else to do, in that case, but head south, where I'll have to catch the ferry to Vesuvius Bay and drive down through the sheep paddocks and rustling woods to find my next celebration of seasonal bounty. There are fall fairs far grander than Saltspring Island's, but few to match it for charm. Here, among the burnished outcrops of rock and tawny hay meadows, life sometimes seems to have more in common with the languid Somerset of Thomas Hardy's England than a fast-paced world filled with chicanery, folly and self-deception learned from television. Of all these small-town fairs, the Saltspring Island fair best exemplifies Gulf Islands tranquillity. There are no stomach-churning rides. Instead of a merry-go-round the kids get to sit on real ponies with names like Fred, and if they seem totally awestruck by the experience—why, the operator just lets them go for a few more circuits for free. The raffle here is not for a gold brick or a furnished house in some cookie-cutter development. It's a truckload of firewood split by the Saltspring Scorpions, the senior boys' basketball team. This is the kind of place where, instead of the House of Horrors, kids are encouraged to clamber through the community ambulance or sit at the wheel of the Coast Guard Auxiliary's Zodiac and pretend they are rescuing another citified sailor who ran aground navigating with a road map and a cell phone.

Saltspring Island: where else can kids learn how to wash a sunburned chicken? (One needs three washtubs, two tablespoons of Cheer, a dash of La France's Blue, a cup of vinegar, bleach and three tablespoons of glycerine. Oh yeah, a soft towel. Nothing's too good for a prize Golden Pencilled Hamburg or a Silver Laced Wyandot.) Who, exactly, is to be found washing chickens? Why, poultry fanciers who want to win with birds like Lisa Lloyd's champion Buff Orpington. And what, precisely, might be the physical attributes of the Madonna or Tom Cruise of Old English Game Hens? Head shape, brightness of eye, the size and colour of the comb. Then the body—does it have depth and width? The handling qualities—if you pinch the abdomen is it soft or filled with hard fat? Pigmentation. Vigour.

Meanwhile, there was cotton candy, courtesy of the Boy Scouts, custom-spun for customers while parents idled in the shade of the orchard where the boughs of ancient apple trees substituted for umbrellas. And then, as blue shadows crept down the hillsides, the gates were finally closed on summer and a stream of Islanders bore away ribbons, flop-eared rabbits, cakes, caged roosters, pickles, homemade ale, loaves of bread, piglets, all those true things that are to be contemplated and improved upon for next year's celebration of what really counts in this life so graced with abundance.

Epilogue: Coming Home

When we left the Coast, the plan called for a summer's work in Alberta then a winter with the rest of our graduating class, bumming around Europe and North Africa spending the loot. I rode my motorcycle to Wong's Emporium and returned with a bouquet of cut carnations. Susan carried them through the four-room beach house on Crescent Road that we rented from Ralph Newton-White. She went out through the room we had dressed up in the marine paint I found on sale at Capital Iron and Metal, past the cheap furniture painted the same sailor blue, beneath the hot water pipes that couldn't be concealed and so were painted bright orange, then down the front steps to the yet unpolluted beach of Foul Bay. I watched her go through the spring rain, this woman I'd just married and about whom I knew less with each day. She went down those long, slippery wooden steps, past the cedar tree she planted and out through the drift logs to lay her wreath on the waters—an offering to Hermes, that distant god of travellers and thieves. Protector, too, of messengers from tyrants and thus, in Susan's logic, reporters, writers, newspapers and other servants of history. Hermes liked his offering. I know that now. Why else would he stretch that summer into nearly twenty years of finding the way home?

A generation of trials and labours, but not punishments: those travels were blessed with discovery. They took us from fabulous Greenland, dreaming under ice two kilometres deep, to the ancient forest of Brocéliande, where they say Merlin still sleeps imprisoned in a cell of crystal rock.

We journeyed from a mile deep in the creaking bedrock of Canada to the mile-high mines of the Coal Branch; from the Stone Age in Labrador to Los Alamos and the laboratories of Armageddon; from the fringes of human habitation on the planet to the leading edges of Western civilization. More important, for a couple of rebellious kids finding their way out of the sixties and into the world, those travels led us to discover in ourselves ways into the heartwood of our country. If we left smug, self-satisfied Victoria as a couple of insular coast colts, we were changed somewhere into citizens and patriots—a word frequently misused and too often held in small repute by those who can't distinguish between chauvinism and simple love of country.

Maybe the change took place in the polar latitudes with the sea ice groaning underfoot and a growing sense of the glorious improbability of the whole enterprise called Canada. I'd been talking with Peter Ernerk, born in an igloo and ignorant of white faces until his sixteenth birthday, although he would later rise to become commissioner of Nunavut. We'd been discussing the mysterious emotional power of rivers like the Fraser, Skeena and Mackenzie. Peter said he'd show me his river. It was 44 below zero and deep in the Arctic night when he took me out on Eclipse Sound. We waited in silence, shuffling our sealskin boots to keep the blood moving. Then it came. The first sunrise of the northern year, still hidden by the horizon but its slanting rays catching the towering glaciers on distant islands until the whole eastern sky glowed where the light spilled along the rim of the world, a swelling river of life-giving light. "That's my river," said Peter. "No trees." And he laughed. A gift of enlightenment. Almost a third of my country is treeless. Our maps call it The Barrens. To Peter it is Nunatsiaq—"the beautiful country." But the light is there for all of us.

Or perhaps my Canada loomed out of Labrador as I looked

westward over the glass-smooth granite that cups Country Cat Pond. From my vantage point the whole country fell away under an immense blue firmament until I felt I could see all the way to Yellowknife—farther away than Europe—but sharing the same granite, under the same sky. Or maybe it came riding head first into the wind out of the Peigan Nation, seeing the shortgrass prairie break like surf against the moonlit reefs and ridges of the Rocky Mountain foothills, the Milky Way pouring across those black, black heavens. Another kind of river. More likely it came at Oyster mouth, just south of Cougar Smith's floathouse at Stories Beach, squinting into December spindrift at the beached ruin of a fighting ship, deciding to go find the true story of K444.

But home is relative. It shifts. And suddenly here we are again, worlds away from that home, yet returning to what is both the end and the beginning of our own country; coming home to the sea of mountains, the rivers like highways from the heartland without end. Circles need to be broken and they demand to be closed. If we began this odyssey with an offering to Hermes, Susan decided, we should end our descent from the Great Plains with an offering to Poseidon, that old ruler of horses and the sea.

So I take the broken oar she's carried with her all these years— her bond to Arbutus Cove and a sea-swept childhood. Just an old splintered oar with the varnish stripped by salt and time. I carry it on my shoulder, up through the aspen woodland until I find this perfect bluff looking out over the muscular brown coil of the North Saskatchewan River, and I drive her splintered oar into the earth. High tide. And I repeat, as instructed, the lines about Odysseus, who travelled so far with his gear that he came in the end to a place "and they thought my oar was a winnowing stick." The prairie wind comes, as it always does, and the leaves begin to dance. Their silver bellies catch the light rippling its way westward, running in front of the breeze. Like a river to the sea. Going home.

Index